About the Author

David Wall writes all kinds of things — everything from Internet books like this one to newspaper columns. He divides most of his writing time between working on an IDG book about the Visual Café Java development environment and writing a novel. In his spare time, David enjoys sailing, collecting Bruce Springsteen concert recordings, and traveling — particularly far afield with a backpack.

David's earlier work includes *The 10 Secrets for Web Success*, a journalistic look at the personalities behind the Web's greatest successes.

ABOUT IDG BOOKS WORLDWIDE

Welcome to the world of IDG Books Worldwide.

IDG Books Worldwide, Inc., is a subsidiary of International Data Group, the world's largest publisher of computer-related information and the leading global provider of information services on information technology. IDG was founded more than 25 years ago and now employs more than 8,500 people worldwide. IDG publishes more than 270 computer publications in over 75 countries (see listing below). More than 90 million people read one or more IDG publications each month.

Launched in 1990, IDG Books Worldwide is today the #1 publisher of best-selling computer books in the United States. We are proud to have received eight awards from the Computer Press Association in recognition of editorial excellence and three from *Computer Currents'* First Annual Readers' Choice Awards. Our best-selling *...For Dummies*® series has more than 25 million copies in print with translations in 30 languages. IDG Books Worldwide, through a joint venture with IDG's Hi-Tech Beijing, became the first U.S. publisher to publish a computer book in the People's Republic of China. In record time, IDG Books Worldwide has become the first choice for millions of readers around the world who want to learn how to better manage their businesses.

Our mission is simple: Every one of our books is designed to bring extra value and skill-building instructions to the reader. Our books are written by experts who understand and care about our readers. The knowledge base of our editorial staff comes from years of experience in publishing, education, and journalism — experience which we use to produce books for the '90s. In short, we care about books, so we attract the best people. We devote special attention to details such as audience, interior design, use of icons, and illustrations. And because we use an efficient process of authoring, editing, and desktop publishing our books electronically, we can spend more time ensuring superior content and spend less time on the technicalities of making books.

You can count on our commitment to deliver high-quality books at competitive prices on topics you want to read about. At IDG Books Worldwide, we continue in the IDG tradition of delivering quality for more than 25 years. You'll find no better book on a subject than one from IDG Books Worldwide.

John J. Kilcullen

John Kilcullen
President and CEO
IDG Books Worldwide, Inc.

IDG Books Worldwide, Inc., is a subsidiary of International Data Group, the world's largest publisher of computer-related information and the leading global provider of information services on information technology. International Data Group publishes over 276 computer publications in over 75 countries. Ninety million people read one or more International Data Group publications each month. International Data Group's publications include: **ARGENTINA:** Annuario de Informatica, Computerworld Argentina, PC World Argentina; **AUSTRALIA:** Australian Macworld, Client/Server Journal, Computer Living, Computerworld, Computerworld 100, Digital News, IT Casebook, Network World, On-line World Australia, PC World, Publishing Essentials, Reseller, WebMaster; **AUSTRIA:** Computerwelt Österreich, Networks Austria, PC Tip; **BELARUS:** PC World Belarus; **BELGIUM:** Data News; **BRAZIL:** Annuário de Informática, Computerworld Brazil, Connections, Super Game Power, Macworld, PC Player, PC World Brazil, Publish Brazil, Reseller News; **BULGARIA:** Computerworld Bulgaria, Networkworld/Bulgaria, PC & MacWorld Bulgaria; **CANADA:** CIO Canada, Client/Server World, ComputerWorld Canada, InfoCanada, Network World Canada; **CHILE:** Computerworld Chile, PC World Chile; **COLOMBIA:** Computerworld Colombia, PC World Colombia; **COSTA RICA:** PC World Centro America; **THE CZECH AND SLOVAK REPUBLICS:** Computerworld Czechoslovakia, Elektronika Czechoslovakia, Macworld Czech Republic, PC World Czechoslovakia; **DENMARK:** Communications World, Computerworld Danmark, Macworld Danmark, PC Privat Danmark, PC World Danmark, PC World Danmark Supplements, TECH World; **DOMINICAN REPUBLIC:** PC World Republica Dominicana; **ECUADOR:** PC World Ecuador; **EGYPT:** Computerworld Middle East, PC World Middle East; **EL SALVADOR:** PC World Centro America; **FINLAND:** MikroPC, Tietoverkko, Tietoviikko; **FRANCE:** Distributique, Golden, Hebdo-Distributique, Info PC, Le Guide du Monde Informatique, Le Monde Informatique, Reseaux & Telecoms; **GERMANY:** Computer Partner, Computerwoche, Computerwoche Extra, Computerwoche Focus, I/M Information Management, Macwelt, PC Welt; **GREECE:** GamePro, Multimedia World; **GUATEMALA:** PC World Centro America; **HONDURAS:** PC World Centro America; **HONG KONG:** Computerworld Hong Kong, PCWorld Hong Kong, Publish in Asia; **HUNGARY:** ABCD CD-ROM, Computerworld Szamitastechnika, PC & Mac World Hungary, PC-X Magazine; **ICELAND:** Tolvuheimur/PC World Island; **INDIA:** Information Systems Computerworld, PC World India, Publish in Asia; **INDONESIA:** InfoKomputer PC World, Komputek Computerworld, Publish in Asia; **IRELAND:** ComputerScope, PC Live!; **ISRAEL:** People & Computers; **ITALY:** Computerworld Italia, Computerworld Italia Special Editions, Macworld Italia, Networking Italia, PC Shopping, PC World Italia, PC World/Walt Disney; **JAPAN:** DTP World, HP Open World Japan, Macworld Japan, Nikkei Personal Computing, Open World Japan, OS/2 World Japan, SunWorld Japan, Windows World Japan; **KENYA:** East African Computer News; **KOREA:** Hi-Tech Information/Computerworld, Macworld Korea, PC World Korea; **MACEDONIA:** PC World Macedonia; **MALAYSIA:** Computerworld Malaysia, PC World Malaysia, Publish in Asia; **MEXICO:** Computerworld Mexico, Macworld, PC World Mexico; **MYANMAR:** PC World Myanmar; **NETHERLANDS:** Computer! Totaal, LAN Magazine, LanWorld Buyers Guide, Macworld, Net Magazine, Totaal! Beurskrant; **NEW ZEALAND:** Absolute Beginner's Guide, Computer Buyer, Computer Industry Directory, Computerworld New Zealand, MTB, Network World, PC World New Zealand; **NICARAGUA:** PC World Centro America; **NIGERIA:** PC World Nigeria; **NORWAY:** Computerworld Norge, Computerworld Privat (Datamagasinet), CW Rapport Norge, IDG's KURSGUIDE, Macworld Norge, Multimediaworld, PC World Ekspress, PC World Nettverk, PC World Norge, PC World's Produktguide, Windows World Spesial; **PAKISTAN:** Computerworld Pakistan, PC World Pakistan; Panama: PC World Panama; **P. R. OF CHINA:** China Computer Users, China Computerworld, China Infoworld, China Telecom World Weekly, Computer & Communication, Electronic Design China, Electronics Today, Electronics Weekly, Game Camp, Game Soft, Network World China, PC World China, Popular Computer Weekly, Software Weekly, Software World, Telecom World; **PERU:** Computerworld Peru, PC World Profesional Peru, PC World Peru; **PHILIPPINES:** Computerworld Philippines, PC World Philippines, Publish in Asia; **POLAND:** Computerworld Poland, Computerworld Special Report, Macworld, Networld, PC World Komputer; **PORTUGAL:** Cerebro/PC World, Computerworld/Correio Informático, Dealer World Portugal, MacIn/PCIn, Multimedia World Portugal; **PUERTO RICO:** PC World Puerto Rico; **ROMANIA:** Computerworld Romania, PC World Romania, Telecom Romania; **RUSSIA:** Computerworld Russia, Mir PK, Sety; **SINGAPORE:** Computerworld Singapore, PC World Singapore, Publish in Asia; **SLOVENIA:** MONITOR; **SOUTH AFRICA:** Computing S.A., InfoWorld S.A., Network World S.A., Software World; **SPAIN:** Computerworld España, COMUNICACIONES WORLD, Dealer World, Macworld España, PC World España; **SWEDEN:** CAP&Design, Computer Sweden, Corporate Computing, MacWorld, Maxi Data, MikroDatorn, Nätverk & Kommunikation, PC/Aktiv, PC World, Windows World; **SWITZERLAND:** Computerworld Schweiz, Macworld Schweiz, PCtip; **TAIWAN:** Computerworld Taiwan, Macworld Taiwan, PC World Taiwan, Publish Taiwan, Windows World; **THAILAND:** Thai Computerworld, Publish in Asia; **TURKEY:** Computerworld Turkiye, MACWORLD Turkiye, PC WORLD Turkiye; **UKRAINE:** Computerworld Kiev, Computers & Software, Multimedia World Ukraine, PC World Ukraine; **UNITED KINGDOM:** Acorn User, Amiga Action, Amiga Computing, Appletalk, Computing, GamePro, GamePro, Macworld, Network News, Parents and Computers, PC Advisor, PC Home, PSX Pro UK, The WEB; **UNITED STATES:** Cable in the Classroom, CD Review, CIO Magazine, Computerworld, Computerworld Client/Server Journal, Digital Video Magazine, DOS World, Federal Computer Week, GamePro World, GamePro, I-Way, JavaWorld, Macworld, Multimedia World, Netscape World Online, Network World, PC Entertainment, PC World, Publish, SunWorld Online, SWATPro Magazine, Video Event, WebMaster; **URUGUAY:** PC World Uruguay; **VENEZUELA:** Computerworld Venezuela, PC World Venezuela; and **VIETNAM:** PC World Vietnam.
7/16/96

Dedication

For my family.

Credits

Senior Vice President,
Group Publisher
Brenda McLaughlin

Publishing Director
Walter Bruce III

Acquisitions Editor
Michael Roney

Software Acquisitions Editor
Tracy Lehman Cramer

Brand Manager
Melissa M. Duffy

Managing Editor
Andy Cummings

Development Editor
Michael Roney

Copy Editors
Jayne Jacobson
Nate Holdread
Nancy Albright

Technical Reviewer
Gus Venditto

Production Director
Andrew Walker

Production Assistant
Christopher Pimentel

Project Coordinator
Ben Schroeter

Supervisor of Page Layout
Craig A. Harrison

Reprint Coordination
Tony Augsburger
Theresa Sánchez-Baker
Elizabeth Cardenas-Nelson

Media/Archive Coordination
Leslie Popplewell
Melissa Stauffer
Jason Marcuson

Production Staff
Mario Amador
Laura Carpenter
Kurt Krames
Mark Schumann

Quality Control Specialist
Mick Arellano

Proofreader
Mary C. Oby

Indexer
Matthew Spence

Acknowledgments

As a publicity stunt, NASA once sent astronaut Gus Grissom to visit the assembly plant where workers were building the Redstone booster that would carry him into space. The plant's entire workforce assembled for Grissom's speech on the cavernous factory floor, anticipating the words of the great man. A huge American flag hung from the rafters. The crowd fell silent as Grissom began to speak.

"Do good work," he said.

That was the extent of his speech. The crowd broke into thunderous applause, knowing that the laconic spaceman had summed up their philosophy of life in three monosyllabic words.

Many people did good work on this book. I owe thanks to Mike Roney, my editor at IDG Books Worldwide, who toiled alongside me as this book took shape. Others deserve credit, too, including copy editor Jayne Jacobson, IDG Books production coordinator Ben Schroeter, and Nate Holdread.

There's a whole community of plug-in developers out there whose work enabled this book to get off the ground. Many thanks to everyone whose plug-ins appear in these pages and especially to those whose plug-ins grace the accompanying CD-ROM. Also, apologies in advance to the developers of any plug-in that escaped my attention. In compiling a work such as this, errors and omissions are bound to occur, try as I did to avoid them. I regret any omissions.

As my opinion of this book wavered like a tree in a stiff breeze, my family and friends kept me encouraged (perhaps, it occurs to me, because I owe money to half of them; but that is another story). My parents, brother, and grandparents have always backed my writing career. Adam Bergman, Adam Bernstein, Lori Lawson, Ellen Marcus, and Bryan and Suzanne Pfaffenberger all provided friendship during the drafting of this book's manuscript, and continue to do so today.

I hope you enjoy this book. Please write me at davidw@lumet.net and share your opinion.

David Wall

Charlottesville, Virginia

Contents at a Glance

Table of Contents

Chapter 4: VRML and Three-Dimensional Imaging 159

Chapter 5: Document and Image Viewers 215

Chapter 7: Navigation **303**

Chapter 8: Utilities **311**

Introduction

Once in a while, a software company comes up with an idea so logical and unselfish that everyone recognizes its significance immediately. Right away, the community of people who follow developments in the computer industry knows that the software company that forwarded the idea has struck on something so cool, it's bound to make computing easier, more fun, more productive, and more profitable for all concerned.

Plug-ins that conform to the Netscape Navigator standard (which you can use on both Netscape Navigator, version 2.0 and greater, and Microsoft Internet Explorer, version 3.0 and greater) are such a development.

When Netscape Communications Corporation issued a press release from its Mountain View, California, headquarters on January 17, 1996, announcing the first 15 plug-ins for its Netscape Navigator Web browser, the Web community cheered. Plug-ins mean the end of often-annoying helper applications that don't integrate with Netscape very well and frequently don't work right. Plug-ins mean that small software developers can work on products that take advantage of Netscape Navigator's technical superiority and Netscape Communications' marketing might. Plug-ins mean that Web surfers can enjoy a new era of sites featuring integrated multimedia, including sound, video, animation, and real-time links to other applications on their desktops. Plug-ins make the Web a better place.

Version 3.0 and above of Microsoft Internet Explorer, the second-most-popular Web browser, support Netscape plug-ins. That is, if you run Microsoft Corporation's Microsoft Internet Explorer 3.0, you'll be able to install and use plug-ins originally designed for Netscape Navigator — the plug-ins discussed in this book and included on the accompanying CD-ROM. The fact that Microsoft, traditionally very snooty about pressing its software design schemes on the software industry as *de facto* standards, has chosen to embrace Netscape's arrangement speaks volumes for the power of open standards and the likelihood of Netscape's continued leadership of the browser market.

The Jeffersonian Browser

You are to be commended for your interest in plug-ins. By buying this book, you've shown that you're committed to putting together a well-appointed browser — a browser for all seasons.

On a promontory to the east of Charlottesville, Virginia, overlooking the University of Virginia and the former railroad town that surrounds it, stands Monticello, the favorite home of Thomas Jefferson. Jefferson's home reflects his varied interests. The entrance hall is filled with biological and anthropological relics from the Lewis and Clark expedition, which he organized. The bookcases in his study, though now carefully maintained by curators, still overflow with volumes in the original French, Latin, and Greek. Monticello's grounds teem with hundreds of varieties of commercial and ornamental plants, the maintenance of which Jefferson carefully monitored.

Perhaps America's only true Renaissance man, Jefferson understood farming, winemaking, careful writing, and the sciences — all while making landmark contributions to government, political philosophy, architecture, and education. He was sufficiently educated to be an expert in a dozen fields. He took the concept of "well-rounded" to the extreme.

Like Jefferson, a good browser can move with ease among an enormous variety of situations. Just as Jefferson may have written letters to James Madison about governmental theory in the morning, designed an innovative mansion in the afternoon, and read the work of Plato in the evening, a copy of Netscape or Microsoft Internet Explorer, outfitted with the proper plug-ins, can handle streaming video at one site, streaming audio at the next, and three-dimensional virtual reality based on the Virtual Reality Modeling Language a couple of sites later. A plugged-in browser is a versatile browser. Like Jefferson's education, which enabled him to accomplish the work of 40 lifetimes in his 83 years, a browser enhanced with plug-ins enables you to get the most out of your Web surfing time.

About this Book

Jefferson went down the road from Charlottesville to the College of William and Mary in Williamsburg, Virginia, for his classical education, then continued his learning throughout his life by reading voraciously, corresponding with the great thinkers of his time, and experimenting on his own in a variety of different fields. Fortunately for you, your browser doesn't have to spend years acquiring the skills it needs, and you don't have to spend hours downloading the plug-ins available on the Web. You have in your hands *Netscape Plug-in Power* and its accompanying CD-ROM. The CD-ROM allows you to outfit your browser with the latest plug-ins — including Macromedia Shockwave and several superb VRML browsers — and the text of this book fills you in on how to use the plug-ins and directs you to the Web sites that take fullest advantage of them.

This book is the definitive compendium of printed information on plug-ins for Netscape Navigator and other browsers that conform to its plug-in specification. It also is the single best reference for questions such as, "Is there a VRML plug-in for the Macintosh?" or "What sites use Macromedia Shockwave for Director in novel ways?" This book is where you should look for the answers to all of your questions about plug-ins.

In addition to this book, there are some excellent Web sites devoted to new developments in browser technology and plug-ins. One of the best plug-ins sites is BrowserWatch's Plug-in Plaza, at `http://www.iworld.com/browserwatch.html`. You'll learn more about Plug-in Plaza and other online plug-in resources in Chapter 1.

Chapter 1 of *Netscape Plug-in Power* deals with general plug-in issues, such as what plug-ins are, how you can find them online, how to use the ones encoded on the CD-ROM that accompanies this book, and how to install and un-install plug-ins on your computer.

Chapters 2 through 8 each cover all the plug-ins in a particular category.

Chapter 2 covers plug-ins that handle sound, for example, TEC Solutions' TEC Player and Progressive Networks' RealAudio Player.

Chapter 3 covers plug-ins that display video and animation, including Macromedia Shockwave for Director and VDOnet's VDOlive.

Chapter 4 teaches you about virtual reality and three-dimensional imaging plug-ins, such as Integrated Data Systems' VRealm, Chaco Communications' VR Scout, and MDL's Chemscape Chime.

Chapter 5 deals with plug-ins that work as document viewers. There you'll find coverage of Adobe's Amber, Inso's Word Viewer, SoftSource's SVF Viewer, and other plug-ins that let you view various file types without a helper application separate from your browser.

Chapter 6 teaches you about communications-related plug-ins. Connect to the world with Galacticomm's Worldgroup Manager, IChat's IChat, and Brainstorm's Groupscape. Inso's CyberSpell checks the spelling in your Netscape electronic mail messages.

Chapter 7 covers navigation plug-ins that enhance the usefulness of your browser. ISYS' HindSite and SmartBrowser's HistoryTree act as high-powered History lists, while InternetConsult's Table of Contents makes it easy to get the scoop on an unfamiliar site.

Chapter 8 encompasses utilities — nifty plug-ins that expand the capabilities of your browser in workmanlike, often subtle ways. You'll learn about plug-ins such as PointCast, which brings a customized news, sports, and features package to your desktop, and EarthTime, which helps you figure out exactly what time it is at the home of the server you're trying to reach.

I've tried to cover every single plug-in available at this writing — in the summer of 1996. Scores more plug-ins undoubtedly will make their debuts in the coming months. Chapter 1 also explains where on the Web you can go to keep up-to-date on the latest plug-in releases and upgrades.

The description of each plug-in covered in Chapters 2 through 8 contains the following sections:

+ **Introduction:** A brief guide to what a plug-in does and how you can use it to make the Web more fun and useful to you. The introduction sometimes tells a little bit about the person or company that created the plug-in and perhaps a bit about the development process.

+ **Installing the Plug-in:** Instructions for getting the latest version of the plug-in. If the plug-in is on the CD-ROM, look at Appendix A for instructions on getting it from there.

+ **Using the Plug-in:** A guide to, well, using the plug-in. If the plug-in being covered in the chapter makes extra controls spring up in your browser window, this section explains what they do and how to use them. If there are tricks to making the plug-in work properly, this section reveals them. If the plug-in works in the background and doesn't let you control anything (as some of the document viewers and sound players do), this section says so, and the chapter moves on to the next issue.

+ **Plugged-In Sites:** A directory of sites that use the plug-in's technology to make their corners of the Web more entertaining, more content-rich, or more attractive. For example, Chapter 2, which covers the RealAudio plug-in, refers you to the National Public Radio site. There you can hear the current editions of "All Things Considered" and other popular NPR programs. The Plugged-In Sites section can also give you ideas about how to use a particular plug-in to enhance a Web site for which you are responsible.

+ **Authoring for the Plug-in:** These sections teach you how to create material to be read by the covered plug-in and attach that material to a Web page with special HTML tags and attributes. You'll learn a little bit about everything from RealAudio Studio, to Macromedia Director, to Adobe Acrobat Distiller here.

Of course, these aren't always comprehensive guides to creating various kinds of site content, since many of these authoring programs are worthy of entire books of their own. You'll find cursory introductions to the more complex authoring tools. Other authoring tools get more complete coverage, especially if they're simple, available free of charge on the Web, or included on the CD-ROM. Space simply does not allow adequate coverage of, say,

Adobe Premiere, one of the best tools out there for creating QuickTime movies and other video presentations. These sections point you in the right direction for further information.

All the plug-in sections also include an information box that allows you to quickly ascertain the essential facts about a plug-in. The boxes look like this:

Plug-in Name: (Duh.)

Creator: The person or company that built and maintains the plug-in

Function: What the plug-in does, for example, "Lets you view Adobe Acrobat documents," or "Displays three-dimensional, manipulable models of complex molecules."

Home Site: The URL at which you'll find the latest version of the plug-in, news of its creator, and other useful information.

Supported Platforms: The computers for which versions of the plug-in exist. Practically all plug-ins have Windows 95 versions; most have Windows 3.*x* versions; a few have Macintosh and Windows NT versions, and a scant handful work with UNIX. You'll find only Windows 3.*x*, Windows 95, and Macintosh plug-ins on the CD-ROM.

Authoring Tool: The program you use to create files to be processed by the plug-in in question. For example, for SoftSource's DWG/OXF Viewer, the authoring tool would be AutoCad.

Good Examples: Some sites you can visit to see exemplary uses of the plug-in's capabilities.

A Note About the Icons

You'll find icons — little pictures that denote special information — scattered throughout the text. Here's a guide to what they mean.

You'll see this little icon next to the main heading of sections that cover plug-ins that are so cool, and can handle so much Web content, that you absolutely *must* install them on your computer. You'll also see this icon in the Table of Contents next to essential plug-ins. Don't miss these treasures!

The CD-ROM icon appears on the title page of chapters that cover plug-ins that appear on the CD-ROM that accompanies this book. You can save tons of time by installing them directly from your CD-ROM drive, without even connecting to the Web. Like the Essential icon, you'll see this icon in the Table of Contents next to plug-ins on the CD-ROM.

Remember, if there's no CD-ROM icon next to the plug-ins that interest you, you should still peruse the CD-ROM. Programs may have been added after the text was completed.

 The Tip icon appears next to information about little-known or subtle tricks you can use to get the most out of your plugged-in browser. Tips often come from little hints I got from the makers of plug-ins; so these can be a real source of expertise-building knowledge.

 The Warning icon appears next to information related to places you can trip up with plug-ins, such as situations in which a particular plug-in tends to crash. Sometimes, stuff identified by the Warning icon comes from traps that I fell into while researching and writing this book — so this icon often contains information you won't find anywhere else. Carefully read text marked with the Warning icon.

The CD-ROM

The CD-ROM that accompanies this book may be more valuable than the book itself. It contains many of the plug-ins discussed in *Netscape Plug-in Power* and stands to save you many hours of downloading plug-ins from the Web. With the enclosed CD-ROM, you can make your browser into a multipurpose, multimedia machine in minutes instead of days.

You'll learn how to install plug-ins from the CD-ROM in Appendix A of this book — a brief write-up called "Using the CD-ROM."

There's also a Web page on the CD-ROM — a file called PLUGINS.HTM. The file, which you can open with your Web browser, points you toward the home sites of all the plug-ins covered in these pages as well as to copies of some of the plug-ins on the disk itself. There also are links to the clearinghouses of plug-in information you'll learn about in Chapter 1, which contain information more current than what could be included on the CD-ROM. You'll read more about the IDG Books *Netscape Plug-in Power* Web site in Chapter 1, and you'll learn the specifics of using the CD-ROM's Web page in Appendix A.

Have Fun!

This book is essentially technical in nature, but it's meant to enhance your Web experience and help you to have fun online. Get the most out of the Web with the help of plug-ins, and let me know how you're doing. Write me at davidw@comet. net.

Plug-in Basics

Remember when, to give your laser printer the capacity to print more fonts, you bought a font cartridge and literally plugged it into a socket on the printer? Or when you were a kid, and some toy of yours just wasn't sufficiently cool on its own and required the presence of some add-on part to achieve truly stratospheric appeal? Are you familiar with the phrase, "Accessories sold separately?" Then you understand plug-ins.

This chapter gives you some background about what plug-ins are, how they work in general, what various purposes they serve, and how they can work for you.

What's a Plug-in?

A plug-in is a program that, instead of functioning on its own, attaches itself to another (usually larger and more complex) program in order to expand the capabilities of the second program. The once-ubiquitous Lotus 1-2-3 spreadsheet program used plug-ins to accomplish special calculation tasks; and Adobe Photoshop, the popular image-editing program, takes plug-ins that enable it to do such things as separate the colors that make up illustrations and filter images through unusual screens. Aldus PageMaker accepts plug-ins that enable it to perform some clever typographic trickery. Often, plug-in modules make programs useful for tasks entirely different from those for which they were specifically designed.

The plug-ins covered in *Netscape Plug-in Power* are expansion modules that attach themselves to Netscape Navigator and Microsoft Internet Explorer, giving those Web browsers special capabilities that aren't part of the basic, unplugged versions of the browsers that you can download from the Netscape and Microsoft Web sites. In some cases, plug-ins make your browser useful in ways its original developer didn't even conceive of — as collaboration-enhancing groupware, for example, or as a communications and diagnostic tool for troubleshooting.

One of the coolest things about plug-ins is that any moderately skilled programmer can design and build one — there's no need for the same companies that make browsers to make all the plug-ins that work with their browsers. Companies such as Heads Off Software and Totally Hip can — and do — make plug-ins that work with Netscape Navigator; and by doing so, they leverage the marketing might of companies many times their diminutive size. Having small, specialized companies work on special-interest plug-ins also frees the large companies — Netscape and Microsoft — to work on the complexities of basic browser programs, a significant challenge in its own right.

Plug-ins and the Web

The Web, though, is especially well suited to programs that use plug-ins. Think about this: Web pages are really just add-on modules for Web browsers. Straight out of the box (or out of the FTP site), and unconnected to the Web, Netscape Navigator isn't much fun. Call up Web sites with it, though, and that program that was all but useless on its own is capable of giving you stock quotes, telling you stories, finding the phone numbers you need, getting you a date, and doing hundreds of other things. The Web is an inherently modular entity, and it makes sense that the tools we use to get around on its sea of information be modular themselves.

Some Web pundits predict a day in the near future when everything on our computers (and on the Internet, which is our computers taken collectively) is modular and interrelated. Your graphical user interface might refer to a code library that resided on a Microsoft or Sun Microsystems computer — meaning that the company that maintained that code library could update it to correct bugs and add features without having to physically ship you a disk of some kind. Under that concept of what the Web is becoming, plug-ins for Web browsers seem like a logical intermediate step toward a totally modular global computing environment.

Better Surfing Through Plug-ins

To some degree, the Web has always been a multimedia phenomenon. Even in the Web's earliest days, you could click on a link to a sound file and, if your browser were properly configured, you'd hear the sound contained in the file. The trouble was, most multimedia couldn't be handled by the browser itself.

The dark days of helper apps

The browser knew only how to recognize files of different kinds and start up whatever application was appropriate for a particular file it encountered. The programs the browser started were called *helper applications*. These programs were completely separate and were related to the browser only by the fact that the browser (usually) could make them start without intervention from the user. They were not integrated with the browser very well — if at all — and they frequently suffered from weird compatibility problems with browsers, data files, and other helper applications.

When you clicked on a multimedia hyperlink in a browser equipped with helper applications (often called *helper apps*), your computer downloaded the information in the file, then "spawned" the helper app. In other words, it started the helper app and loaded the newly downloaded file into it. The arrangement looked something like Figure 1-1, which shows NET TOOB, a program often used as a helper application for video files, handling a Video for Windows file for Netscape. After the helper app finished its job, you had to manually close it in order to get back to your browser and your Web session.

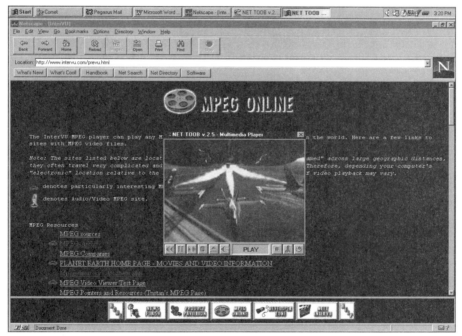

Figure 1-1: A helper application.

The preceding paragraph assumes that you had the needed helper application installed on your machine. Frequently, you'd come across a multimedia file on the Web that, according to the textual description, was something you wanted — but you'd have to spend ten minutes finding, downloading, and installing the appropriate helper app on your computer. This was a hassle and made Web multimedia fairly rare.

Helper apps aren't dead, by the way, they're just on their way out. Given a choice between a helper app and a plug-in, go with the plug-in, which brings you to the next topic.

Plug-ins to the rescue

Enter plug-ins, a simpler, more streamlined means of handling content that the browser's core code can't process. Plug-ins eliminate several of the hassles of helper apps.

Because they become part of the browser itself, plug-ins do the following:

✦ Integrate themselves into the browser's user interface, and are therefore relatively easy to learn to use.

✦ Usually don't require you to diddle with often-obscure file-type associations.

✦ Don't require you to manually close them when you're done using them.

✦ Won't fail when you move directories around on your hard disk.

✦ Often save you from having to find the helper applications you need, since the right plug-in for an application will download if you give the word.

Figure 1-2 shows PreVU, a plug-in, playing an MPEG video file. You can't see anything unusual? Exactly — the ability to handle MPEG files became part of Netscape when mBED was installed.

Figure 1-2: A plug-in-equipped browser playing a video file.

Because most of them are more or less *transparent*, — that is, they don't over-shadow your browser the way helper applications often do — plug-ins make it easier for Web site designers to make the Web a truly multimedia experience. Even those plug-ins that cause windows with controls and other special features to appear on your screen don't conflict with page design as much as a separate application does. Web page designers can integrate the controls and frames that are part of plug-in operation into their pages because they can control precisely where and when (and often *if*) those controls appear in the browser window. The presence of plug-ins also widens the palette of media with which site designers may express their content.

If every Web surfer has a properly equipped browser — or at least a browser that can easily accept expansion modules — site designers can feel free to use snazzier designs. The phenomenon of plugged-in publishing is somewhat similar to the phenomenon of color television, in that as more and more people came to own color televisions, show producers felt freer to broadcast things that depended on color.

Plug-ins versus ActiveX Controls

In exploring expansion modules for Web browsers, you'll soon hear about ActiveX Controls. Though similar in function to plug-ins that comply with the Netscape standard, ActiveX Controls are significantly different. Here's the basic scoop on plug-ins in comparison to ActiveX Controls:

   ✦ Plug-ins work with both Netscape Navigator and Microsoft Internet Explorer.

   ✦ ActiveX Controls work only with Microsoft Internet Explorer and are there-fore useless to Macintosh users.

   ✦ There are many more plug-ins than ActiveX Controls.

Developed by Microsoft to work only with its Microsoft Internet Explorer, ActiveX Controls give new capabilities to the basic Explorer program. There are ActiveX Controls that enable Explorer to show videos and others that expand its capabilities to play audio files. Installing ActiveX Controls is significantly more automatic than installing plug-ins.

Many of the plug-in developers you read about in this book also make ActiveX Controls that do the same things. If you run Explorer, you may be better off using the ActiveX Control because it's probably better integrated with Explorer than the plug-in. Otherwise, Explorer users can install Netscape-standard plug-ins just like a Netscape Navigator user.

Finding and Using Plug-ins

As you set out to build the perfect plugged-in browser, you'll need some information about where to go to get plug-ins. This section gives you some ideas about where to look for the latest Netscape expansion modules.

You don't always have to take the initiative in installing plug-ins. When your browser tries to load a page that contains information for a plug-in with which your browser is not equipped, you'll see a window similar to the one in Figure 1-3. Clicking on the More Info button takes you to the Netscape plug-ins page — which you'll learn about in just a moment.

Even if you don't actually try to load a plug-in-savvy page from a Web site, you'll often come across plug-ins that you can install or link to on the same site. For example, many virtual reality sites that employ Virtual Reality Modeling Language (VRML) to render three-dimensional navigable spaces have, on their plain-HTML welcome pages, links to the files you use to install VR Scout or WIRL (both covered in Chapter 4). You can follow these links, install the plug-ins, then return to the VRML site at which you started and browse with the aid of your newly acquired VRML-capable plug-in.

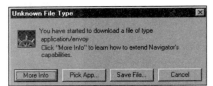

Figure 1-3: The Unknown File Type dialog box, which appears when you try to retrieve information for a plug-in your browser doesn't have.

But the best policy, as the Boy Scouts say, is to be prepared. By outfitting your browser with many plug-ins before you set out on a multimedia jaunt across the Web, you save yourself the hassle of stopping your surfing to download and install plug-ins. To preserve the continuity of your surfing in the future, you ought to arm your browser with plug-ins before you really need to.

Where to go for plug-ins? The CD-ROM that accompanies this book is an excellent resource. It contains many of the best plug-ins available, and you don't have to traverse the Web and wait for interminable downloads. You can just load the plug-ins right off the CD-ROM and onto your hard disk — take a look at Appendix B for more details on how to use the CD-ROM. You can also open PLUGINS.HTM, a file on the CD-ROM, with your browser and follow the links there to the home sites of plug-ins that aren't on the disk itself. Between the download time you'll save by using the plug-ins actually on the CD-ROM and the search engine time you'll save by using PLUGINS.HTM, the CD-ROM is a valuable resource to you in your quest to prepare your browser for all sorts of fun and productive applications.

Because it is a fairly static tool, prepared and burned on polycarbonate at a single point in time, the CD-ROM will eventually be out of date. It is then that you'll want to turn to the online resources dedicated to plug-ins and their uses. These Web sites serve as handy central locations for information about the latest plug-ins and the most recent improvements to the old standby plug-ins.

Add one or more of these sites to your browser's list of bookmarks or favorite places and check back every week or so. That way, you'll keep informed about plug-in news without wasting tons of time.

Some of the best plug-ins sites include the following:

✦ BrowserWatch Plug-ins Plaza (http://www.browserwatch.com/plug-in.html)

✦ This book's companion site (http://www.idgbooks.com/idgbooksonline)

✦ Netscape's plug-ins page (http://home.netscape.com/comprod/mirror/navcomponents_download.html)

✦ C|Net's plug-ins page (http://www.cnet.com/Content/Reviews/Compare/Plugin/) and reviews page (http://www.cnet.com/Content/Reviews/index.html)

✦ Yahoo!'s plug-ins listing (http://www.yahoo.com/Computers and Internet/Internet/World_Wide_Web/Browsers/Netscape_Navigator/Plug_Ins/)

This section takes you on a guided tour of these sites, which are your first line of defense against browser obsolescence!

BrowserWatch Plug-in Plaza

Hands down the best plug-in news monitor on the Web at this writing, Plug-in Plaza — like this book — represents a comprehensive compendium of information about scores of plug-ins. At Plug-in Plaza, you'll find information about what platforms a particular plug-in works with (Windows 3.x, Windows 95, standard Macintosh, Power Macintosh, or UNIX), where to find the plug-in's home site on the Web, and where to go to see the plug-in in action.

A production of *BrowserWatch* — which, in its own right, is an excellent publication to monitor for news of browsers and the companies that make them — Plug-in Plaza (http://www.browserwatch.com/plug-in.html) consistently has more up-to-date information about plug-ins (both available and forthcoming) than any other site, including Netscape's own site.

One of the neatest things about Plug-in Plaza is its succinct, table-based design. You can locate the table for the plug-in that interests you and immediately get all the basic information. This isn't the place to get much more insight than what fits into a hastily written sentence or two, but the tables contain links to sites with more information, if you want it. Plug-in Plaza exploits the flexibility of the Web by spreading the burden of providing information among several parties to you, the surfer, who stands to benefit from this superb collection of knowledge.

 Plug-in Plaza's maintainers keep their site so up-to-date, they frequently don't fit new entries into the alphabetical sequence of existing entries. If you don't see the plug-in you want in its alphabetical place, check the end of the list — the odds are good it was added recently and hasn't yet been collated into the sequence.

BrowserWatch Plug-in Plaza appears in Figure 1-4.

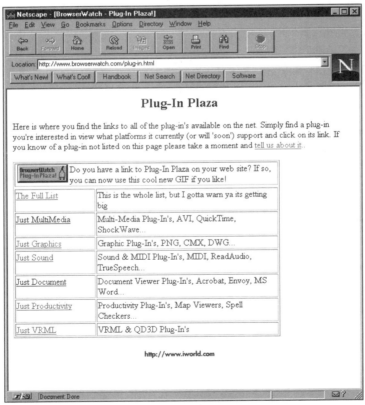

Figure 1-4: BrowserWatch Plug-in Plaza (`http://www.browserwatch.com/plug-in.html`).

IDG Books Online site

The IDG Books Online site (http://www.idgbooks.com) features excerpts and useful sample software from a wide range of book titles, including those of particular interest to Webmasters, HTML scripters, and anyone who browses the Web for fun or profit. The *Netscape Plug-in Power* page includes updated information and pointers for plug-ins. Figure 1-5 shows the IDG Books Online site.

Netscape's site

This site, which you'd think would be the mother of all plug-in emporia, places a distant second to Plug-in Plaza in terms of comprehensiveness and currency. Even though it's maintained by the people who sell Netscape Navigator and invented browser plug-ins, Netscape's plug-in site (http://home.netscape.com/comprod/products/navigator/version_2.0/plugins/index.html) doesn't mention many of the latest plug-ins and has only limited information about the modules that it does cover.

Figure 1-5: IDG Books Online (http://www.idgbooks.com).

In place of Plug-in Plaza's table-based layout, Netscape's plug-in index has a paragraph of text about each plug-in. This is a good thing, since you get a better idea of what each plug-in does from the longer write-ups than you can get from Plug-in Plaza's laconic blurbs. On the other hand, you don't get the consistency of presentation that characterizes Plug-in Plaza. Though most of the paragraphs have both a link to the plug-in's home page and a link to some sample pages that use the plug-in's special capabilities, the links aren't as consistently placed as they are in the BrowserWatch site, making them harder to find. At the bottom of each paragraph, you'll see a list of the platforms on which the paragraph's plug-in works.

Figure 1-6 shows the Netscape plug-ins page.

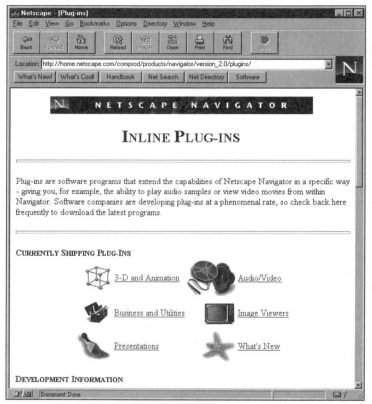

Figure 1-6: The Netscape plug-ins page (`http://home. netscape.com/comprod/products/navigator/ version_2.0/plugins/`).

The main appeal of Netscape's plug-in index is that this is the page you get when your browser tries to call up a page that features plug-in content it does not recognize. When you try to work with an unknown data type that Netscape suspects requires a plug-in, it will refer you to this page so you can sift through the selections in search of the plug-in that will handle the new kind of data. (You'll learn about the process later in this chapter.)

C|Net

C|Net shines not in its comprehensiveness, but in its thorough treatment of the plug-ins it covers. Just as you'd go to the phone book for limited information about a person but call up their home page if you wanted a more in-depth look at their personality, you should use the C|Net resources for expanded reviews of plug-ins, both new and old.

There are two C|Net resources worth mentioning in the context of plug-ins. The first, shown in Figure 1-7, is the C|Net plug-ins page (`http://www.cnet.com/Content/Reviews/Compare/Plugin/`). This page is a pale replica of the Netscape plug-in index and an even weaker jab at the authority of BrowserWatch Plug-in Plaza. Still, the C|Net compendium has a sort of cool interface (in the form of the graphic at the bottom of the plug-in page), and there's always the possibility that C|Net, whose news-gathering organization is one of the best on the Web, could scoop the other sites with news of a new plug-in. If you've heard a rumor that a new plug-in has been released by a software publisher, it's worth paying a visit to C|Net's guide page.

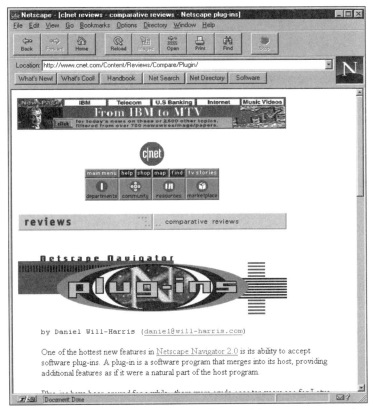

Figure 1-7: The C|Net plug-ins page (`http://www.cnet.com/Content/Reviews/Compare/Plugin/`).

The other worthwhile C|Net resource is the site's reviews page (`http://www.cnet.com/Content/Reviews/index.html`). There you'll find news and reviews of all kinds of computer stuff, from new scanning hardware, to new Web sites, to new plug-ins. This isn't a dedicated plug-ins page, but plug-in news shows up there with sufficient frequency to make it a worthwhile place to visit in your quest for the latest and greatest expansion modules for your browser. And who knows, you might actually learn something about something other than plug-ins — C|Net's coverage of the Web and the computer-products market is some of the best anywhere. The C|Net reviews page appears in Figure 1-8.

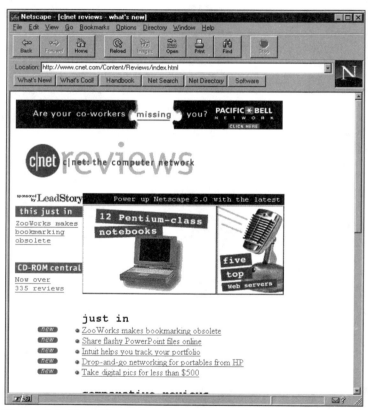

Figure 1-8: The C|Net reviews page (`http://www.cnet.com/Content/Reviews/index.html`).

Yahoo!

Less likely to break the news of a plug-in's release than the other sites, Yahoo! nonetheless stands ready to help you find the plug-ins you need. Take a look at the plug-ins branch of the Yahoo! tree (`http://www.yahoo.com/Computers_and_Internet/Internet/World_Wide_Web/Browsers/Netscape_Navigator/Plug_Ins/`). You'll find a few plug-ins there. However, the descriptions of the functions of each plug-in are very short (if there are any at all), and there's no information about the platforms with which each plug-in is compatible. Yahoo!'s plug-in branch is pictured in Figure 1-9.

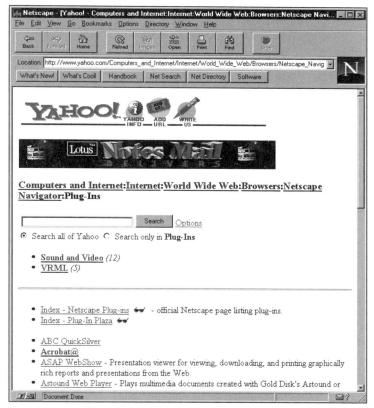

Figure 1-9: Yahoo!'s plug-ins listings (`http://www.yahoo.com/Computers_and_Internet/Internet/World_Wide_Web/Browsers/Netscape_Navigator/Plug_Ins/`).

Is the Yahoo! plug-in page very useful? Not really. But it's one more place to look; and, again, it's possible that this backwater portion of the plug-in universe could get news of a newly released product before the other sites do. Many people say Yahoo! is the best subject tree on the Web, which means that it devotes its effort to cataloging lots of Web sites, not handling special-interest cases such as plug-ins.

It's handy to know that while browsing Yahoo! — which you, like many Web surfers, may even use as your home page — you can drop in and see what's new in the plug-in arena. Still, the other plug-in resources are better bets for serious plug-in search-and-install operations.

Installing and Uninstalling Plug-ins

What happens when you've found a plug-in that you'd like to install on your machine? You want to integrate the plug-in into your browser, and thereby make your browser more flexible and useful. How can you do it?

Also, what happens when a plug-in outlives its useful life span, and the space it ties up on your hard disk outweighs any benefit you get from having it there? How do you uninstall a plug-in? This section answers both questions.

Installing plug-ins

Appendix A shows you how to install the contents of the CD-ROM. You'll learn about downloaded files in this section.

Specific procedures for installing particular plug-ins are part of each plug-in's write-up in subsequent chapters. You'll find the details of getting, decompressing, and running setup programs in Chapters 2 through 8.

Here are some general tips:

✦ When you download a file, save it in a temporary directory by itself. That way the downloaded file won't interfere with decompressed files in the same directory.

✦ Always shut down your browser after downloading a plug-in and restart it only after the plug-in has installed completely. When your browser restarts (and only when it restarts), it looks for new plug-ins.

✦ The best plug-in-distribution scheme is an executable file that runs the setup program as soon as you run the file. Other plug-ins come as self-extracting archives that require you to run a setup program (usually called SETUP) after you run the downloaded file to extract its contents. To extract the contents of still other downloaded files, you have to use a program such as WinZip or StuffIt, and then run the setup file.

To decompress archived files, you'll need an archive program for your machine. Fortunately, free versions of such programs are all over the Web. Windows users can get the evaluation version of WinZip at `http://www.blackrhino.com/winzip_x.htm`. Macintosh jockeys can get the shareware version of StuffIt Lite at `http://www.aladdinsys.com/`.

Uninstalling a plug-in

Most plug-ins come with an uninstall program that undoes what the setup program did. By running the uninstall program, you can usually remove all traces of a plug-in on your disk and on your desktop. You'll find a plug-in's uninstall program in the folder in which the plug-in resides or, in the case of Windows 95 systems, in a folder that branches from the Start menu.

When you run an uninstall program, try to automate its function as much as possible, since the program probably has a good idea of the location of its components. If there's an Automatic Uninstall option presented to you, take it.

Many plug-ins, though, don't have accompanying uninstall programs. In that case, you need to go through your hard disk and manually delete the files the plug-in installation routine put there.

Look for files to delete in the PLUGINS folder in your NETSCAPE/NAVIGATOR/PROGRAM folder. Delete any sub-folders named after the plug-in you want to ax and delete any library files (DLL files on Windows machines or plug-in files on Macintoshes) that bear the name of the offending plug-in. (Sometimes these files have obscure names.) You can verify the .DDLs that correspond to a particular plug-in via the About Plug-ins command in your browser. Shut down and restart your browser, and the plug-in should be gone.

A recent HTML standards-setting conference resolved to replace the <EMBED> tag with<OBJECT>, a new tag that serves the same purposes, plus some new ones. Soon, you may have to use the <OBJECT> tag instead of the <EMBED> tag.

Authoring for Plug-ins

The appeal of most plug-ins is that they allow you to display unusual kinds of information on your Web pages. You can use a plug-in, for example, to fit MPEG movie clips into your pages or to display Microsoft Word documents. You need to create those files before you embed them, and that requires at least one specialized program.

Explaining how to use authoring programs isn't the function of this book — and many of the programs you use to create content for plug-ins are so complex, they have entire books devoted to them. Instead, *Netscape Plug-in Power* tells you which program you should use to create material in the information box at the opening of each plug-in section. This book assumes you either know how to use popular programs such as AutoCAD and Macromedia Director, or know where to look for instructions. In the case of less well-known as Powersoft's media.splash, the "Authoring for..." section gives some basic information, and directs you to further information on the Web.

To actually attach the files you create to Web pages, you'll have to learn a little new HTML. The important tag here is <EMBED>. It's used very much like the <IMG> tag, which is used to embed GIF and JPEG still graphics in Web pages. <EMBED> has three mandatory attributes and can handle several more if specific plug-ins require them.

The basic attributes are the following:

   + **SRC.** Defines the URL (filename, directory and filename, or full Internet URL) of the file to be embedded (as does the <IMG> tag).
   + **HEIGHT.** Defines the height, in pixels, of the space to be opened for the embedded file.
   + **WIDTH.** Defines the width, in pixels, of the space to be opened for the embedded file.

A typical usage of the <EMBED> tag, with the three mandatory attributes, is:

```
<EMBED SRC="JBOAT.MPG" HEIGHT=200 WIDTH=400>
```

That tag would open a rectangle 400 pixels wide and 200 pixels tall and fill it with the contents of JBOAT.MPG, an MPEG movie. You might use that example code to call the PreVU plug-in.

Building a Plug-in

Netscape Plug-in Power is meant to help you find and use plug-ins that are available on the Web. But because these plug-ins may not fit your needs exactly, it may be worth your time and money to hire a team of developers to build a plug-in that does.

On the other hand, the market for plug-ins is expanding constantly; and the odds are excellent that if you need a certain kind of plug-in for your browser, someone else does too — and might even pay for copies. With the explosion in the number of corporate intranets based on Internet and Web protocols, more people are using Web browsers to access corporate information on building-sized networks every day. If you design a plug-in that helps communicate a certain kind of engineering data or transmits files from an obscure presentation-graphics package over a network, the odds are quite good that someone else needs software for the same purpose. You can earn goodwill from the Web community by making your new plug-in freely available to the public or (much less likely) make some money by selling it.

There's another way around the MIME type problem that isn't as graceful as re-configuring your server and may slow your site's performance slightly, but it does the job. You may want to do this if your ISP is uncooperative or if you can't figure out how to get MIME type information into your server, and you are in a hurry.

MIME type difficulties arise only when a MIDI file is transferred via the Hypertext Transport protocol (HTTP). You can get around the problem by using File Transfer Protocol (FTP) instead. Put the file you want to embed on an FTP server (not a Web server), and use the following <EMBED> statement, assuming that you're working with a MIDI file in directory /MUSIC on FTP server "ftpserver.foo.com":

```
<EMBED SRC="ftp://ftpserver.foo.com/music/FANDANGO.MID
       WIDTH=200 HEIGHT=50>
```

That does the trick — not gracefully, but in a hurry.

The details of building a plug-in are beyond the scope of this book. This section serves only to give you some general background information about the programming architecture behind plug-ins and to direct you to more information in the event you want to start programming plug-ins. If you're interested in putting together a Netscape plug-in, you should make sure you have the proper background — basically, familiarity with Microsoft Foundation Class programming techniques. You should also have and be able to use a good C++ development package such as Microsoft Visual C++.

The plug-in API

How do small companies design programs to work with the big-name browsers? Aren't the browsers' inner workings closely held trade secrets?

Plug-in developers know how to make their products work with the browsers in the same way the makers of Windows and Macintosh programs know how to make their products work within their respective operating systems. Just as Microsoft maintains a set of technical specifications — called an Application Program Interface (API) — that defines how programs must share system resources while running under Windows, Netscape maintains an API that specifies how plug-ins work with its browser (Microsoft decided to make version 3.0 of its browser accept plug-ins that conform to the Netscape API, instead of writing its own). The advantage of public APIs such as the one for Netscape plug-ins is that they enable outside developers (Heads Off and Totally Hip, for example) to get the information they need to write useful programs (plug-ins, in this case) while protecting proprietary information that outside developers don't need.

Take a look at the Netscape Plug-in Guide at `http://home.netscape.com/eng/mozilla/2.0/handbook/plugins/index.html`, which includes all the information in the Netscape plug-in API.

If you're going to develop plug-ins for multiple platforms (Macintosh, Windows 95, and UNIX, for example), you need to be aware of the differences in the plug-in APIs among those operating systems. The Macintosh and UNIX APIs have slightly more powerful features than the APIs for Windows 3.1 and Windows 95. The Netscape Plug-in Guide explains the differences among the APIs.

The Plug-in Software Development Kit

You'll probably want a copy of the Netscape Plug-in Developers Software Development Kit (SDK) to ease the plug-in creation process a bit, since coding by hand and manually checking for compliance with the appropriate API adds monumental quantities of time to your plug-in development process.

The Netscape SDK is a set of programming tools that helps you design and code plug-ins that comply with the Netscape plug-in API. You'll find the SDK in both Macintosh and Windows versions at `http://home.netscape.com/comprod/development_partners/plugin_api/index.html`.

The Netscape Plug-in SDK includes these components:

✦ A compiler

✦ A debugger

✦ A complete copy of the API and some other technical documentation

✦ Some sample code that can serve as the framework for your projects

Bear in mind that the SDK won't make plug-in development much easier if you're not a skilled C++ programmer. You can compare the SDK to a surgeon's instruments: They're quite useful in properly trained hands, but they're useless to someone untrained to use them.

A Word From The Experts

Vijay Mukhi, Sonal Kotecha, and Shashank Tripathi have assembled an overview of plug-in programming at `http://www.neca.com/~vmis/plugins.html`. Their guide is full of wit and useful information and should be your first stop as you research plug-in programming.

Sound

Sound and the Web go together well. You can incorporate sound into your Web pages and achieve a whole new dimension in coolness, but without the galactic bandwidth demands that attend video, animation, and virtual reality. It's not hard to record and edit sounds, and lots of sounds are in the public domain. In short, you can dramatically increase your site's appeal — or your surfing enjoyment, if that's your angle — by getting clued in to plug-ins that expand your browser's audio capability.

The plug-ins in this chapter handle sounds. With these tools installed on your computer, you can hear everything from the music of the Doors, to the sound of a baby crying, to little click and chirps that accompany animated sequences. With sound-enhanced Web pages, you'll be guaranteed to get some oohs and ahs from those who visit your site — without getting the angry words that so often result from bandwidth-greedy animation and video clips.

New versions of Netscape Navigator — versions 3.0 and later — come with a plug-in called LiveAudio that plays MPEG, .AU and .WAV audio files. LiveAudio is okay for some applications, but it's pretty crude in many ways, especially if you plan to work with large audio files. One of the main shortcomings of LiveAudio is that it doesn't stream data — you must wait for the entire file to download before you hear anything. The plug-ins in this chapter are more sophisticated plug-ins that make your browser work better.

When you're using your favorite sound-editing program to create sounds for your Web site, remember that short is better. Even when you're creating sound for plug-ins such as Crescendo Plus and RealAudio that *stream* sound files (that is, play the files as they are downloaded rather than wait until the download is complete before beginning to play the files), big files can be ponderous. For one thing, they'll take bandwidth away from the other information on your pages; meaning that your visitors may have to wait longer for the still graphics to download because a sound clip is wending its way from server to browser in the background.

Besides, Web surfers are a furtive bunch — they're not going to hang around your site long enough to listen to all of Aaron Copland's *Appalachian Spring*. A better bet is to design a short, memorable instrumental or vocal jingle to associate with your site — and perhaps loop it. Check out The Secret Organization's site (http://www.secret.org/). I don't know what the Organization does, but its looped three-second drum clip will stick in your mind and remind you of the mysterious nature of the site. The Secret Organization's sound comes to you via a Java applet, but you could achieve the same effect with carefully chosen plug-ins.

Crescendo

Creator: LiveUpdate

Function: Plays MIDI files embedded in Web pages

Home Site: http://www.liveupdate.com/crescendo.html

Supported Platforms: All Windows and Macintosh systems

Authoring Tool: Any program that generates MIDI sound files, such as Cakewalk

Good Examples: Glen Flood Music Productions at http://www.frontiernet. net/~gmflood/; the Café Internet at http://www.novagate.com/ ~cafeinternet/; Susan Hudgins' home page at http://oz.net/~susanh/ (see Figure 2-1)

Crescendo brings the Musical Instrument Digital Interface (MIDI), the granddaddy of all electronic music file formats, into the age of the Web. With LiveUpdate's Crescendo, Web page publishers can attach musical backgrounds — what radio people would call "beds" — to Web pages. Cooler still, Crescendo lets page designers hand control of the music over to site visitors with a CD player-like control panel. With Crescendo's control panel, surfers who encounter a Crescendo-enhanced site can turn off the sound if they don't want to tie up bandwidth or scan back and forth through a selection for a passage that interests them. Crescendo is a publisher's dream that doesn't impinge on the freedom of Web users.

As testament to the virtues of Crescendo, scores of sites that employ it already have sprung up. Crescendo seems to be especially popular on the home pages of amateur and professional musicians who use the plug-in to share their work with Web users. This is a real service: Music that wouldn't make it out of the garage without the Web is getting global exposure, thanks to LiveUpdate and its excellent product.

Plug-in Power Rating: ★★★★

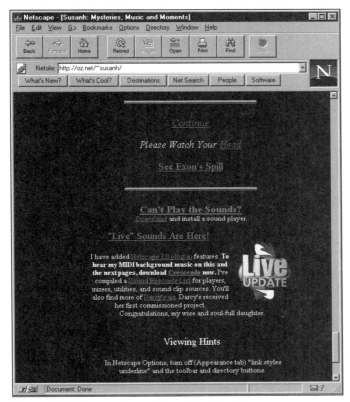

Figure 2-1: Crescendo on Susan Hudgins' home page.

At the core of Crescendo is the MIDI file format, a long-standing, popular means of encoding music electronically. Simply put, MIDI works by assigning a number to each of 128 musical instruments, voices, and sound effects. A violin, for example, is instrument number 41, while a church organ is instrument 20, and a gunshot is "instrument" 128. A MIDI file contains instructions that amount to, "Play a D-flat on instrument 20 while playing a C on instrument 41. Then, after three-quarters of a second, have instrument 20 change to C-sharp . . ." and so on.

The trouble with MIDI is that in order for MIDI-encoded music to sound right, you need a high-end sound card. A *wavetable-synthesis* sound card is programmed with exactly the right tone for each of the 128 MIDI instruments. An *FM synthesis* sound card — the less-expensive kind that most people, other than serious musicians, have — can depict each of the MIDI instruments, but not as accurately as a wavetable-synthesis card. FM-synthesized instruments sound much more tinny and "computerish" than wavetable-synthesized sounds.

So, if you're playing a MIDI-encoded Brahms symphony with Crescendo, and it sounds more like the ice cream truck than the National Symphony Orchestra, don't blame MIDI or the plug-in you're using to play it. Understand that it's your sound card that's causing the problem.

Installing Crescendo

To install Crescendo on a Windows 95 or Windows 3.*x* system:

1. Point your browser at `http://www.liveupdate.com/dl.html`. Fill in the two blanks with your name and e-mail address and click on the Submit button. Then click on the icon representing your operating system.

2. On the page that appears next, click on one of the three download sites. If one site doesn't work, it's probably overloaded. Try another.

3. Save the downloaded files to a new folder by themselves.

4. Shut down your browser.

5. Double-click on the new executable file in the folder you just created. You'll see a WinZip dialog box. Accept the defaults outlined in this box and click on the Unzip button. Click on the OK button when the extraction program tells you it unzipped four files correctly.

6. Scan the README.DOC file that appeared on your screen for any new information.

7. Move the file NPMIDI32.DLL (for Windows 95 and Windows NT) or NPMIDI16.DLL (for Windows 3.x) to your browser's PLUGINS folder.

8. Restart your browser. Crescendo should be installed and ready to go.

To install Crescendo on a Macintosh system:

1. Point your browser at `http://www.liveupdate.com/dl.html`. Fill in the two blanks with your name and e-mail address and click on the Submit button.

2. Click on the icon for MacOS.

3. On the page that appears next, click on one of the three download sites. If one site doesn't work, it's probably overloaded. Try another.

4. Use StuffIt, StuffIt Lite, or StuffIt Expander to decompress the file you download. If you don't have a StuffIt program, get a copy of StuffIt Expander at `http://www.aladdinsys.com/obstufex.htm`.

5. Shut down your browser.

6. From the Crescendo folder that your StuffIt program created when it decompressed the downloaded material, drag the Crescendo 2.0 file (the filename may have changed by the time you download Crescendo) to the plug-ins folder in your browser's folder.

7. Restart your browser. Crescendo will be ready for use.

 In order to run Crescendo on the Macintosh, you need to have QuickTime 2.1 or later installed on your machine. You can get QuickTime from Apple at http://quicktime.apple.com

Using Crescendo

As is the case with most sound plug-ins, using Crescendo is normally very easy — you just call up a Crescendo-enabled page and the plug-in handles all the work of translating the data in the MIDI file into sound emanating from your speakers. (Of course, you have to make sure your speakers are on — an important step that gets neglected dozens of times.) Unlike most of the other plug-ins in this chapter, though, Crescendo gives page designers the option of including a control panel that lets page visitors control the music much as they would control a song playing on their CD player. In fact, the Crescendo control panel looks a lot like a CD player's control panel. By employing this metaphor (one that's familiar to most people who work on computers), Crescendo increases its ease-of-use by several orders of magnitude. Figure 2-2 shows the Crescendo control panel (on the Café Internet page) with labels on its various parts.

Here's a brief explanation of what each of the buttons on the control panel does:

✦ **Rewind.** Starts playing the musical passage at the beginning.

✦ **Back 10 seconds.** Starts playing the musical passage 10 seconds before the current point.

✦ **Pause.** Stops playing. To release a pause, you can click on either the Pause button or the Play button.

✦ **Play.** Begins playing.

✦ **Forward 10 seconds.** Starts playing the musical passage 10 seconds after the current point.

✦ **Help.** Takes you to a page on LiveUpdate's site that leads you to the Crescendo technical support area (if you have purchased Crescendo Plus and have the necessary password) or to a page on which you can order Crescendo Plus.

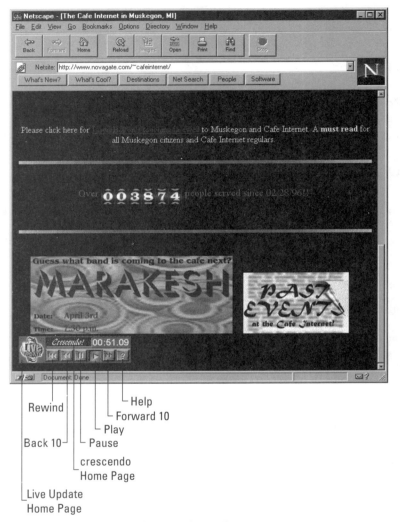

Figure 2-2: The Crescendo control panel.

In addition to the buttons, there are two other clickable regions on the Crescendo control panel. When clicked on, the script "Crescendo!" above the control buttons takes you to the Crescendo home page (http:\\www.liveupdate.com\ crescendo). The LiveUpdate logo on the left side of the control panel, when click oned, takes you to the LiveUpdate corporate home page (http://www. liveupdate.com).

Plugged-in sites

Because Crescendo is the first and best implementation of streamed MIDI music, it is used in scores of pages on the Web. The most comprehensive listing of these pages is part of the LiveUpdate site at `http://www.liveupdate.com/ sites.html`. LiveUpdate also features a Cool Site of the Day at `http://www. liveupdate.com/sod.html`. That page features past Cool Sites, too.

Here are a few jewels from the LiveUpdate list:

✦ The Chicagoland Car-Finder (`http://www.chicagocar.com/`). Visit this site even if — perhaps especially if — you're not trying to buy or sell a motor vehicle in the Chicago area. In addition to the Crescendo-based embedded music, the Car-Finder has lots of other sharp Web tricks, including animated buttons and a live clock. And no, the imitation LED level bar below the Crescendo control panel isn't linked to the music. It's just a series of still images shown in sequence. Nonetheless, it's pretty nifty, and it emphasizes the audio aspect of the page with a visual element. Figure 2-3 shows the Chicagoland Car-Finder.

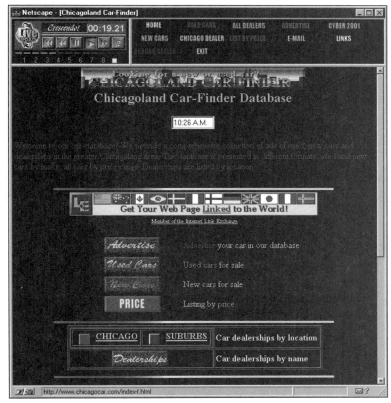

Figure 2-3: The Chicagoland Car-Finder.

✦ And In the Dark (http://www.surfsouth.com/~brad/). A guide to the music of "Roxette, Enya, Julee Cruise, The Beatles, Pink Floyd, Chris Isaak, Collective Soul and Vivaldi." It's good to see that Brad McCall, the maintainer of this site, has limited musical tastes. His site uses Crescendo (without the control panel) to play a brief snippet of background music that loops over and over.

✦ The Journey home page (http://webcom.net/~sdlake/journey.html). Ah, Journey. Big 1980's flashback. This is a standard band-fan page, with news about the group's members and links to other Web resources. The page incorporates a complete MIDI version of Journey's "Faithfully" that sounds really silly on an FM-synthesis sound card, but probably sounds great on a wavetable card.

Authoring for Crescendo

Acquiring MIDI files is a piece of cake — they're all over the Web in archives, and building your own is as easy as getting and learning how to use some MIDI-aware sound-editing software. Cakewalk Music Software (http://www.cakewalk.com/) and SoundTrek (http://www.soundtrek.com/) make good MIDI software.

Embedding MIDI files for Crescendo is just like embedding multimedia files for any other plug-in. You use the <EMBED> tag, with SRC, WIDTH, and HEIGHT attributes, to define where Crescendo's control panel will appear, and what sound file it will be linked to. A typical <EMBED> usage for Crescendo looks like this:

```
<EMBED SRC="FANDANGO.MID" WIDTH=200 HEIGHT=50>
```

Note that the control panel is 200 pixels wide and 50 pixels high. If you do not want the control panel to appear on your site, you should specify WIDTH=0 and HEIGHT=2.

Don't forget to configure your server to handle MIME types and audio/midi, audio/x-midi, application/x-midi, and audio/x-midi with filename extensions .MID and .MIDI.

Crescendo Plus

Creator: LiveUpdate

Function: Plays MIDI files embedded in Web pages just like regular Crescendo — but Crescendo Plus uses streaming technology

Home Site: http://www.liveupdate.com/crescendo.html

Supported Platforms: All Windows and Macintosh systems

Authoring Tool: Any program that generates MIDI sound files, such as Cakewalk

Good Examples: The Kool Kat Club at `http://isis.infinet.com/koolkat/index.html`; the Café Internet at `http://www.novagate.com/~cafeinternet/`; Glen Flood Music Productions at `http://www.frontiernet.net/~gmflood/`

Crescendo Plus is the for-a-fee version of the excellent Crescendo plug-in, discussed above. The two products are similar, with the following key exceptions:

✦ Crescendo Plus employs streaming technology, meaning a MIDI file starts to play before it downloads completely. This is the main difference between Crescendo and Crescendo Plus, and it's an important one.

✦ In Crescendo Plus, you can right-click on or long-click on the control panel and get a Save As command that lets you save a MIDI file to disk.

✦ Crescendo Plus has a volume control and a button that lets users disable looping.

✦ Crescendo Plus costs $19.95, U.S.

Plug-in Power Rating: ★★★★

Installing Crescendo Plus

You use precisely the same technique as you do when installing Crescendo, except that you must buy the software. Check out your options — including a secure server to which you can transmit a credit card number — at `http://www.liveupdate.com/buy.html`.

Using Crescendo Plus

Although Crescendo Plus works basically the same as Crescendo, there are two differences:

✦ With the volume control, you can adjust the playback volume of the music.

✦ With the loop button, you can stop a selection from looping (that is, playing over and over again).

Plugged-in sites

Any site that works with Crescendo works better with Crescendo Plus.

Authoring for Crescendo Plus

With Crescendo Plus, authoring is exactly the same as it is for Crescendo, MIME, and other similar programs.

EchoSpeech

Creator: Echo Speech

Function: Plays compressed speech

Home Site: http://www.echospeech.com/plugin.htm

Supported Platforms: All Windows systems. The company says Macintosh variants will be available soon

Authoring Tool: The EchoSpeech Coder Program (at http://www.echospeech.com/coder.htm)

Good Examples: The Los Angeles Dodgers' home page at http://www.dodgers.com/; the Duke Nukem 3D page at http://www.3drealms.com/duke3d.html; Radio Hope at http://www.radiohope.org/; the American Comedy Platoon at http://members.gnn.com/acplatoon/acp1.htm (see Figure 2-4)

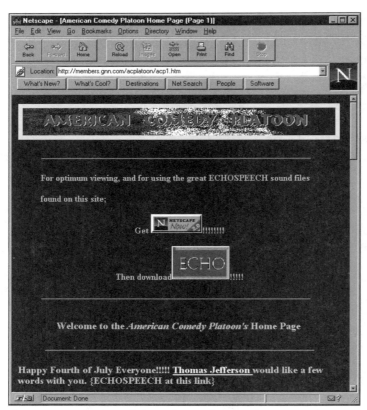

Figure 2-4: EchoSpeech in action at the American Comedy Platoon site.

EchoSpeech isn't just another audio player plug-in — it's a carefully designed system for transmitting recorded human speech across the Web. Though it hasn't really caught on since the May, 1996 release of its current version, EchoSpeech includes one of the most important elements of Web success: technical innovation.

EchoSpeech uses a nifty algorithm that looks at the contents of .WAV files and interprets them in the way the human vocal apparatus would. It then reduces the .WAV-encoded sound information to a much smaller, proprietary .ES format tailored to the EchoSpeech plug-in.

Can you encode music with EchoSpeech technology? Yes, but it doesn't sound very good. Since the EchoSpeech Coder Program looks at sounds and tries to reproduce them as the human voice would, music tends to fall outside its capabilities. Imagine trying to generate the sounds of a five-piece rock band with your voice, and you'll understand the situation.

In brief, EchoSpeech works very well to encode voices, but not so well for music. It's a good choice for Web pages that must instruct, persuade, or entertain with voice communication.

Plug-in Power Rating: ★★★

Installing EchoSpeech

To attach EchoSpeech to your browser:

1. Point your browser at `http://www.echospeech.com/plugin2.htm`.

2. Click on the link for the version of EchoSpeech you want: the 32-bit version for Windows 95 and Windows NT, or the 16-bit version for Windows 3.*x*.

3. When your browser asks where you want to save the file you're downloading (either NPE32_12.EXE or NPE16_12.EXE) specify your browser's PLUGINS directory.

4. Shut down your browser.

5. Double-click on the file you downloaded. Accept the default settings in the WinZip Self-Extractor dialog box by clicking on the Unzip button. The program will extract a file called NPECHO32.DLL (for Windows 95 and Windows NT) or NPECHO16.DLL (for Windows 3.*x*).

6. After the file unzips, click on the OK button in the confirmation dialog box and close the WinZip Self Extractor dialog box.

7. Restart your browser. EchoSpeech will be ready to go.

Using EchoSpeech

When you call up a page with an embedded EchoSpeech voice, the plug-in will begin to do its work right away, automatically. The important part of an EchoSpeech-enabled page, as far as the voice is concerned, is the yellow "EchoSpeech — The Voice of the Web" box. The box appears in Figure 2-5.

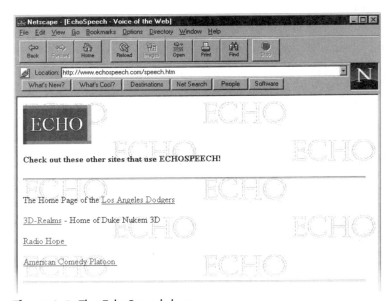

Figure 2-5: The EchoSpeech box.

Clicking on it in various ways controls the behavior of the EchoSpeech plug-in:

   ✦ To pause while playing the sound file, click on the box.

   ✦ To un-pause the sound file, click on it again.

   ✦ To restart the sound file after it has finished playing, click on the box.

   ✦ To access the Echo Speech home page, right-click on the box.

That's all there is to using the EchoSpeech plug-in once it's installed as part of your browser.

Plugged-in sites

Few sites have chosen EchoSpeech for voice encoding purposes, even though it's an excellent means of encoding and transmitting voice. It seems that most Webmasters have chosen general-purpose sound-encoding solutions, such as RealAudio, rather than single-purpose voice encoders.

Still, a few brave site designers have opted to go with EchoSpeech to encode voice data on their Web pages. Some of these have only a few sentences encoded with EchoSpeech; others have more elaborate offerings. The number of sites with EchoSpeech content surely will grow in the coming months.

Here are some of the early EchoSpeech offerings:

✦ The Los Angeles Dodgers' home page (`http://www.dodgers.com/`). The announcer says, "Welcome to Dodger Online, the official Web site of the Los Angeles Dodgers." You can get game summaries at `http://www.dodgers.com/audio/replay.es` — altogether, an excellent resource for Dodgers fans too distant to get the team's daily radio broadcasts. Figure 2-6 shows the Dodgers' welcome page — including welcomes in five different languages.

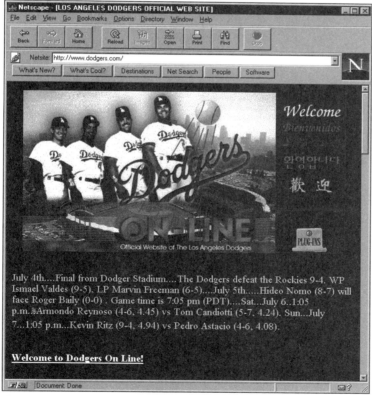

Figure 2-6: The Los Angeles Dodgers' home page (`http://www.dodgers.com/`), home of EchoSpeech clips.

✦ Radio Hope (http://www.radiohope.org/). A web radio station featuring "the voice of a lost generation." There was only one EchoSpeech clip on this site at this writing, and it included lots of music and therefore sounded weird. Basically, Radio Hope is a sort of Christian media outlet that tries to tell the stories of people with some serious problems — addictions, depression, and the like. It's a pretty cool Web site, in any case. Figure 2-7 shows Radio Hope.

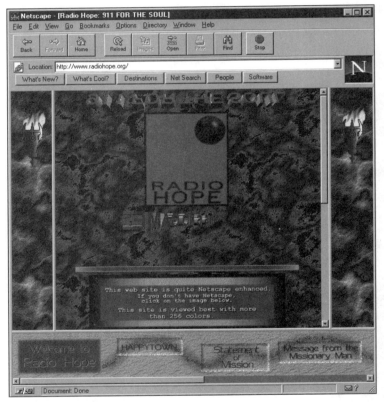

Figure 2-7: Radio Hope.

✦ The American Comedy Platoon (http://members.gnn.com/ acplatoon/acp1.htm). Just one little clip on this page — a spoof of President Clinton lampooning Hillary about the Whitewater scandal. It's dittohead humor from a Republican comedy troupe.

Authoring for EchoSpeech

To publish EchoSpeech content on your pages, you must begin with a high-quality PCM-format .WAV file sampled at 11 kilohertz with 16-bit samples. Then, using the simply named EchoSpeech Coder Program available via a link from `http://www.echospeech.com/plugin.htm`, you translate the .WAV file into EchoSpeech's unique .ES format. The Coder Program is simple — you just specify source and output files and click on an Encode button. You can read more about the Coder Program at `http://www.echospeech.com/coderhlp.htm`.

Using the `<EMBED>` tag, you attach your .ES file to a Web page. Here's an example:

```
<EMBED SRC="GREETING.ES" WIDTH=200 HEIGHT=50>
```

In this example, the file GREETINGS.ES is designated to be played by EchoSpeech, and the yellow EchoSpeech box is 200 pixels wide by 50 pixels high.

 Configure your Web server to recognize MIME type `audio/echospeech`, which uses the .ES file extension.

Alternately, you can put your EchoSpeech files on a public FTP server and use the full FTP URL in your `<EMBED>` statements, like this:

```
<EMBED SRC="ftp://ftpserver.foo.com/voice/GREETING.ES WIDTH=200
       HEIGHT=50>
```

That's a shortcut around the problem, but it works.

Koan

Creator: Sseyo

Function: Plays MIDI files and music in the Koan format

Home Site: `http://www.sseyo.com/`

Supported Platforms: All Windows systems

Authoring Tool: Koan Pro

Good Examples: Passenger, at `http://www.sseyo.com/passeng.html`; the Koan File Gift Box at `http://www.sseyo.com/koangbox.html`

Claiming that Koan files of less than one kilobyte can play for more than eight hours, Sseyo is betting on Koan to be the Next Big Thing in network music (see Figure 2-8). Brian Eno, producer of David Bowie and U2 albums and expert in ambient music, has released an experimental collection of music recorded in the Koan format. Named for the mantra-like chants of Buddhist monks, Koan offers excellent compression ratios and high-fidelity playback of music.

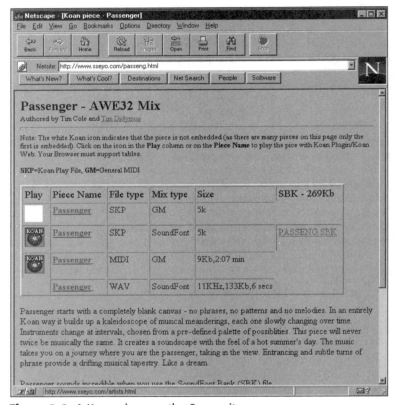

Figure 2-8: A Koan piece on the Sseyo site.

The Koan plug-in hasn't yet been proven, but you don't have to count on the Koan scheme's catching on in order to use the plug-in. The Koan plug-in plays ubiquitous MIDI files, too — making it a worthy competitor of several of the other plug-ins described in this chapter.

Plug-in Power Rating: ★★

It's not a bad idea to download the Koan Web Application from the Sseyo Web site, too. The Web application is a standalone Windows program that gives you extra control over the music that's playing via the plug-in.

Installing Koan

To install Koan on your Windows 95 or Windows 3.x system:

1. Point your browser at `http://www.sseyo.com/browser.html`.

2. In the table on that page, choose the file you want — either KNP1016.EXE for Windows 3.x, or KNP1032.EXE for Windows 95 and NT. Click on the link to that file.

3. Save the file you're downloading to a directory by itself.

4. After the download is complete, shut down your browser.

5. Double-click on the file you downloaded. It's a self-extracting WinZip archive. When the file finishes the decompression process, close the windows that WinZip opened.

6. If you're installing Koan on a Windows 3.x machine, run SETUP16.EXE. For Windows 95 or Windows NT, run SETUP32.EXE.

7. The installation program will ask you to confirm the components you want to install. Click on the Do the Install! button to install the named Koan components.

8. You'll see a dialog box asking you to confirm that it's OK to install Koan components in a directory called KOANWEB. Click on the Yes button if that's all right, or change the directory and click on Yes.

9. You'll get another dialog box, asking you to confirm that you want to install the Koan plug-in. Click on Yes.

10. Yet another dialog box will appear, asking you to find your NETSCAPE.EXE file (at this writing, Koan wasn't aware of the plug-in capabilities of Microsoft Internet Explorer). Hunt through your directory trees until you find the file, highlight it, and click on OK.

11. Click on Yes when the install program asks you to confirm the location you just selected.

12. Click on OK when the install program tells you that installation is complete, then read and clear the license agreement.

13. Restart your browser. Koan will be ready to go.

Using Koan

Using Koan couldn't possibly be easier. When you call up a page with an embedded Koan file, you start to hear the music coming from your speakers. The page looks like the one shown in Figure 2-9. You can click on the Koan icon in the center of the page to stop the music, and click on it again to restart it.

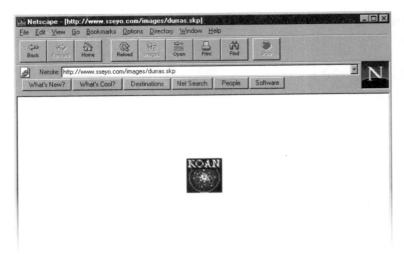

Figure 2-9: Koan playing a music clip.

If you want more control over the music that's playing, download the Koan Web Application from the Sseyo site. It's a helper application, really, but it's handy for playing a clip as you move from site to site and for altering the volume and other aspects of the music that's playing.

Plugged-in sites

Music in the Koan format isn't very popular on the Web — in fact, you'll be hard-pressed to find it anywhere but on the Sseyo Web site. There, there's a whole page devoted to free Koan music at `http://www.sseyo.com/koangbox.html`. That page, called the Koan File Gift Box, appears in Figure 2-10.

You can also order Koan music through the mail. Generative Music 1, Brian Eno's first album in the Koan format, gets a lot of attention on the Sseyo site. Check it out at `http://www.sseyo.com/genmus1.html`.

Koan plays standard MIDI files, too; so if you can't find enough Koan-format music to suit your appetite, you can turn to the MIDI archives. There are better dedicated MIDI players discussed in this chapter, though; and if that's all you want, you're better off with one of those.

Authoring for Koan

Creating Koan files requires the Koan Pro Authoring System, a program designed to output music both in the proprietary Koan format and in MIDI format. There's a write-up about Koan Pro at `http://www.sseyo.com/kprobroc.html`, and a link at the bottom of that page through which you can download a demo version of the authoring program (the full version costs 140 British pounds — about $200 U.S.).

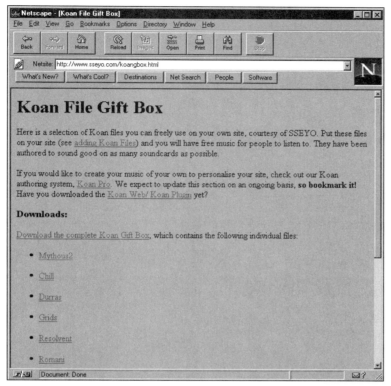

Figure 2-10: The Koan File Gift Box.

Once you've created Koan or MIDI files, you're faced with the task of embedding them in your Web pages. The <EMBED> tag is the tool to use. A typical Koan-file <EMBED> statement looks like this:

```
<EMBED SRC="SPACE.SKP" WIDTH=32 HEIGHT=32 AUTOSTART=TRUE>
```

That statement embeds a Koan icon 32 pixels square in a Web page and tells file SPACE.SKP to start automatically when the page is loaded. AUTOSTART also can be false, in which case, the file won't play until the surfer clicks on the icon.

There's one more attribute that you can use in <EMBED> statements for Koan: ALIGN. Set ALIGN to any of the following values:

- ✦ RIGHT, to push the icon to the right side of the page
- ✦ LEFT, to push the icon to the left side of the page
- ✦ TOP, to push the icon to the top of the page

✦ `MIDDLE`, to center the icon on the page

✦ `BOTTOM`, to push the icon to the bottom of the page

ListenUp

Creator: Bill Noon

Function: Gives some voice-recognition capability to your browser, letting you navigate from link to link by pronouncing key words and phrases

Home Site: `http://snow.cit.cornell.edu/noon/ListenUp.html`

Supported Platforms: Power Macintosh only, though Bill Noon says he'll compile a version for other Macintoshes if you ask him (`wn10@cornell.edu`)

Authoring Tool: ListenUp is based on Apple's PlainTalk speech recognition software, and requires MacOS version 7.5 or later. With those components installed on the computers that download your ListenUp-enabled Web pages, you can author pages for ListenUp with any text editor.

Good Examples: Only a couple: A single-page site at `http://snow.cit.cornell.edu/noon/ListenUp_test.html` and a multipage site at `http://snow.cit.cornell.edu/noon/ListenUp2_test.html`

The cool thing about the computer community, and particularly its network component, is the whangingly fun stuff that hobbyists come up with. Working on his own, without the support of a software company — and more to discover how plug-ins work than anything else — Bill Noon built ListenUp, a Macintosh plug-in that lets you navigate from page to page, not with a mouse, but with your voice (see Figure 2-11).

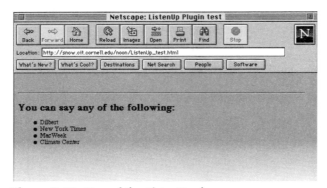

Figure 2-11: One of the ListenUp demo pages.

For example, if you were looking at a ListenUp-aware page on your screen and saw the words "visit Yahoo!" highlighted as a hyperlink, you could speak the word "Yahoo!" into your Mac's microphone and your browser would open the Yahoo! link. Think of the applications for personal hotlists — especially those of people with better control over their voices than their arms.

Bill Noon, in his experimentation, has created a real "gee-whiz" plug-in that everyone will enjoy.

Plug-in Power Rating: ★★★

Installing ListenUp

To install ListenUp on your Power Macintosh:

1. Make sure you have MacOS version 7.5 or later and PlainTalk Speech Recognition version 1.4.1 or 1.5a1 installed on your machine. You can download PlainTalk from Apple at `ftp://ftp.info.apple.com/Apple.Support.Area/Developer_Services/`.

2. Point your browser at `http://snow.cit.cornell.edu/noon/ListenUp.html`.

3. Click on the link (near the top of the page) for your version of PlainTalk. Noon's kind of hidden the links to the downloadable plug-in files in the list of requirements for running ListenUp.

4. Use StuffIt, StuffIt Lite, or StuffIt Expander to decompress the file you download. If you don't have a StuffIt program, get a copy of StuffIt Expander at `http://www.aladdinsys.com/`.

5. Shut down your browser.

6. Drag the ListenUp file to the plug-ins folder in your browser's folder.

7. Restart your browser. ListenUp will be ready for use.

Using ListenUp

Getting ListenUp to work for you is as easy as opening your mouth and speaking. Though your Mac may crash if the verbal command for accessing a link is too complex, that's a problem to be addressed on the publisher's side, not the surfer's side.

Using ListenUp is highly dependent upon how the designer of a page sets up his or her information. Specifically, the page has to tell you what to say in order to access specific links. Figure 2-11 is a good example — you can pronounce "Dilbert" and see the Dilbert site, or say "New York Times" to call up the Times Online site.

Make sure you speak clearly into your computer's microphone and try to minimize background noise as much as you can.

Note that there's no icon or other graphic in the little box that's reserved for the embedded ListenUp plug-in. That's coming soon, Noon says — along with some more handy features and increased reliability.

Plugged-in sites

Aside from the single demo page shown in Figure 2-11, there's only one other ListenUp-aware site on the Web. It's at `http://snow.cit.cornell.edu/noon/ListenUp_test2.html` and was also created by Noon. This page appears in Figure 2-12.

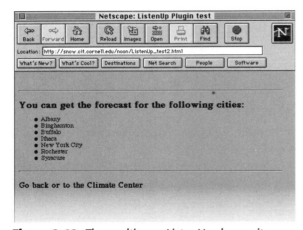

Figure 2-12: The multipage ListenUp demo site.

This site lets you use your voice to navigate to weather forecasts for each of seven cities in New York, then speak your way back to the main menu page.

Authoring for ListenUp

Since PlainTalk does all the hard work involved in ListenUp's operation, authoring for ListenUp isn't complicated. To make a page ListenUp-savvy, you have to insert an `<EMBED>` statement and create a simple script file.

The `<EMBED>` statement is minimally complex — it's just a `SRC` attribute, a `WIDTH` attribute, and a `HEIGHT` attribute. Here's a typical ListenUp `<EMBED>` statement:

```
<EMBED SRC="CMD.PTLK" WIDTH=1 HEIGHT=1>
```

That statement references the script file CMD.PTLK and makes the embedded box one pixel wide by one pixel high. You should make the box as small as possible until there's something to go inside it.

Creating the script is simple, too. You just list the verbal commands in quotes and equate them to the URLs you want the browser to access when each one is spoken, and PlainTalk does the rest. Here's an example:

```
# A sample script for ListenUp (the pound sign denotes
      a comment).
"Yahoo"=http://www.yahoo.com
"Deja News"=http://www.dejanews.com
"Big Book"=http://www.bigbook.com
```

That script, saved in plain text as CMD.PTLK and placed in the same folder as the Web document containing the `<EMBED>` tag above, would call up Yahoo when a user said "Yahoo" into his microphone, Deja News when he said "Deja News," and so on. It's a lot of fun to build a site based on ListenUp.

Publishers need to be aware of a couple of glitches in ListenUp's operation.

First, you get your server administrator to define MIME type `plugin/listenup` and associate it with the `.PTLK` file extension.

Second, you can only define 100 spoken phrases for each ListenUp-enabled Web page. This isn't a problem, because any page with more than 100 links would be impossible to navigate anyway.

MIDIPlug

Creator: Yamaha

Function: Plays MIDI music — and gives Web surfers a great deal of control over how it sounds

Home Site: `http://www.yamaha.co.jp/english/xg/html/midhm.html`

Supported Platforms: Power Macintosh and all Windows systems

Authoring Tool: Any program that can generate MIDI music files

Good Examples: Lots of clips that branch from `http://www.yamaha.co.jp/english/xg/html/3-6/no5.html`; a page that integrates graphics and MIDI music at `http://www.yamaha.co.jp/english/xg/html/photo/no6.html`

Computer people like to attach the phrase "yet another" to new instances of old inventions, for example, "yet another mail handler" or "yet another word processing program." Yamaha's MIDIPlug is yet another MIDI plug-in — totally serviceable and an okay choice for playing MIDI music, but nothing spectacular. Figure 2-13 shows MIDIPlug playing a clip on the Yamaha site.

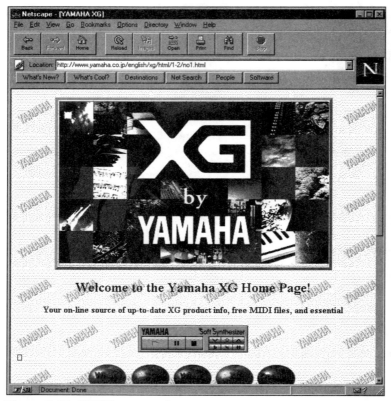

Figure 2-13: MIDIPlug at work.

Plug-in Power Rating: ★★

Installing MIDIPlug

To install MIDIPlug on your Windows system:

1. Point your browser at http://www.cyber-bp.or.jp/yamaha/ index_e.html.

2. Click on the link that says "Please register as a user." You'll need the number you get on the registration screen to download the software.

3. After you fill in the (lengthy) registration form, click on the Register button at the bottom of the page. You'll end up back at `http://www.cyber-bp.or.jp/yamaha/index_e.html` and you'll receive an e-mail message containing the user identification and the password you entered.

4. Click on the link for the version of MIDIPlug you want. You'll see a dialog box that asks for your user identification and password. Enter the values you entered on the registration page and click on OK.

5. Read the license agreement and, if you agree to its terms, click on the Agree button. The file will begin to download.

6. The file you're downloading is a .ZIP compressed file. If you've set up WinZip as a helper application on your browser, the distribution file will download, and WinZip will start automatically. If you have not set up WinZip as a helper application, you should do so — start by getting WinZip from `http://www.blackrhino.com`.

7. Have WinZip extract the contents of the file you downloaded to an empty temporary directory.

To install MIDIPlug on your Power Macintosh:

1. Point your browser at `http://www.cyber-bp.or.jp/yamaha/index_e.html`.

2. Click on the link that says "Please register as a user." You'll need the number you get on the registration screen to download the software.

3. After you fill in the (lengthy) registration form, click on the Register button at the bottom of the page. You'll end up back at `http://www.cyber-bp.or.jp/yamaha/index_e.html` and you'll receive an e-mail message containing the user identification and password you entered.

4. Click on the link for the Macintosh version of MIDIPlug. You'll see a dialog box that asks for your user identification and password. Enter the values you entered on the registration page and click on OK.

5. Read the license agreement, and, if you agree to its terms, click on the Agree button. The file will begin to download.

6. Use StuffIt, StuffIt Lite, or StuffIt Expander to decompress the file you download. If you don't have a StuffIt program, get a copy of StuffIt Expander at `http://www.aladdinsys.com/obstufex.htm`.

7. Shut down your browser.

8. Drag the MIDIPlug file to the plug-ins folder in your browser's folder.

9. Restart your browser. MIDIPlug will be ready for use.

Using MIDIPlug

MIDIPlug is a full-featured MIDI player, meaning that it (usually, according to the whim of the page author) gives you a control panel that lets you alter the way an embedded file plays back. Figure 2-14 shows the MIDIPlug control panel, with its important parts labeled. When you call up a MIDIPlug-enabled page, music may or may not start playing immediately. Whether it does or not, you control it with this panel.

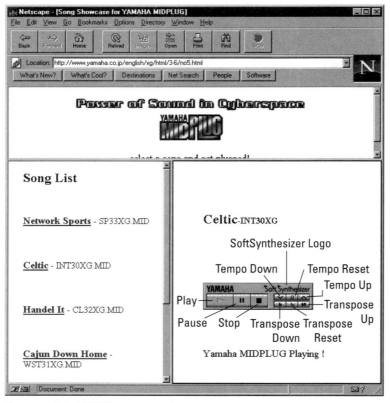

Figure 2-14: MIDIPlug's controls.

The important parts of the console are

+ **Play.** Starts the music.

+ **Pause.** Temporarily stops the music.

+ **Stop.** Halts the music and prepares to start again at the beginning.

✦ **Tempo Down.** Slows the pace of the music. This button turns green when the tempo has been decreased.

✦ **Tempo Reset.** Returns the pace of the music to its original level.

✦ **Tempo Up.** Boosts the pace of the music. This button turns green when the tempo has been increased.

✦ **Transpose Down.** Drops the music's key one semitone. This button turns green when the key has been lowered.

✦ **Transpose Reset.** Returns the key of the music to its original level.

✦ **Transpose Up.** Ups the music's key one semitone. This button turns green when the key has been increased.

✦ **Soft Synthesizer Logo.** Click on here for a pop-up menu containing the commands represented by the buttons.

Plugged-in sites

You'll find lots of MIDI music customized for MIDIPlug at `http://www.yamaha.co.jp/english/xg/html/3-6/no5.html`. From that page, you can choose any of a dozen links that will take you to music-enhanced pages.

One such page appears in Figure 2-15. It's a demonstration of integrating graphics with the MIDIPlug plug-in.

Authoring for MIDIPlug

You can create MIDI files to be played by MIDIPlug with any of a score (no pun intended) of music-editing programs. Once you've generated a MIDI file that you want to embed in your Web pages, use the `<EMBED>` tag to define how your file appears on the page.

A typical MIDIPlug `<EMBED>` statement looks like this:

```
<EMBED SRC="JOPLIN.MID" WIDTH=196 HEIGHT=49 AUTOSTART=TRUE
       REPEAT=TRUE>
```

That line of code reserves a rectangle 196 pixels wide and 49 pixels high for the control panel (those are its ideal proportions). You can hide the panel by setting `HEIGHT=0`.

The `AUTOSTART=TRUE` attribute tells MIDIPlug to start playing JOPLIN.MID as soon as the page is loaded, without waiting for intervention from the Web surfer. `REPEAT=TRUE` guarantees that the clip will loop — play over and over again.

Figure 2-15: MIDIPlug playing a music file.

MIDIPlug requires some server MIME type adjustment, too. Make sure the server is configured for MIME type audio/midi or audio/x-midi, associated with filename extension .MID.

MIDIPlugin

Creator: Arnaud Masson

Function: Plays MIDI music — with some special Karaoke features that let you sing along with your machine

Home Site: http://www.planete.net/~amasson/midiplugin.html

Supported Platforms: Power Macintosh

Authoring Tool: Any program, such as Cakewalk, that generates MIDI output

Good Examples: Daryl Lee's MIDI page at `http://pandora.library.ucsb.edu/~lee/midi`; Arnaud's MIDIPlugin page `http://www.planete.net/~amasson/midiplugin.html`

Not to be confused with MIDIPlug (above), MIDIPlugin is a player for embedded MIDI music that doubles as a simple Karaoke machine (see Figure 2-16). Karaoke, you may know, is a bar game in which the words to a song appear on a prompt screen as music plays in the background, and you get to imitate your favorite singing stars. MIDIPlugin lets you imitate Sonny and/or Cher to your heart's content without running the risk of appearing on an emotionally damaging videotape. Of course, you may irritate your neighbors; but that's another issue.

Developed by Arnaud Masson, MIDIPlugin illustrates that hobbyists can have an impact on the state of the art on the Web. This is a useful and fun plug-in that you'll enjoy having as part of your Web-surfing toolkit.

Plug-in Power Rating: ★★

Installing MIDIPlugin

To install MIDIPlugin on your Macintosh:

1. Point your browser at `http://www.planete.net/~amasson/midiplugin.html`.
2. Scroll down to the Downloading section of the page. Click on the link there. You may have to try a couple of times, because Arnaud's server is in France and it's apparently quite busy.
3. Use StuffIt, StuffIt Lite, or StuffIt Expander to decompress the file you download. If you don't have a StuffIt program, get a copy of StuffIt Expander at `http://www.aladdinsys.com/obstufex.htm`.
4. Shut down your browser.
5. Drag the MIDIPlugin file from the MIDIPlugin folder to your plug-ins folder.
6. Restart your browser. MIDIPlugin will be ready for use.

Using MIDIPlugin

Once again, the simple beauty of plug-in technology comes to the fore with MIDIPlugin's ease-of-use. When you call up a page that's equipped with embedded references to MIDIPlugin, you'll see a control panel similar to the one that appears in Figure 2-16.

This control panel parallels exactly the control panel on a typical CD player: both have (from left to right) a Stop button, a Play button, and a Pause button. The slider below the three buttons is a volume control — moving it to the right makes the music louder. As you move the slider, the simulated-LED bar graph below lights to match the position of the volume slider.

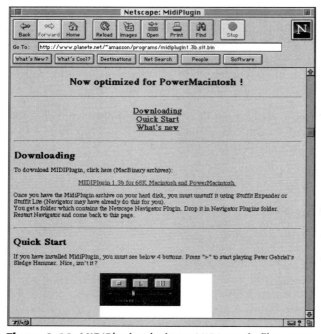

Figure 2-16: MIDIPlugin playing a MIDI music file.

Though Masson says his plug-in works as a Karaoke machine, I have neither managed to get it to work that way, nor contacted Masson (who is serving his obligation to the French military at the moment) to ask what's going on.

Plugged-in sites

You'll find a couple of cool clips (Peter Gabriel's "Sledgehammer" and the Eagles' "Hotel California") on the MIDIPlugin home Page (http://www.planete.net/ ~amasson/midiplugin.html). The Eagles' tune allegedly is outfitted to run in Karaoke mode.

You may also want to look at Darryl Lee's MIDI page (shown in Figure 2-17) at http://pandora.library.ucsb.edu/~lee/midi. Darryl has assembled a variety of hymns and other religious music on his page, and the page provides a fine text of MIDIPlugin and your sound hardware.

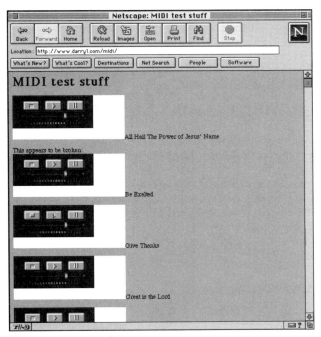

Figure 2-17: Darryl Lee's MIDI page.

Authoring for MIDIPlugin

You can create MIDI files with any of a dozen music-editing programs, and public-domain MIDI clips exist all over the Web. Getting MIDI music with which to use MIDIPlugin is not a challenge.

The trouble arises when you try to embed your MIDI file in a Web page. Documentation on how to do this is sparse or nonexistent. You can embed a MIDI file with this code:

```
<EMBED SRC="TUNE.MID" WIDTH=200 HEIGHT=80>
```

That statement does not, however, exploit any special attributes that MIDIPlugin may be able to handle, and it does not take advantage of MIDIPlugin's alleged Karaoke feature. Keep an eye on the MIDIPlugin home page for better documentation when Masson completes his military service.

MidiShare NetPlayer

Creator: GRAME

Function: Plays MIDI and QuickTime music files

Home Site: http://www.grame.fr/english/MidiShare.html

Supported Platforms: All Macintosh systems

Authoring Tool: MidiShare, or any program that generates MIDI or QuickTime music

Good Examples: La Rhétorique des Doigts at http://www.grame.fr/english/MidiShare.html; MIDI archives all over the Web

Part of a suite of MIDI tools, MidiShare NetPlayer is a slick implementation of a tired theme: the MIDI music player (see Figure 2-18). With its clever interface, MidiShare NetPlayer makes an attractive option for everyday Web surfing with the Macintosh. The plug-in's real strength lies, though, in its integration with the other tools in the MidiShare suite — making this plug-in an even more appealing choice for music professionals who need to capture, modify, and republish MIDI music.

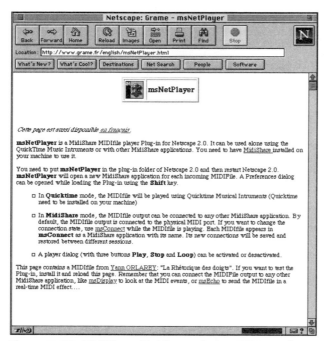

Figure 2-18: MidiShare NetPlayer playing MIDI music.

Plug-in Power Rating: ★★★

Installing MidiShare NetPlayer

To install MidiShare NetPlayer on your Macintosh, you must first install the MidiShare main program. To do that:

1. Point your browser at `http://www.grame.fr/english/ MidiShare_mac.html`.

2. Click on the link labeled MidiShare Kit.

3. Use StuffIt, StuffIt Lite, or StuffIt Expander to decompress the file you download. If you don't have a StuffIt program, get a copy of StuffIt Expander at `http://www.aladdinsys.com/obstufex.htm`.

4. Drag the MidiShare file extracted by StuffIt to your Control Panel folder.

5. Shut down and restart your computer. The MidiShare icon should appear at startup. You're now ready to download and install the MidiShare NetPlayer plug-in.

To install the plug-in:

1. Point your browser at `http://www.grame.fr/english/ msNetPlayer.html`.

2. Scroll to the bottom of the page and click on the link labeled Download msNetPlayer for Macintosh.

3. Use StuffIt, StuffIt Lite, or StuffIt Expander to decompress the file you download.

4. Shut down your browser.

5. Drag the NetPlayer file into your plug-ins folder.

6. Restart your browser. The MidiShare NetPlayer plug-in is ready for use.

Using MidiShare NetPlayer

It's another fire-and-forget MIDI player — unless you have more of the MidiShare tools residing on your Macintosh.

In its most basic implementation (the version that comes with this book on the accompanying CD-ROM), MidiShare NetPlayer has a Play button, a Stop button, and a Pause button, just as a standard CD player does. You can use MidiShare NetPlayer that way, but its real power becomes evident when you combine the power of the plug-in with the greater capabilities of the other MidiShare tools that GRAME sells for money.

With MidiShare Echo, for example, you can modify the characteristics of the file the plug-in is playing by adding reverberation, decreasing the volume, or doing any of a dozen other things. With MidiShare Connect, you can redirect the output from the plug-in into a file, a musical instrument, or any other MIDI device you've connected to your machine.

 When MidiShare NetPlayer is loading, press and hold the Shift key to call up the Preferences menu. With this menu, you can switch between the MIDI slate of instruments and the QuickTime collection of instruments. You must have QuickTime installed on your Macintosh for the QuickTime instruments to be available.

Plugged-in sites

As a generic MIDI player, you can take MidiShare NetPlayer all over the Web, looking for things to play. If your machine is outfitted with some of the MidiShare composing tools, you can break down the clips you capture and figure out what makes them sound the way they do.

Take a look at the Samply the Best MIDI Archive at `http://www.attache.nl/ tayfun/`, also shown in Figure 2-19. Samply the Best contains a huge collection of MIDI samples (hence the name), and you can play them all with MidiShare NetPlayer.

Figure 2-19: The Samply the Best MIDI Archive.

Authoring for MidiShare NetPlayer

MidiShare NetPlayer handles the task of playing standard MIDI music files, and they're all over the Web. They're also easy to create from scratch, using any of a dozen or more music editors that recognize the MIDI format.

To embed a MIDI file in a Web page, use a statement such as this one:

```
<EMBED SRC="TUNE.MID" WIDTH=100 HEIGHT=64 LOOP=TRUE
       AUTOSTART=TRUE>
```

That statement gives the MidiShare NetPlayer a space 100 pixels wide by 64 pixels high in which to put the control panel connected to the file TUNE.MID. LOOP=TRUE tells the plug-in to play TUNE.MID over and over, and AUTOSTART=TRUE tells the plug-in to start playing TUNE.MID as soon and the browser loads the page in which the clip is embedded.

Yep, it's the MIME type problem again. Here are the settings for MidiShare NetPlayer:

```
MIME type = audio/midi or audio/x-midi
filename extension = .mid
```

Rapid Transit

Creator: FastMan

Function: Plays CD-quality music compressed (at a ratio of 40-to-1 or better, the company says) with the Rapid Transit authoring tool

Home Site: http://monsterbit.com/rapidtransit/

Supported Platforms: Windows 95. FastMan had a Macintosh plug-in at one time, but it was unreliable, and the company withdrew it until it could be improved. They say the Mac version will be back soon. Keep your eye on http://monsterbit.com/rapidtransit/RTMacplg.html

Authoring Tool: Rapid Transit Encoder, which is temporarily not available

Good Examples: The 10,000 Maniacs at http://monsterbit.com/rapidtransit/maniacs.lcc; Linda Ronstadt at http://monsterbit.com/rapidtransit/linda.lcc (see Figure 2-20).

Figure 2-20: Rapid Transit playing Linda Ronstadt.

Claiming to be the solution to the problem of communicating high-quality voice and music recordings over the Web, Rapid Transit offers a unique scheme for file transfer. Instead of using streaming technology, as many of the other plug-ins in this chapter do, Rapid Transit uses a powerful compression procedure to shrink plain old .WAV files by factors of 40 or more, then transmit them to surfers' computers and quickly decompress them for playing. Rapid Transit's compression truly is impressive and probably represents a viable alternative to more-popular, streaming-based sound-encoding technologies. Upcoming versions of Rapid Transit will include streaming in addition to huge compression ratios.

Unfortunately, at least in the early beta that was available at this writing, Rapid Transit is crippled by a clunky user interface (there's no way to get sounds to play in the background while you look at a Web page's other contents, for example). You're forced to look at the product's logo while the plug-in does its stuff. It's still deep in beta-testing, though, and these problems are being worked out.

In brief, Rapid Transit is a good idea whose implementation surely will improve over time.

Plug-in Power Rating: ★★

Installing Rapid Transit

To install Rapid Transit on a Windows 95 system:

1. Point your browser at `http://monsterbit.com/rapidtransit/`
2. Click on the Download the RT player (Netscape Plug-in) link.
3. Save RTPLUG.EXE to a temporary directory by itself.
4. Shut down your browser.
5. Double-click on RTPLUG.EXE. It is a self-extracting .ZIP archive, and it will leave a large DOS window on your screen when it has finished unpacking files. Close the DOS window.
6. Run the file SETUP.EXE, which appeared in the temporary directory from which you ran RTPLUG.EXE. Follow the installation program's instructions.
7. Restart your browser. The Rapid Transit plug-in will be ready to go.

Using Rapid Transit

Rapid Transit isn't a streaming sound-encoding technology at this writing; so when you click on a link to a Rapid Transit song, the first thing you'll see is a dialog box with a bar graph that represents the plug-in's progress in downloading the Rapid Transit file. You can see this bar-graph dialog box in Figure 2-21.

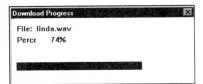

Figure 2-21: The Rapid Transit Download Progress dialog box.

Don't use the X button in the top-right corner of the Download-Progress dialog box to abort the download! If you try, you'll crash your browser and be left with part of the download-progress bar graph in the corner of your screen. If you start to download a Rapid Transit file accidentally, too bad — you'll have to wait for it to finish before you can move on.

After the sound file finishes downloading (the file is in .LCC form as it crosses the network, but the Rapid Transit plug-in decompresses it into .WAV form immediately after it comes to rest on your hard drive), you'll see the Rapid Transit logo on your screen. Take a look at it in Figure 2-22.

Figure 2-22: The Rapid Transit logo — what you see while a file plays.

The file you downloaded doesn't start playing automatically. To get it to play, you must right-click somewhere in your browser window and choose Play Downloaded File from the pop-up menu. When the clip is playing, you can stop it by right-clicking on and choosing Stop Playing from the pop-up menu. The pop-up menu appears in Figure 2-23.

You'll note that the pop-up menu has a third option on it — the one that says Play Other WAV Files. That option does precisely what you think. If you choose it, you'll get a standard Windows file-selection menu from which you can select another file to play via Rapid Transit.

The "Play Other WAV Files" option is actually quite handy, since Rapid Transit doesn't check to see what files already reside in your PLUGINS directory, which is where Rapid Transit deposits each of the files it downloads before it downloads the same file again. Rather than wait for even a short download, use the Play Other WAV Files option to return to files you've already downloaded.

Be aware that Rapid Transit puts .WAV files into your PLUGINS folder, and doesn't delete them automatically. If you're not careful, .WAV files will collect there, taking up hard drive space and ultimately harming the performance of your computer. Make sure you clean out sound files from your PLUGINS folder from time to time, especially if you use Rapid Transit a lot.

Figure 2-23: The Rapid Transit pop-up menu.

Plugged-in sites

The best place to go for Rapid Transit music is the Rapid Transit music selection menu at `http://monsterbit.com/rapidtransit/RTMusic.html`. There, you'll find links to Rapid Transit-encoded music of all kinds, from classical to country — and a deliciously ambiguous category called eclectic.

Here are some of the best Rapid Transit tunes on the Web. Many of them, particularly the rock and country songs, are under copyright; so it's unclear how long they will remain on the FastMan site:

✦ **The 10,000 Maniacs — Because the Night** (`http://monsterbit.com/rapidtransit/maniacs.lcc`): The same remake of the Springsteen hit you heard on the radio all the time a couple of summers ago. There's a little bit of screechiness in this file — but remember, I worked with an early beta version, and the crowd noise may confuse the encoding algorithm.

✦ **Linda Ronstadt — Desperado** (`http://monsterbit.com/rapidtransit/linda.lcc`): A single verse of this classic made popular by the Eagles. Rapid Transit compresses the thirty-second passage of music to 0.07 megabytes for transmission across the Net — a compression ratio of 44:1!

✦ **Steve Martin on Language** (http://monsterbit.com/rapidtransit/ martin.lc): Listen to one of the comedy kings of the last 20 years talk about the fun of international travel. Travel hint: When confronted with a French taxi driver who does not understand English, it is not helpful to address him in English — even if you affect a French accent on top of the words.

Authoring for Rapid Transit

Right now, you can't. The company sent out a bunch of copies of the Rapid Transit Encoder some time ago, but it's since stopped. Keep your eye on http://monsterbit.com/rapidtransit/RTMore.html for updates about the availability of the Rapid Transit Encoder.

RealAudio

Creator: Progressive Networks

Function: Plays high-quality sound, encoded in RealAudio format, almost as fast as it downloads

Home Site: http://www.realaudio.com/products/player2.0.html

Supported Platforms: All Windows, Macintosh, and UNIX systems

Authoring Tool: RealAudio Encoder (RealAudio Server is required to transmit data over the Web, too)

Good Examples: WBAL-AM at http://www.wbal.com; National Public Radio at http://www.npr.org; ABC News at http://www.realaudio.com/contentp/abc.html

No one had heard of streaming audio — or streaming anything else — before RealAudio came out in early 1995. It's the most popular streaming audio solution on the Web, used by everyone from ABC News to Radio HK, one of the first and best radio stations to broadcast worldwide on the Web. RealAudio isn't the invention of a freelance hacker or a struggling garage operation. It's the *de facto* standard for encoding voice and music in situations in which keeping the surfer entertained and informed, not audio quality, is the highest concern.

But even audio fidelity is becoming less of an issue with RealAudio, as successive versions of the encoding scheme boast ever-greater sound quality. When the first version of RealAudio hit the Web, the things it played sounded as though they were broadcast from a distant AM radio station. Now, it sounds like the AM station is right down the block, and sometimes the sound quality approaches that of an FM signal. Though it faces lots of competition from the other sound technologies described in this chapter, RealAudio still holds the lead in the battle for network sound supremacy. Figure 2-24 shows the National Public Radio site, one of the best and most popular RealAudio-enabled Web sites.

Plug-in Power Rating: ★★★★

Figure 2-24: RealAudio on the NPR site.

Installing RealAudio

To install the RealAudio plug-in on your Windows 95 or Windows 3.*x* system:

1. Point your browser at `http://www.realaudio.com/products/
   player2.0.html`.

2. Scroll to the bottom of the page and fill in the registration form. Specify your operating environment, processor type, and connection speed.

3. Click on the Go to download and instructions page button.

4. On the page that appears after you click on the button, click on the link to the download site that's best for you. Site 1 is intended for European surfers and people on the East Coast of the United States; Site 2 is best for U.S. West Coast Web users and people in Asia, Australia, and South America.

5. Save the file you download by itself in a temporary directory.

6. Shut down your browser.

7. Double-click on the file you just downloaded. You'll find that RealAudio is one of the easiest-to-install plug-ins out there — all you do is follow the instructions in the installation program that starts when you run the down-loaded file. The installation program takes care of everything, including restarting your browser for you. Once you complete the installation routine, you'll see the RealAudio player (a helper application that comes with the plug-in) as it plays a message of thanks from Progressive Networks. After that, the RealAudio plug-in is ready for use.

To install RealAudio on a Macintosh system:

1. Point your browser at `http://www.realaudio.com/products/player2.0.html`.

2. Scroll to the bottom of the page, and fill in the registration form. Specify your operating environment, processor type, and connection speed.

3. Click on the Go to download and instructions page button.

4. On the page that appears after you click on the button, click on the link to the download site that's best for you. Site 1 is intended for European surfers and people on the East Coast of the United States; Site 2 is best for U.S. West Coast Web users and people in Asia, Australia, and South America.

5. Shut down your browser.

6. Use StuffIt, StuffIt Lite, or StuffIt Expander to decompress the file you down-loaded. If you don't have a StuffIt program, get a copy of StuffIt Expander at `http://www.aladdinsys.com/obstufex.htm`.

7. Double-click on the RealAudio Installer file that sprang from the compressed archive. The installer program takes care of the nitty-gritty details of making your browser RealAudio-capable.

8. Restart your browser. You're ready to use RealAudio.

Using RealAudio

Having been the first on the scene with streaming sound, RealAudio knows a thing or two about how to present audio information. Many sites still use RealAudio as a helper application, possibly because their designers like having the RealAudio controls float as a separate application, away from the contents of the Web page itself. Other page designers embed controls in their pages, while still others hide the RealAudio paraphernalia altogether and have pages with music that plays automatically in the background.

Using the RealAudio controls is just like using the controls on a CD player, except for the slider bar that lets you move back and forth through a RealAudio recording (it's a pretty slick alternative to Fast-Forward and Rewind buttons).

Plugged-in sites

The Web sites that use RealAudio now probably number in the hundreds. Take a look at Progressive Networks' Timecast site at `http://www.timecast.com/` — one of the best. Timecast lets you select from a list of audio news and features sources — including ABC Radio News, ABC Radio Sports, Air Force Radio News, the Dow Jones Investors' Network, and the @Computerworld Minute — and play them in sequence, giving you a complete rundown of the news that interests you. You can also register with Timecast; so all you need to do is enter your user identification when you visit the site in order to get the news package you want. Timecast appears in Figure 2-25.

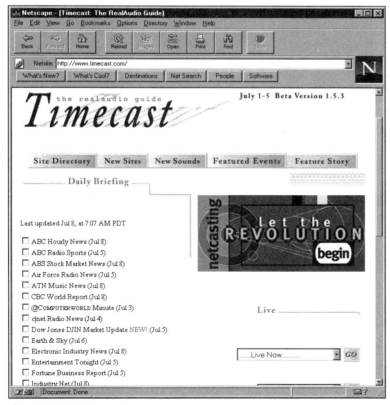

Figure 2-25: Timecast.

Some other notable RealAudio-enabled sites:

✦ ABC Radio News (http://www.realaudio.com/contentp/abc.html), which resides on the RealAudio site, is worthy of note by itself. Updated hourly, this is the same broadcast you hear on the radio. It's a great thing for people who like ABC Radio's hourly news digest, but who don't have a radio near their computers. Since this site uses the RealAudio helper application, you can start the newscast, then surf away to other sites as you listen to the news. Figure 2-26 shows the ABC Radio news page.

Figure 2-26: ABC Radio News.

✦ Word (http://www.word.com/) uses RealAudio to artistic ends. A magazine, Word has text articles — but they're enhanced with embedded RealAudio music that plays in the background as you read. Recently, an article about growing up in poverty featured a RealAudio blues tune; and the somewhat degraded sound quality that characterizes RealAudio clips only added to the experience because it made the clip sound as if it were emanating from a cheap AM radio. The Word welcome page appears in Figure 2-27.

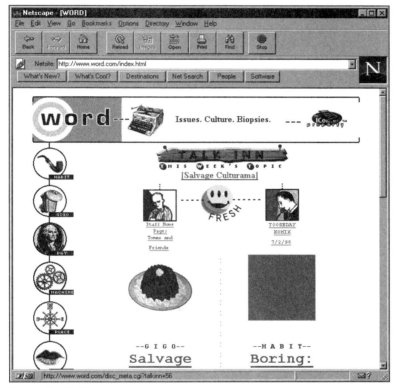

Figure 2-27: Word.

✦ WBAL-AM (http://www.wbal.com/). Baltimore's mega-powerful news and talk radio station has always had a large listening area — but now it has a global signal, thanks to RealAudio. Point your browser at this site and get audio from all of WBAL's on-air personalities mere seconds after it goes out over the air in Baltimore. Figure 2-28 shows the WBAL site.

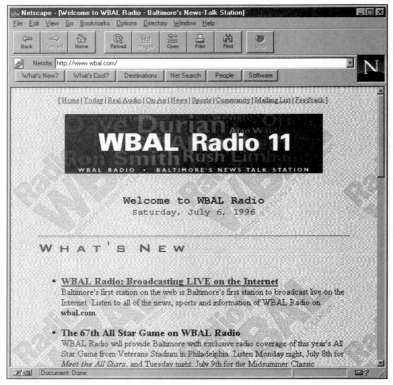

Figure 2-28: WBAL-AM on the Web.

Authoring for RealAudio

Creating RealAudio files is the job of the RealAudio Encoder, available at
`http://www.realaudio.com/products/encoder.html`. RealAudio Encoder
takes sound files in any of several popular formats, including .WAV and .AU, and
converts them to the proprietary RealAudio format.

One of the cool things about authoring for the RealAudio plug-in is the many
options Web page publishers have in the way of on-page controls. RealAudio lets
you embed what amounts to a complete copy of the RealAudio Player helper
application in your Web pages. But it also lets you embed just the control panel
portion, and also lets you embed the Start and Stop buttons by themselves. Here's
a guide to the HTML coding involved in each of those options.

To embed both the Stop and Play buttons independently, you need two separate
`<EMBED>` statements (you can put just the Play button on your page with a single

<EMBED> statement, by the way, though your site's visitors may find it inconsiderate that you enabled them to start a sound clip without giving them the power to stop it, short of leaving the page).

Here's the code required for the Play button (see Figure 2-29):

```
<EMBED SRC="JAZZ.RPM" ALIGN=BASELINE WIDTH=40 HEIGHT=20
       CONTROLS=PlayButton CONSOLE="JAZZ2">
```

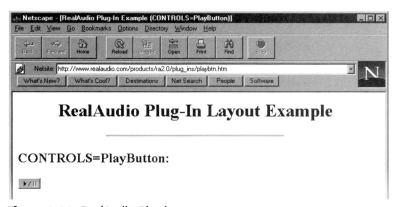

Figure 2-29: RealAudio Play button.

In this statement, a Play button 40 pixels wide and 20 pixels high controls the file JAZZ.RPM. The CONSOLE attribute, which is duplicated in the <EMBED> statement for the Stop button, below, declares that the two buttons work together to control the same audio file. ALIGN=BASELINE tells your browser to line up the bottom of the button with the bottom of the text to the left and right of it.

Here's the code required for the Stop button:

```
<EMBED SRC="JAZZ.RPM" ALIGN=BASELINE WIDTH=40 HEIGHT=20
       CONTROLS=StopButton CONSOLE="JAZZ2">
```

Again, the button is defined as a 40-by-20-pixel rectangle, aligned with the baseline of the surrounding text, that is part of console JAZZ2 — which enables it to work with the Play button discussed above.

To embed the control portion of the RealAudio panel — that is, to embed the Play button, Stop button, and slider bar, as shown in Figure 2-30 — here's the code you should insert into your Web page:

```
<EMBED SRC="SAX.RPM" WIDTH=200 HEIGHT=35 CONTROLS=CONTROLPANEL>
```

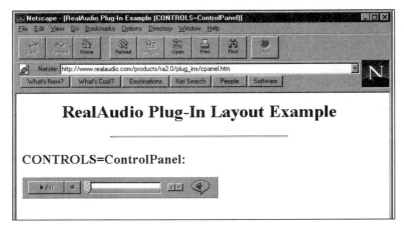

Figure 2-30: The RealAudio controls.

The statement above puts everything but the volume control and the information boxes into a Web page. Unless you're intent on displaying author and copyright information in the RealAudio boxes, the control portion of the panel is probably the best compromise between giving surfers sufficient control over the sound clip and not surrendering gigantic portions of your page to something over which you have no design control. After all, most people will control volume with the knob on their speaker, not the RealAudio volume slider that's the only functional component excluded from the CONTROLPANEL value for the CONTROLS attribute. Note that the CONTROLPANEL attribute creates a display that fits best into a rectangle 35 pixels high and 200 pixels wide.

If you want to include on your Web page all the RealAudio controls, including the volume slider and the information boxes, use this statement:

```
<EMBED SRC="MAMBA.RPM" WIDTH=300 HEIGHT=135 CONTROLS=ALL>
```

The results of the ALL value for the CONTROLS attribute appear in Figure 2-31. Note that the ALL attribute creates a display that fits best into a rectangle 135 pixels high and 300 pixels wide.

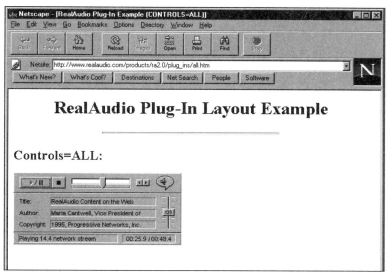

Figure 2-31: The full RealAudio display.

ShockTalk

Creator: Digital Dreams

Function: Adds speech-recognition capabilities to Macromedia's Shockwave for Director plug-in (covered in Chapter 3)

Home Site: http://www.surftalk.com/

Supported Platforms: All Macintosh systems

Authoring Tool: Macromedia Director and Speech Xtra

Good Examples: The Capital Quiz at http://www.surftalk.com/shocktalk/uscq.html; Speakable Links at http://www.surftalk.com/SurfTalk/index.html

Shockwave for Director (which you'll read about in the next chapter) is pretty impressive by itself. It adds sound and interactive animations to Web sites. But what if you could interact with Shockwave for Director not just with your mouse but with your voice, too? ShockTalk makes that possible.

By taking advantage of Apple's PlainTalk speech-recognition scheme (as many of the Macintosh plug-ins in this chapter do), ShockTalk brings huge new functionality to your browser without adding megabytes of code to your hard disk. With this plug-in, you can order a Shockwave for Director presentation to move forward or back, or select an option from an on-screen menu, with your voice. It's a truly cool bit of programming that every Shockwave for Director publisher should evaluate.

Plug-in Power Rating: ★★

Installing ShockTalk

To install ShockTalk on your Macintosh system, you must have Shockwave for Director and PlainTalk installed on your computer. If you don't have PlainTalk, get it from Apple at `http://www.speech.apple.com/`. You can read about Shockwave for Director and how to get it in Chapter 3 of this book.

At this writing, ShockTalk won't work with the PowerPC version of Shockwave for Director. In order to use ShockTalk on a Power Mac, you must install the Standard Macintosh version of Shockwave for Director. This works just fine as a temporary fix, and Macromedia (the maker of all the Shockwave products) says version 5 of Shockwave for Director will work well with ShockTalk.

To install ShockTalk on your computer:

1. Point your browser at `http://www.surftalk.com/shocktalk/index.html`.

2. Click on the link (in the list of things required to use ShockTalk) that simply says, "ShockTalk."

3. Use StuffIt, StuffIt Lite, or StuffIt Expander to decompress the file you download. If you don't have a StuffIt program, get a copy of StuffIt Expander at `http://www.aladdinsys.com/obstufex.htm`.

4. Shut down your browser.

5. Drag the ShockTalk file that StuffIt extracts from the archive to your plug-ins folder.

6. Restart your browser. You're ready to use ShockTalk.

Using ShockTalk

A good page design should make clear how to use a particular ShockTalk presentation. Typically, you'll see a page similar to the one shown in Figure 2-32, with a Director animation in one region and a list of speakable commands elsewhere on the page.

Figure 2-32: ShockTalk at work on the U.S. Capital Quiz.

In the case of the Capital Quiz, the state-capitals test that appears in Figure 2-32, you have five commands at your disposal. When the presentation prompts you for the name of, say, Iowa, you can respond with a correct or incorrect answer; or you can instruct the program to "repeat question," move on to the "next question," tell it that "I don't know," request that "you tell me," or ask that it "stop quiz."

Depending upon how you have set up PlainTalk on your computer, you may have to hold down a keyboard button in order to get the computer to listen to you; or you may have to announce your name before speaking a command ("David, I don't know"). There's PlainTalk documentation on the Web at http://www.sims. berkeley.edu/~jwang/AV/PlainTalk/ that explains these issues in greater detail.

Plugged-in sites

Besides the Capital Quiz, you can explore a speech-navigable version of the Digital Dreams Web site. Starting from http://www.surftalk.com/SurfTalk/ index.html, which appears in Figure 2-33, you can move from page to page using only voice commands — at least until you leave the Digital Dreams site.

To follow a link, announce clearly, "Link to. . ." and then the text that defines the link on the Web page. You'll move to the page that the site designer attached to the link whose text you spoke.

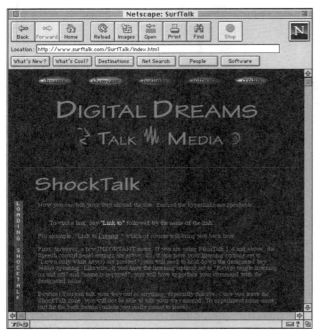

Figure 2-33: The ShockTalk speakable links demo.

Authoring for ShockTalk

Authoring for ShockTalk is little different from creating any other presentation with Macromedia for Director. Essentially, you build a Director movie, then modify it with a Lingo program that connects the movie to PlainTalk and explains which audio commands are supposed to do which tasks. There's an example Lingo script at http://www.surftalk.com/Hi-Res/asrxtra.html.

Lingo — you'll see if you visit that page — isn't as straightforward as the rest of the Director presentation-making process. Adding the Lingo script to your movie bears more resemblance to programming in BASIC than to working with graphical elements and sound. You'll probably have to learn a lot by trial and error as you experiment with Lingo and its applications to ShockTalk.

After you've built a movie and a Lingo script, you use Speech Xtra (also at `http://www.surftalk.com/Hi-Res/asrxtra.html`) to combine the two and generate a finished product, ready for use by ShockTalk.

Embedding a ShockTalk-enhanced movie in a Web page is exactly the same as embedding a standard Shockwave for Director presentation in a Web page. Learn how to do that in Chapter 3.

Speech Plug-in

Creator: William H. Tudor

Function: Reads aloud the contents of an embedded text file

Home Site: `http://www.albany.net/~wtudor/speechinfo.html`

Supported Platforms: All Macintosh systems running Mac OS 7.0 or higher

Authoring Tool: Any text editor

Good Examples: William Tudor's own page, at `http://www.albany.net/~wtudor`

William Tudor's Speech Plug-in takes advantage of the Macintosh's PlainTalk technology, which translates ASCII text into a synthesized human voice. By using PlainTalk, Speech Plug-in requires that a Web server transmit only svelte ASCII text, rather than bloated sound-file information, across communications lines. Speech Plug-in makes it easy to create fun, informative Web sites without resorting to complex sound-sampling schemes.

Plug-in Power Rating: ★★★

Installing Speech Plug-in

To install Speech Plug-in on your Macintosh:

1. Point your browser at `http://www.albany.net/~wtudor/speechinfo.html`.
2. Click on the link that says, "Download the MacOS version 1.0 of the Speech Plug-in."
3. Use StuffIt, StuffIt Lite, or StuffIt Expander to decompress the file you download. If you don't have a StuffIt program, get a copy of StuffIt Expander at `http://www.aladdinsys.com/obstufex.htm`.
4. Shut down your browser.

5. Drag the icon labeled Speech from the Speech folder you just decompressed to your browser's plug-ins folder.

6. Restart your browser. The Speech Plug-in is ready for use.

Using Speech Plug-in

Speech Plug-in is commonly termed "transparent to the user." That is, once you have installed it correctly, you need only call up a Speech Plug-in-enabled site to hear it work. There are no settings, controls, or other potentially confusing aspects of Speech Plug-in's operation.

When you call up a site that's outfitted for speech, you may have to wait a few seconds while PlainTalk starts. Then, you'll hear the speech pronounced, slowly and deliberately, in an accent that may sound somewhat odd.

If you want to change the voice in which Speech Plug-in and PlainTalk read embedded ASCII, open the Speech control panel in your Control Panels folder. There, you can choose from among several voices.

Plugged-in sites

The only page designed specifically for Speech Plug-in was William Tudor's own home page, shown above in Figure 2-34. Other Speech Plug-in-aware sites may be out there — look out for pointers on Tudor's page.

Authoring for Speech Plug-in

The essential part of a site enhanced for Speech Plug-in is an ASCII text file, generated with SimpleText or some other text editor. The text file should contain the exact script you want the synthesized PlainTalk voice to read when your page is called up by a distant browser. Be sure to save your text file with the filename extension .SPC.

Remember that while PlainTalk is good, it is not perfect; and you should avoid unusual words in your script. If you have to include a name or other proper noun that might challenge PlainTalk, you may want to write it out phonetically — you should write the name of Duke University basketball coach Mike Krzyzewski as "Shashefsky" (that's the way it's pronounced).

Then, to attach your text file to your Web page, use a statement such as this one:

```
<EMBED SRC="TALK.SPC" WIDTH=10 HEIGHT=10>
```

PlainTalk takes care of the rest.

Speech Plug-in requires that your Web server be configured to handle MIME type `text/x speech`, with the filename extension `.SPC`.

Also, `WIDTH` and `HEIGHT` attributes in the `<EMBED>` statement must have values of at least 10 each to prevent Netscape Navigator from crashing.

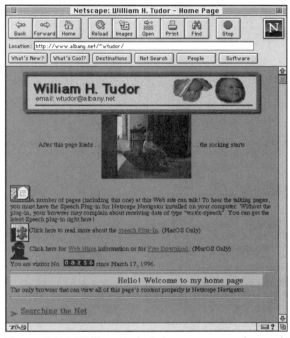

Figure 2-34: William Tudor's home page, enhanced for Speech Plug-in.

Talker

Creator: MVP Solutions

Function: Reads the contents of a text file

Home Site: `http://www.mvpsolutions.com/PlugInSite/Talker.html`

Supported Platforms: All Macintosh systems

Authoring Tool: Any text editor

Good Examples: The Interactive Humor Database at `http://humor.ladir.com/bin/SearchSpeech.html`; The Adventures of Stubby Cottontail at `http://www.lifelong.com/carnivalworld/stubby/stubbyhp.html`; Bananaman's Poem of the Day at `http://www.ithaca.edu/banana/` (see Figure 2-35)

Figure 2-35: Bananaman's Poem of the Day, a Talker-enabled site.

Talker uses the Macintosh's PlainTalk text-to-speech technology to bring sound to the Web just as Speech Plug-in does. With a simple text file and functions that are built into the latest versions of the MacOS, you can bring entertainment, instructional materials, and audio persuasion to your Web site with extreme ease.

Plug-in Power Rating: ★★★

Installing Talker

Before installing Talker, make sure you have MacOS version 7.5 or later and PlainTalk Speech Recognition version 1.4.1 or 1.5a1 installed on your machine. You can download PlainTalk — in English and Mexican Spanish — from Apple at `ftp://ftp.info.apple.com/Apple.Support.Area/Developer_Services/`.

To install Talker on your Macintosh:

1. Point your browser at `http://www.mvpsolutions.com/PlugInSite/Talker.html`.

2. Scroll down the page, and click on the click on here to download link in the How to Make This Page Talk section.

3. Use StuffIt, StuffIt Lite, or StuffIt Expander to decompress the file you download. If you don't have a StuffIt program, get a copy of StuffIt Expander at `http://www.aladdinsys.com/`.

4. Shut down your browser.

5. Drag the Talker file out of the folder StuffIt just decompressed and drop it into your browser's plug-ins folder.

6. Restart your browser. Talker is ready to go.

Using Talker

Using Talker is a no-brainer — just call up a Talker-wise site, wait a few seconds for the text to download and PlainTalk to spool up, and sound will start to emanate from your machine's speakers.

If you want to stop a page's talking, press and hold down the Esc key.

Plugged-in sites

There are quite a few sites designed to work with Talker. Check out the directory on the MVP Solutions site at `http://www.mvpsolutions.com/PlugInSite/Talker.html#otherlinks`.

Here are a few especially clever Talker sites:

✦ **The Interactive Humor Database** (`http://humor.ladir.com/bin/SearchSpeech.html`). They say the essence of a joke is in the delivery. If that's true, these jokes all fall flat, since the droning monotone of the PlainTalk text-to-speech engine is hardly one to inspire laughter. Still, the concept — that of having the computer read jokes to site visitors — is pretty cool. Beware of the abundant salty humor, by the way. The Interactive Humor Database appears in Figure 2-36.

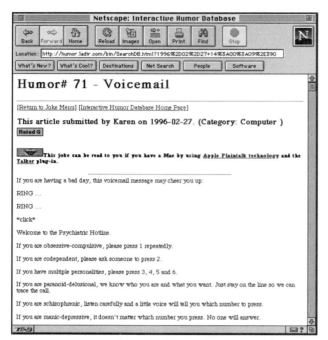

Figure 2-36: The Interactive Humor Database.

✦ **The Adventures of Stubby Cottontail** (http://www.lifelong.com/ carnivalworld/stubby/stubbyhp.html). What a great idea — an illustrated, audio-enhanced children's book on the Web! At the Stubby site, kids and their folks can read about the adventures of hapless Stubby and his friends; and kids who are learning to read get help from the Talker voice. There's also a parallel story about Stubby in Spanish. The welcome page appears in Figure 2-37.

Authoring for Talker

Building a Talker-wise Web page is essentially a matter of creating a text file that contains the text you want the plug-in to speak, then using the <EMBED> tag to attach that text file to an HTML document.

Using SimpleText or another text editor, create a text document and save it with the filename extension .TALK. Then insert a statement similar to this one into the Web page you're endowing with sound:

```
<EMBED SRC="REPORT.TALK" WIDTH=10 HEIGHT=10>
```

Figure 2-37: The Adventures of Stubby Cottontail.

In that example, the text file REPORT.TALK is attached to a Web page for reading. The 10-by-10-pixel plug-in box will contain nothing, but it has to be that size to prevent browser crashes and other troublesome behavior.

ToolVox

Creator: Voxware

Function: Plays proprietary ToolVox speech files in .VOX format

Home Site: http://www.voxware.com/download.htm

Supported Platforms: All Windows systems and Power Macintosh

Authoring Tool: ToolVox Encoder

Good Examples: Technobabble review of Voxware at http://www.voxware.com/ voxdemo.htm; John F. Kennedy's inaugural address at http://www.voxware.com/ voxdemo.htm (see Figure 2-38); The Computer Karaoke Homepage at http://www. teleport.com/~labrat/karnews.shtml; UFO reports at http://medianet. nbnet.nb.ca/ufo/nextpage.htm#questions

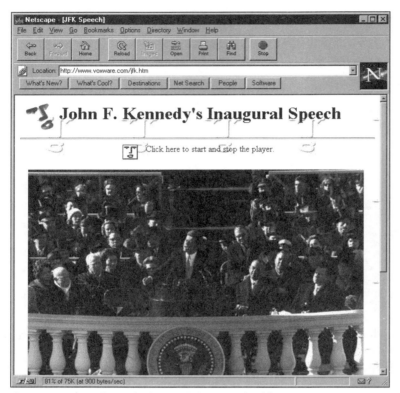

Figure 2-38: ToolVox playing JFK's inaugural address.

With the capability to encode a minute of speech or singing into 18 kilobytes of data, VoxWare's ToolVox makes it hard to justify producing Web pages that appeal to only the eye. By adding ToolVox sound to your pages, you can dramatically increase their effectiveness and attractiveness without wasting tons of bandwidth on enormous files in .WAV or .AU format.

Similar in design to EchoSpeech (discussed earlier in this chapter), ToolVox uses a custom program to interpret voices recorded in generic formats (such as .WAV), and outputs them in a proprietary format optimized for the Web. By filtering the voices through an algorithm that's designed especially to encode the sound of the human voice in tiny files, ToolVox manages to communicate sound while using less bandwidth than many still graphics.

Plug-in Power Rating: ★★★

Installing ToolVox

To install ToolVox on your Windows system:

1. Point your browser at `http://www.voxware.com/download.htm`.

2. Depending upon which operating environment you use, click on either the Windows 95 or Windows 3.1 link under the ToolVox Player heading.

3. Fill in the registration form and click on the Continue button.

4. At the bottom of the page that appears after you complete the registration form, click on the link that's connected to the download site closest to you. At this writing, the two download servers are in Princeton, New Jersey, and Seattle, Washington.

5. Save the file you download by itself in a temporary directory.

6. Shut down your browser.

7. Double-click on the file you downloaded. ToolVox's excellent installation program will start. It automatically identifies your browser files and installs each of its files in the proper place.

8. Restart your browser. ToolVox will be ready to go.

To install ToolVox on your Macintosh system:

1. Point your browser at `http://www.voxware.com/download.htm`.

2. Click on the Mac OS link under the ToolVox Player heading.

3. Fill in the registration form and click on the Continue button.

4. At the bottom of the page that appears after you complete the registration form, click on the link that's connected to the download site closest to you. At this writing, the two download servers are in Princeton, New Jersey, and Seattle, Washington.

5. Shut down your browser.

6. Use StuffIt, StuffIt Lite, or StuffIt Expander to decompress the file you download. If you don't have a StuffIt program, get a copy of StuffIt Expander at `http://www.aladdinsys.com/`.

7. Double-click on the installer program that your decompression program extracted from the downloaded archive. The installer does the work of setting up the plug-in for use.

8. Restart your browser. ToolVox is ready for use.

Using ToolVox

There are three ways you'll encounter ToolVox while you're surfing the Web. Each gives you a different degree of control over the sound coming from your computer's speakers, ranging from none to lots.

Some sites feature ToolVox speech as a background phenomenon — there's not necessarily an icon on the page that tells you it's ToolVox sound you're hearing, and the sound just plays in the background without any attention from you. You can't start it and you can't stop it.

Other pages, such as the one in Figure 2-38 with John F. Kennedy's Inauguration Address embedded in it, give you a ToolVox icon with which to control the sound. Click on the icon once and the sound starts; click on it again and the sound stops.

Still other pages give you a full ToolVox control panel similar to the one shown in Figure 2-39. Much like a CD player's control panel, the full suite of controls lets you start, stop, and rewind the clip and speed or slow its playback rate.

Plugged-in sites

Looking for a cool site at which you can use your ToolVox plug-in? Check out VoxWare's directory of talking sites at `http://www.voxware.com/coolsite.htm`.

Here are a couple of sites you may want to visit early in your ToolVox career:

✦ **The Computer Karaoke Homepage** (`http://www.teleport.com/ ~labrat/karnews.html`). An excellent, supremely logical application of ToolVox. The maintainer of this site — which features sing-along MIDI clips for use with several of the other plug-ins in this chapter — uses ToolVox to communicate site news to surfers. An experiment to perform: Read the text-based site news at the bottom of the page, then listen to the ToolVox version. Reading the screen isn't fun, is it? Figure 2-39 shows the ToolVox-enhanced announcements page at the Computer Karaoke Homepage site.

✦ **Internet Radio** (`http://www.internet-radio.com/`). Using a variety of sound schemes, Internet Radio communicates news, sports, features, and music to surfers. Sites such as this one make you wonder about the future of broadcast radio.

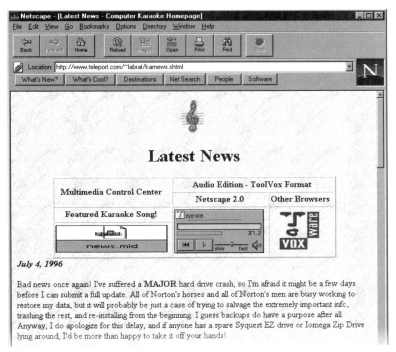

Figure 2-39: The Computer Karaoke Homepage.

Authoring for ToolVox

To make a ToolVox file, start with a clear .WAV or .AIF recording of one person speaking or singing. It's okay to have several people speak or sing in sequence, one at a time, but try to avoid having more than one voice making noise at a given instant — this will confuse the ToolVox encoding algorithm and reduce sound quality.

When you have a suitable .WAV or .AIF file, run it through the ToolVox Encoder, also available at `http://www.voxware.com/download.htm`. The result will be a .VOX file — a Web-ready version of your original ponderous recording, compressed by a factor of 50 or more.

To embed that file in a Web page, use this basic syntax:

```
<EMBED SRC=WELCOME.VOX PLAYMODE=AUTO VISUALMODE=PLAYER
       HEIGHT=82 WIDTH=160>
```

That statement embeds the file SPEECH.VOX in a 82-by-160-pixel space in a Web page. The other attributes affect the appearance and performance of the sound file, and each can take any of several values. Here's a summary:

The PLAYMODE parameter describes when the sound file plays. Its potential values are

+ USER. The file does not play until someone clicks on the Play button or the ToolVox icon.

+ AUTO. The file begins to play as soon as the page is loaded.

+ CACHE. The file doesn't stream. Instead, it downloads completely, then waits for someone to click on the icon or the Play button.

The VISUALMODE deals with display issues. Its potential values are

+ ICON. Instead of a control panel, an icon appears on the Web page. A surfer clicks on the icon to start and stop playback. Set HEIGHT and WIDTH to 27 to get a small ToolVox icon; set both the dimensions to 50 for a large icon.

+ PLAYER **or** EMBED. Embeds the entire control panel in the Web page. Set HEIGHT=82 and WIDTH=160 if you use one of these two equivalent parameters.

+ BACKGROUND. Nothing appears on the Web page, but if you set PLAYMODE=AUTO, the file plays automatically in the background.

+ FLOAT **(Windows)** or PLAYER **(Macintosh)**. Puts the ToolVox controls in a separate window, such as a helper application.

TrueSpeech

Creator: DSP Group

Function: Plays TrueSpeech audio files

Home Site: http://www.dspg.com/plugin.htm

Supported Platforms: All Windows systems

Authoring Tool: Windows 95 Sound Recorder

Good Examples: The TrueSpeech home page at http://www.dspg.com/plugin.htm; Kiwi Internet Radio at http://www.mfmarketing.com/mfmarketing/rinz.htm

Benefiting from extreme ease in making its proprietary-format data files (you use the Sound Recorder that comes with Windows 95 and Windows NT), TrueSpeech is a great way to encode music and noise — not just speech — for transmission over the Web. A simple user interface, high sound quality, and simple but flexible `<EMBED>` statements make TrueSpeech a technical rival to the best of the plug-ins.

Figure 2-40 shows TrueSpeech's intuitive control panel on the home page of DSP Group, the audio software company that developed TrueSpeech.

Plug-in Power Rating: ★★★

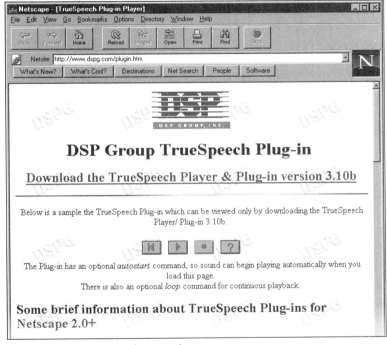

Figure 2-40: TrueSpeech at work.

Installing TrueSpeech

To install TrueSpeech on your Windows 95 system,

1. Point your browser at `http://www.dspg.com/allplyr.htm`.
2. Click on the button marked Download TrueSpeech Player Ver. Win95.

3. Read the license agreement, fill in the registration form at the bottom, and click on the Download Software button.

4. Save the TrueSpeech archive file by itself in a temporary directory.

5. When the file has downloaded completely, shut down your browser.

6. Double-click on the file you just downloaded. The self-extracting archive files will unpack all the files it contains, including one called SETUP.EXE.

7. Double-click on SETUP.EXE. Follow the prompts, and the installation program will take care of the details of installing the TrueSpeech plug-in on your computer.

8. Restart your computer. You can start using TrueSpeech.

Using TrueSpeech

Like many of the plug-ins in this chapter, TrueSpeech uses the metaphor of a CD player to describe its controls. There are four buttons on the TrueSpeech control panel (see Figure 2-40). From the left, they are:

✦ **Rewind.** Starts the clip over at the beginning.

✦ **Play.** Starts playback.

✦ **Stop.** Halts playback.

✦ **Help.** Calls up the ToolVox help pages on the DSP Group site.

Plugged-in sites

Looking for nifty TrueSpeech-savvy sites? Look no further than DSP Group's Official (Cool) Sites Using TrueSpeech page at `http://www.dspg.com/cool.htm`. There you'll find a frequently updated list of the best TrueSpeech content on the Web.

One of the best sites on the list is Kiwi Internet Radio, at, which is shown in Figure 2-41. This radio station, based in Te Awamutu, New Zealand, offers a mixed bag of programming. It even solicits contributions from surfers — the ultimate interpretation of "all-request radio."

Also take a listen to the TrueSpeech files at the Chicken Soup of the Day site, at `http://www.positive-place.com/chickensoup/dailysoup.htm`. The authors of *Chicken Soup for the Soul*, a best-selling book of happy stories, read aloud from their work. The stories run from mushy to sappy; but when you're in the mood, you're in the mood.

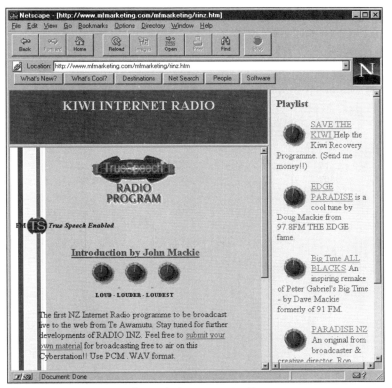

Figure 2-41: TrueSpeech at Kiwi Internet Radio.

Authoring for TrueSpeech

The neat thing about creating TrueSpeech content for your Web pages is that you can do it with something you probably have on your hard drive right now — Sound Recorder. Since DSP Group developed Sound Recorder for Microsoft, they were able to build support for their .TSP file format into the native sound application of Windows 95 and Windows NT. It was a boon for them — and for you.

To make a .TSP file, open (or record) a PCM .WAV file with Sound Recorder. Then choose File, Save As from the menu bar, click on the Change button at the bottom of the dialog box, and select DSP Group TrueSpeech from the list box. Then click on Save, and you have a .TSP file that's ready for embedding in a Web page.

The embedding process isn't hard, either. Here's the basic syntax:

```
<EMBED SRC="FILENAME.TSI" HEIGHT=60 WIDTH=200 AUTOSTART=TRUE
        LOOP=TRUE>
```

The standard TrueSpeech controls (the ones that appear in Figure 2-40) need a 60-by-200-pixel box. AUTOSTART determines whether a TrueSpeech file starts automatically when the page in which it's embedded is loaded; it can be set to TRUE or FALSE. LOOP determines whether the clip plays over and over; it, too, can be set to either TRUE or FALSE.

Yep, it's that pesky MIME type problem again. This time, you need to configure your server to recognize MIME type audio/tsplayer, with filename extension .TSI.

Video and Animation

It's been called the Holy Grail of the Web: the ability to serve video and animation on demand. Imagine being able to call up a Web site and instruct the server there to send you last night's *Seinfeld*, followed by your favorite cartoon from 1978 and a Letterman show from two years ago. When that becomes possible, entertainment will be a different animal entirely. Power will return to the viewers after being held by the advertisers and network programmers for so long.

The plug-ins you'll learn about in this chapter bring video-on-demand a little closer to reality. These plug-ins let you call up a Web site and see areas of video and animation embedded in pages. The effect is stunning, especially when you consider that Java, which remains a somewhat crude language, can't yet render interactive animations as elaborate as those that plug-ins can handle. These plug-ins go beyond the capability of LiveVideo, the video plug-in that comes with Netscape Navigator 3.0.

Most of the plug-ins in this chapter, like many of the sound players in Chapter 2, use a technology called *streaming*. Simply put, streaming means that the plug-in starts playing a file sent to it by a server before the file has been moved entirely to your computer. That is, a QuickTime movie plug-in that employs streaming will play the first part of a movie while it downloads subsequent parts from the Web, and the Astound plug-in will show the first frame of a presentation long before it has downloaded the last one. Streaming saves you from having to wait for huge multimedia files to download — a real advantage for everyone, since those who put multimedia presentations on the Web want someone to view them and get upset if people surf away rather than wait for a long download.

Even with streaming, video and animation files can be ponderous. Until the average Internet connection gets faster, video and animation may best be left to corporate intranets, where they're great for marketing materials, videoconferencing (though check out Chapter 6 for more information on that), and training. Since corporate intranets typically have much higher data-transfer rates than modem connections, they're much better suited to moving vast amounts of data than telephone-based network connections.

Action

Creator: Open2U

Function: Plays embedded MPEG-1 movie files

Home Site: http://www.open2u.com/action/action.html

Supported Platforms: Windows 95 and Windows NT systems

Authoring Tool: Any video editor that generates MPEG-1 output, such as Open2U's ActionStudio (there's information about ordering ActionStudio at http://www.open2u.com/action/)

Good Examples: The demonstration page that comes with the Action installation package: ACT_DEMO.HTM in your PLUGINS/ACTION directory. There are surprisingly few MPEG-1 video archives on the Web.

Action is a good no-frills MPEG-1 video player. It downloads quickly, installs with little hassle despite its crude setup program, and has some of the simplest and most intuitive controls found on any video plug-in. You'll be generally pleased by most aspects of Action's performance. On the other hand, the plug-in — at least the beta release I worked with at this writing — seems to suffer from poor playback quality, even when it's working with files on the same machine as the browser to which it's attached. Video sometimes pauses momentarily, and sound sometimes includes pops and static on top of the recorded music or voice. Action does not support streaming and plays only old-technology MPEG-1 files. Because of these shortcomings, Action faces serious competition from PreVU, another MPEG video plug-in that's discussed later in this chapter.

Despite the technical troubles with early versions of the plug-in, Action has a lot going for it. Backed by an excellent technical-support staff (some of my electronic-mail queries to Open2U were handled within an hour of the time I sent them), Action is a good MPEG-1 video plug-in choice.

Plug-in Power Rating: ★★

Installing Action

To install Action on your Windows 95 system:

1. Point your browser at `http://www.open2u.com/action/action.html`.

2. Click on the download link. Save ACTION32.EXE by itself in a temporary folder.

Don't rename the file you download from the Open2U site — accept ACTION32.EXE or whatever other filename the Save As dialog box suggests. The Action installation program is picky about the name of the downloaded file and will get confused if you change it.

3. Shut down your browser after the file downloads completely.

4. Run ACTION32.EXE, which is Action's installation program. The installation routine is quite crude: You have to manually type in your plug-ins directory or find it by clicking through a directory tree with your mouse. The plug-ins directory for Netscape Navigator users is C:/Program Files/ Netscape/Navigator/Program/Plugins; the one for Microsoft Internet Explorer users is C:/Program Files/Plus!/Microsoft Internet/Plugins, assuming that drive C is your hard disk.

5. Restart your browser. Action should come to life anytime you access a page with embedded MPEG video.

In order to work properly, your display must be set to show 256 colors. Action won't work right if you've configured your monitor and video card for 16 or 16.7 million colors. Adjust your display's palette by choosing Settings, Display from the Start menu.

Using Action

When you open a Web page with embedded MPEG video, Action automatically goes to work displaying the clip — after it finishes downloading the clip in its entirety. The downloading process can take a while if the MPEG clip is large or if your connection to the Web is slow. The problem isn't as severe if you're down-loading video from another computer on a local area network or other small-scale, high-speed intranet.

Remember, Action only works with MPEG-1 files, which are pretty scarce on the Web. If your browser doesn't seem to be downloading anything, it's probably not. Try PreVU on the file.

Plugged-in sites

There aren't many Web pages with MPEG-1 video that's tailored to Action. One of the best examples at this writing is in ACT_DEMO.HTM, the demonstration page that comes with Action. You'll find it in your Action directory (usually …PLUG-INS/ACTION). The demonstration page — in which a globe spins and the word Open2U flies and spins — appears in Figure 3-1.

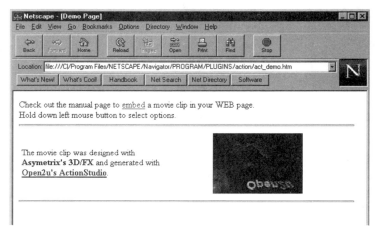

Figure 3-1: The Action demonstration page.

Authoring for Action

Generating MPEG video clips that Action can handle is a huge topic — the subject of quite a few books, in fact. To generate MPEG clips, you'll want to use a good video-editing program such as Adobe Premiere or Open2U's ActionStudio. You may need a sound-editing program such as Waveform Hold and Modify (WHAM) to work with the audio tracks of your movies.

Once you've generated an MPEG video clip (usually in the form of a file with an .MPG or .MPEG extension), you'll have to use the <EMBED> tag to attach the file to a Web page. The <EMBED> tag enables browsers with the Action plug-in designated for playing MPEG video to automatically refer to their Action routines upon encountering embedded MPEG files.

The basic syntax for the <EMBED> tag is <EMBED SRC="FILENAME" WIDTH=X HEIGHT=Y>, where FILENAME is the name of the MPEG video file you want to embed (you can express it as a full Web URL if it's not stored in the same directory as the HTML file that contains the <EMBED> tag), X is the WIDTH of the display window in pixels, and Y is the HEIGHT of the display window in pixels.

Action recognizes several other attributes in the <EMBED> tag in addition to the three mandatory attributes:

✦ AUTOSTART. If you specify AUTOSTART=TRUE in the <EMBED> tag, your MPEG movie will begin playing as soon as the page finishes loading. Otherwise, the clip won't play until you click on the Play command.

✦ LOOP. Adding the LOOP=TRUE attribute to the <EMBED> tag instructs the plug-in to repeat the clip over and over until the Web page is closed.

✦ SYNC. Specifying SYNC=ON guarantees that the audio portion of your clip plays in synchronization with the visual portion of your clip. You should usually specify SYNC=ON.

✦ SIZE. To make your video clip appear twice as large as it is encoded in the MPEG file, add SIZE=DOUBLE to your list of attributes.

If you use the SIZE=DOUBLE attribute, don't forget to adjust your HEIGHT and WIDTH attributes accordingly. If your video clip has frames that are 100 pixels high by 200 pixels wide, and you use the SIZE=DOUBLE attribute, you'll have to make sure you have the attributes HEIGHT=200 and WIDTH=400. Otherwise, you'll see only a corner of your video's frames displayed.

✦ COLOR. If you specify COLOR=MONO, your video clips will run in grayscale (black and white) instead of in color. This won't save any download time, though the creative effect sometimes adds a lot to a presentation.

Therefore, a fully decked-out <EMBED> tag for Action would look like this:

```
<EMBED SRC="GIRAFFE.MPG" HEIGHT=400 WIDTH=600 AUTOSTART=TRUE
       LOOP=TRUE SYNC=ON SIZE=DOUBLE COLOR=MONO>
```

That tag would cause a file called GIRAFFE.MPG to display at twice its normal size of 300 pixels wide by 200 pixels tall (therefore requiring WIDTH and HEIGHT attributes of 600 and 400, respectively), in grayscale, with sound synchronized with video. The clip would start playing as soon as its page loaded and would play repeatedly until the page was closed.

Animated Widgets

Creator: InternetConsult

Function: Plays embedded animations

Home Site: http://www.InternetConsult.com/

Supported Platforms: Windows 95

Authoring Tool: None

Good Examples: http://www.InternetConsult.com/animplug.html (the only example)

Animated Widgets is little more than a novelty (see Figure 3-2). Though Widgets download very quickly and run smoothly, Brad Klein of InternetConsult built this plug-in as an experiment in plug-in coding, and there isn't even an authoring tool for it. At the moment, this plug-in is essentially useless. Brad points to Table of Contents, a much cooler InternetConsult plug-in you'll learn about in Chapter 7, as a better example of what he, his company, and plug-in technology can do.

Unless you discover some sort of use for Animated Widgets that Brad and I can't fathom, you'll want to pass on this plug-in in favor of mBED or other similar plug-ins covered in this chapter.

Plug-in Power Rating: ★

Installing Animated Widgets

Installing Animated Widgets (if you want to install it for some reason) is easy:

1. Download the file NPANM32.EXE from http://www.InternetConsult.com/animplug.html. Make sure you save the file in your PROGRAM FILES/NETSCAPE/NAVIGATOR/PLUG-INS folder. (Your browser should default to that directory if you installed your copy of Netscape in accordance with the defaults.)

2. Open a window for your PLUG-INS folder and double-click on the icon for NPANM.EXE. It will extract a .DLL file — a file your browser can refer to in special situations — from itself.

3. Exit your browser, then restart it. Animated Widgets will be available for use.

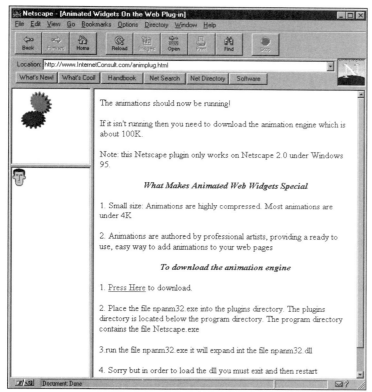

Figure 3-2: Animated Widgets on the job (`http://www.InternetConsult.com/animplug.html`).

Using Animated Widgets

Using this simple plug-in is even less brain-intensive than installing it. Point your browser at `http://www.InternetConsult.com/animplug.html`, the only page on the Web at this writing that requires Animated Widgets. You'll see a couple of animations on the left side of the screen: a pair of whirling gears and a blabbering cartoon face. Click on an animation to stop its movement; click on it again to restart it. That's all there is to Animated Widgets.

Authoring for Animated Widgets

You can't do it. I wrote Brad Klein, the head of InternetConsult and the developer of Animated Widgets, asking when a widget creator will be available. He replied laconically, "When someone gives me some money to do it." Inquire further at the InternetConsult Web site (http://www.InternetConsult.com/) if you're interested in bankrolling an authoring tool.

Astound Web Player

Creator: Gold Disk

Function: Plays Astound and Studio M multimedia

Home Site: http://www.golddisk.com/awp.html

Supported Platforms: All Macintosh and Windows systems

Authoring Tool: Astound or Studio M demo versions which can be accessed at http://www.golddisk.com/awp/create.html. You use Astound Web Installer (at the same URL) to embed Astound and Studio M files in your Web pages.

Good Examples: Several animated banners (http://www.golddisk.com/ marshall/webdemo.html); a promotion page for a restaurant (http://www. golddisk.com/awp/sample/spagwest_demo/spagwest.asn); an animated Gold Disk home page (http://www.golddisk.com/awp/sample/ alternate_home_page_demo/gdhome.asn)

By enabling its users to control the pace of Web presentations, Astound Web Player strikes a blow for interactivity and user-friendliness. Streaming multimedia technology enables Astound Web Player to speed up the delivery of huge Web presentations. Ideal for viewing marketing and instructional material, Astound Web Player handles files created with Gold Disk's Astound and Studio M products — demos of which may be had on the Gold Disk site, as can the full version of Astound Web Player itself. Astound and Studio M multimedia exhibits can include sound, animation, user interaction in the forms of buttons and hyperlinks, and snazzy effects such as wipes and dissolves.

Astound Web Player has some pretty cool technical features. Its marketing materials sound like a veritable litany of Web buzzwords. To wit:

Astound Web Player uses streaming, which means it can show you one part of a presentation while it downloads another part. This feature means you can start watching the first part of an Astound or Studio M presentation before the entire presentation has finished traversing the network. That's especially handy when viewing large presentations.

Astound Web Player can handle presentations that occupy the entire window of a browser; so you can make your whole page a multimedia extravaganza for

Astound Web Player-equipped browsers. Also worthy of note is that it's easy to designate alternate pages for people who visit your page with something other than Netscape Navigator and cannot handle plug-in material.

 Some of the most annoying bugs include the fact that the music in Astound and Studio M presentations, playing in a browser window, will continue to play when you change to another program. It's really annoying to be watching a presentation with Astound Web Player, then toggle over to Word or some other program and still have the presentation's music playing. This holds true even when the other application plays sounds — the two sounds play at the same time. What's more, playing the music when you've hidden the browser window taxes your computer's processing power and can slow down your machine's operation.

Plug-in Power Rating: ★★★

Installing Astound Web Player

To install Astound Web Player on your Windows 95 system:

1. Visit the plug-in's home page at `http://www.golddisk.com/awp.html`.
2. Click on the links that match your computer and browser and save the downloaded file in a directory by itself.
3. After the file downloads completely, shut down your browser.
4. Run the downloaded file, and the Astound Web Player will go about the task of attaching itself to your browser. You'll be asked to specify where on your hard disk you want the Astound files to reside — the defaults are probably just fine.
5. Restart your browser. Astound should be ready to go.

To install Astound Web Player on your Macintosh or Power Macintosh system:

1. Visit the plug-in's home page at `http://www.golddisk.com/awp.html`.
2. Click on the links that match your computer and browser and save the downloaded file in a temporary folder by itself.

Using Astound Web Player

Like most plug-ins, using Astound Web Player couldn't be much easier once you've installed it. When you visit a site that wants to send Astound or Studio M data to your computer, at first you'll see a field of Astound logos, often with a gray bar at the bottom. Such a display appears in Figure 3-3. Wait a minute for the first part of the presentation to download. Remember, you won't have to wait for the whole, possibly ponderous, presentation to arrive at your computer. Astound Web Player's streaming technology saves you from that fate.

When Astound Web Player is downloading data from the Web, you'll see a gray bar at the bottom of the placeholder graphic. The gray bar holds percentage figures that show how much of a file has downloaded. The status bar appears in Figure 3-3.

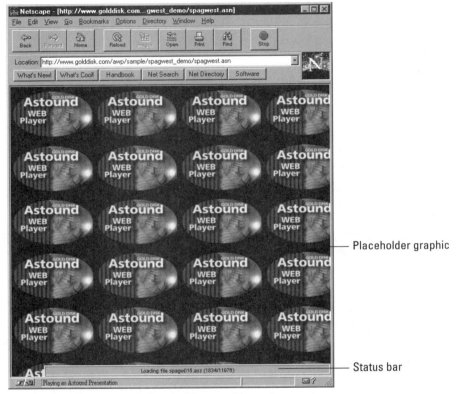

Placeholder graphic

Status bar

Figure 3-3: The Astound placeholder graphic and status bar.

Plugged-in sites

Astound Web Player hasn't yet made its way into common usage, but Gold Disk has put up some pretty cool demonstrations of the capabilities of its product. The company's Webmasters have accumulated links to all the demonstrations on the Sample Astound Web Projects page (http://www.golddisk.com/awp/demos. html). From that page, it's a snap to access several impressive (and often wacky) Astound-enabled pages.

A presentation (http://www.golddisk.com/marshall/webdemo.html) shows how some well-known Web sites (including Apple's and Netscape's) would look if enhanced with Astound technology. The results are fantastic. A still illustration of the enhanced Apple page appears in Figure 3-4. This presentation also is an excellent way to get an overview of Astound Web Player's capabilities.

Figure 3-4: Gold Disk's idea for an Astound-enhanced Apple Computer home page (http://www.golddisk.com/ marshall/webdemo.html).

You can find an advertisement for Cactus Leone's, a "Spaghetti Western" restaurant that serves refried risotto and burritos parmigiana, at (http://www. golddisk.com/awp/sample/spagwest_demo/spagwest.asn). This may be a fictional establishment (thankfully), but their Web people sure know how to put on a show with Astound. Part of the presentation appears in Figure 3-5.

Authoring for Astound Web Player

Creating Astound and Studio M presentations requires (surprise!) Astound or Studio M. You can download demonstration copies of these programs from the Gold Disk Web site at http://www.golddisk.com/awp/create.html. The demonstration programs are fully functional for 30 days but stop working after the trial period. Gold Disk sells full-fledged copies of Astound and Studio M.

Figure 3-5: The Cactus Leone's Astound-based advertisement
(http://www.golddisk.com/awp/sample/spagwest_demo/
spagwest.asn).

To attach a file to a Web page for the use of Astound Web Player, you use the
<EMBED> tag. Astound's syntax for the tag is one of the simplest of all plug-ins,
since it uses only the three mandatory attributes: SRC, WIDTH, and HEIGHT.

A typical Astound <EMBED> tag looks like this:

```
<EMBED SRC="DEMO.ASN" HEIGHT=500 WIDTH=200>
```

That tag would play the Astound presentation with the filename DEMO.ASN in a
box 500 pixels high and 200 pixels wide.

If you want your Astound or Studio M presentation to occupy the entire browser
window, don't embed the presentation at all. Instead, set it up as a hyperlink to
the presentation file. The following tag:

```
<A HREF="DEMO.ASN">Here's an Astound presentation</A>
```

would yield hyperlinked text ("Here's an Astound presentation") that, when
clicked on, would cause the Astound slide show to fill the entire browser window.
This method has the added advantage of working with browsers that do not
understand the <EMBED> tag but have Astound configured as a helper application.

ClearFusion

Creator: Iterated Systems

Function: Plays Video for Windows (.AVI) files containing video and animation

Home Site: http://webber.iterated.com/coolfusn/download/cf-loadp.htm

Supported Platforms: All Macintosh systems and Windows 95

Authoring Tool: Any video editor that will generate .AVI files, such as Adobe Premiere

Good Examples: Jurassic Park (http://www.acm.uiuc.edu/rml/Mpeg/Avi/); Apollo space clips (http://128.165.1.1/solarsys/raw/apo/); figure skating (http://haskell.cs.yale.edu/sjl/skate-images/kevin/jumpspin.html); MTV Japan (http://www.meshnet.or.jp/MTVJAPAN/program/menu.html)

Windows' native video file type is Video for Windows, with its .AVI extension. ClearFusion enables you to transfer these files across the Web and play them immediately (more or less, depending on the speed of your network connection). This plug-in allows for data streaming (which reduces download time) and provides simple but effective controls for adjusting the playback of video (see Figure 3-6). Streaming is ClearFusion's advantage over LiveVideo, which comes with Netscape Navigator 3.0 and also plays .AVI files.

Plug-in Power Rating: ★★★

Installing ClearFusion

To install ClearFusion in a Windows 95 system:

1. Point your browser at http://webber.iterated.com/coolfusn/download/cf-loadp.htm and start downloading the file CF20W32.EXE. Save the file in an empty temporary directory.

2. Run CF20W32.EXE. It's a self-extracting archive file and will expand itself. Just close the DOS window when the title bar says, "Finished."

3. Run SETUP.EXE, which should have appeared in your temporary directory when you expanded the archive. Unless you have an unusual situation, accept all the options, which will install the plug-in into standard locations on your hard disk.

4. Restart your browser. ClearFusion will be ready to go.

No instructions for installing ClearFusion on a Macintosh are available at this writing.

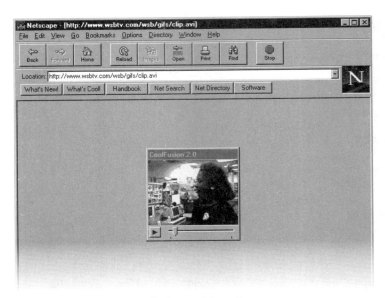

Figure 3-6: ClearFusion playing a video clip.

Using ClearFusion

When you click on a link to an .AVI file, ClearFusion will spring into action without any special attention from you. You'll see a small window appear in your browser window, and the video clip will begin to play there. You can click on the title bar of the ClearFusion window and drag it anywhere you want, just as you would do with any other window on your desktop.

The ClearFusion window has a number of controls that enable you to adjust the way the plug-in plays video and animation. The most basic control is the Start/Stop button that appears in the lower-left corner of the ClearFusion window. If there is a triangle icon on this button, click on the button and the clip will start to play. A square icon means that clicking on the button will cause the clip to stop. In reality, if you're using a dialup connection to retrieve video clips from the Internet, you'll find that as data downloads, the video playback pauses quite a bit anyway.

Figure 3-7 shows the ClearFusion control menu that appears when you right-click on (in Windows systems) or long-click on (on Macintoshes) the video frame. You can start and stop the video and make adjustments to ClearFusion's various options via the pop-up menu.

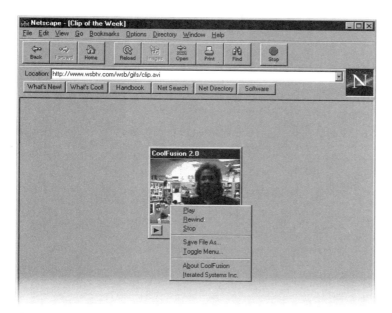

Figure 3-7: The ClearFusion control menu.

ClearFusion only works well with .AVI files that aren't compressed (or are "compressed" at a ratio of 1:1). If a clip you're viewing flashes or flickers while downloading, it's probably compressed. Future versions of ClearFusion may solve the compression problem.

The sites recommended in the ClearFusion information box all feature uncompressed clips.

Plugged-in sites

Want to see what ClearFusion will do? Take a look at these sites:

✦ **Jurassic Park** (http://www.acm.uiuc.edu/rml/Mpeg/Avi/). Here, you'll find scenes from the mega-popular dino-thriller.

✦ **Apollo space clips** (http://128.165.1.1/solarsys/raw/apo/). Video clips from America's man-on-the-moon program. One of these clips, playing in ClearFusion, appears in Figure 3-8.

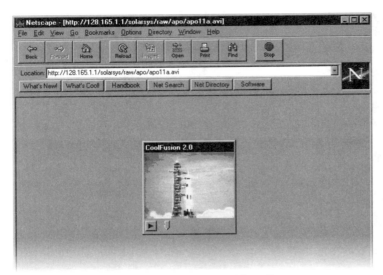

Figure 3-8: ClearFusion playing a NASA video clip.

✦ **Figure skating** (http://haskell.cs.yale.edu/sjl/skate-images/
kevin/jumpspin.html). Spins, camels, and death drops. ClearFusion playing one of these clips appears in Figure 3-9.

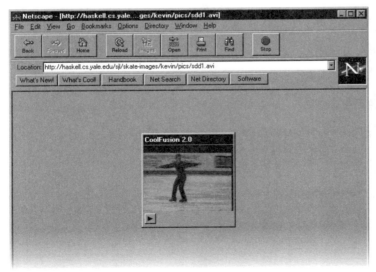

Figure 3-9: ClearFusion playing a figure skating video.

✦ **MTV Japan** (http://www.meshnet.or.jp/MTVJAPAN/program/menu.html). Clips from the Japanese incarnation of everyone's favorite catatonia-inducing network.

Authoring for ClearFusion

You can generate cool .AVI clips for your own site with any video editing program that will output in .AVI format. Adobe Premiere is an excellent choice for video editing on both Windows and Macintosh computers.

To add a Video for Windows (.AVI) clip to your Web page, use the <EMBED> tag. A typical use is <EMBED SRC="AIRPLANE.AVI" WIDTH=176 HEIGHT=144>, where AIRPLANE.AVI is the file to be played; and WIDTH and HEIGHT are the size, in pixels, of the ClearFusion window that appears when the clip plays.

Emblaze

Creator: Interactive Media Group

Function: Displays still pictures and (silent) animation very smoothly at data-transfer rates as low as 14.4 Kbps

Home Site: http://Geo.inter.net/Geo/technology/emblaze/downloads.html

Supported Platforms: All Macintosh and Windows systems

Authoring Tool: Emblaze Creator, on the Web at http://www.Geo.Inter.net/technology/emblaze/creator.html

Good Examples: You'll find a directory of Emblaze sites at http://www.Geo.Inter.net/technology/emblaze/animations.html. Some of the best include an animated clock at http://www.Geo.Inter.net/technology/emblaze/animations/clock.html, some animated graphs at http://www.Geo.Inter.net/technology/emblaze/animations/graphs.html, and an animated version of the old navigation bar from the Netscape site at http://www.Geo.Inter.net/technology/emblaze/animations/penguin.html.

Unveiled at a Cannes trade show in February, 1996, Emblaze boasts some of the best animation performance for low-speed connections to the Web. Though it doesn't yet support sound, Emblaze allows you to create animations that run smoothly on 14.4 Kbps modem connections and with hardly any delay at all on 28.8 Kbps and faster connections. Emblaze can display still graphics drawn in Emblaze Creator, but its real strength is in animation.

Installing Emblaze

To install Emblaze on a Windows 95 or Windows 3.1 system:

1. Point your browser at `http://Geo.inter.net/Geo/technology/emblaze/downloads.html` and download NPBLZ32.DLL for a Windows 95 system, or NPBLZ16.DLL for a Windows 3.*x* system. Be sure you save the file in the PLUG-INS subdirectory of the directory containing your browser's program files.

2. Shut down and restart your browser. Emblaze will be ready to go.

To install Emblaze on a Macintosh system:

1. Point your browser at `http://Geo.inter.net/Geo/technology/emblaze/downloads.html` and download the version of PLUG.SIT.HQX for either a standard Macintosh or a Power Macintosh.

2. Use StuffIt Expander to decompress the archive file (you may have already configured your browser to start StuffIt automatically). A file called EmblazeFAT will emerge from the archive file.

3. Move EmblazeFAT to your PLUGINS folder.

4. Shut down and restart your browser. Emblaze will be ready to go.

Using Emblaze

Using Emblaze is a real zero-brainer. You call up a document containing an Emblaze still picture or animation, and the plug-in does the rest. There are no controls to use or adjustments to make. Emblaze runs smoothly and without complication.

The one shortcoming of Emblaze is that you can't leave a site while an Emblaze animation is playing, and there's no way to stop animations before they've run their course. If you want to leave a site, you must wait until the embedded animation finishes playing.

Plugged-in sites

There's a directory of example Emblaze pages at `http://www.Geo.Inter.net/technology/emblaze/animations.html`, and links to some of the best Emblaze-enabled pages on the Web at `http://www.Geo.Inter.net/technology/emblaze/world.html`.

The Emblaze clock, at `http://www.Geo.Inter.net/technology/emblaze/animations/clock.html` and pictured in Figure 3-10, shows some of the things Emblaze can do. The clock's hands spin; then the humanoid clock spins around, gestures with its thumb to the left side of your screen, and dances off-screen.

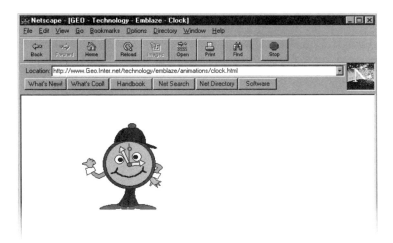

Figure 3-10: The Emblaze clock animation.

The Emblaze business animation, at http://www.Geo.Inter.net/technology/emblaze/animations/graphs.html and pictured in Figure 3-11, shows some of the less frivolous applications of Emblaze. In this example, columns in a column chart grow, and bars wiggle across a bar chart.

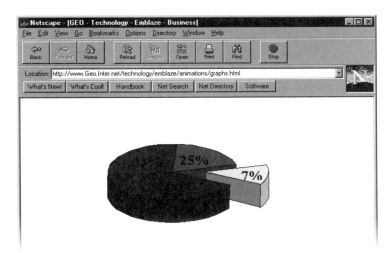

Figure 3-11: The Emblaze business animation.

Don't miss the 46 Things That Never Happen in Star Trek page, either. It's at
`http://www.Geo.Inter.net/technology/emblaze/animations/fish.html`
and is pictured in Figure 3-12. There's a really cool animation of colorful fish that,
as the page notes, "has absolutely nothing to do with the text of this page," but
which illustrates what Emblaze can do.

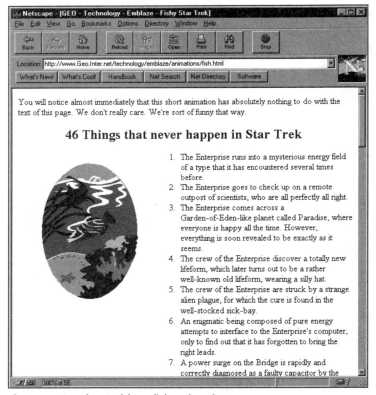

Figure 3-12: The Emblaze fish animation.

Authoring for Emblaze

To create Emblaze animations and still pictures, you need a copy of Emblaze
Creator. Aim your browser at `http://www.Geo.Inter.net/technology/`
`emblaze/creator_downloads.html` and download Emblaze Creator. At this writing, it's available only for Macintosh computers, though the program's output may
be read by any computer for which there is an Emblaze plug-in (that is, any
Windows or Macintosh machine).

Note that if you're going to use Emblaze Creator to build animations for your Web site, you're required by the program's license agreement to put the Emblaze logo and a link to the Emblaze home page on your Web page.

The HTML for embedding Emblaze pictures and animations in your page is similar to the code used for other plug-in material. You use the `<EMBED>` tag with `WIDTH` and `HEIGHT` attributes that specify how much space the browser should allocate for the plug-in display.

For example, the following tag would result in the animation CAT.BLZ being displayed in a box 300 pixels high and 450 pixels wide:

```
<EMBED SRC="cat.blz" HEIGHT=300 WIDTH=450>
```

mBED

Creator: mBED Software

Function: Plays *mbedlets* — animations that can jazz up a Web page with motion

Home Site: `http://www.mbed.com/`

Supported Platforms: All Macintosh and Windows systems

Authoring Tool: The Incredible Mbedable Machine, available at `http://www.mbed.com/machine.html`

Good Examples: The mBED Software home page (`http://www.mbed.com/home.html`); SilkPresence (`http://www.silkpresence.com/silkpresence/`); Fingerstyle Guitar Online (`http://www.cstone.net/~crispy/acoustic.html`)

One of the easiest ways to create animation for your Web site, mBED provides everything you need to author animations — called mbedlets — on the Web. That means you can go to mBED Software's Web site, find the Incredible Mbedable Machine, and manipulate its controls to generate the sort of animation you want. You can then save that animation to your site, making it available to anyone who visits your pages with the mBED plug-in.

The Web-based Incredible Mbedable Machine is a demonstration version of the mbedlet design tools that mBED sells, but it's plenty powerful for the designer of a personal home page or a simple corporate site. The Web version of the design tool isn't overwhelmingly powerful, but it's powerful enough for a lot of uses and hints at a great future for embedded animation.

In brief, mBED is a complete, Web-based animation solution. The generosity of mBED Software is incredible, since the company's officials have put all this plug-in technology on the Web for anyone to use and are receiving only goodwill and free advertising in return for their efforts.

Plug-in Power Rating: ★★★★

Installing mBED

To install mBED in a Windows 95 or Windows 3.*x* system:

1. Point your browser at `http://www.mbed.com/noembed/download.html` and download the file MBED32.EXE (for Windows 95) or MBED16.EXE (for Windows 3.*x*). Save the file in an empty temporary directory.

2. Run the file you downloaded. It's a self-extracting archive file and will expand itself. Just close the DOS window when the title bar says, "Finished."

3. Run SETUP.EXE, which should have appeared in your temporary directory when you expanded the archive. Unless you have an unusual situation, accept all the options; this will install the plug-in into standard locations on your hard disk.

4. Restart your browser. mBED will be ready to go.

To install mBED on a Macintosh system:

1. Point your browser at `http://www.mbed.com/noembed/download.html` and click on the link for either Power Macintosh or 68K Macintosh.

2. If you have StuffIt configured correctly as a helper application, it will automatically open the archive file and store its contents in the Temporary folder in your browser's folder. Move the uncompressed file to the Plugins folder in your browser's folder.

3. Restart your browser; mBED will be ready to go.

Using mBED

You don't "use" mBED; it just kind of happens when you call up an mBED-aware site after installing the mBED plug-in. When you open a Web page with mbedlets in it, you'll briefly see an mBED placeholder logo that temporarily fills the space an mbedlet will fill while that mbedlet downloads. The mBED placeholder graphic appears in Figure 3-13.

Figure 3-13: The mBED placeholder graphic.

After the mbedlet downloads, it goes about its business without any attention from you. Some mbedlets work a little like Java applications, in that they can have menu bars, drop-down menus, sliders, and interactive animation. To see what happens when you do certain things, use your mouse to play around with specific mbedlets. You may be surprised by what you discover.

Plugged-in sites

Some of the best mbedlets appear on the mBED Software site itself. There's an animated version of the company's home page at `http://www.mbed.com/home.html` that features flying balls and a sun and moon that rise and set in the arc formed by the arms of the bright yellow man in the mBED logo. The animated mBED Software home page appears in Figure 3-14.

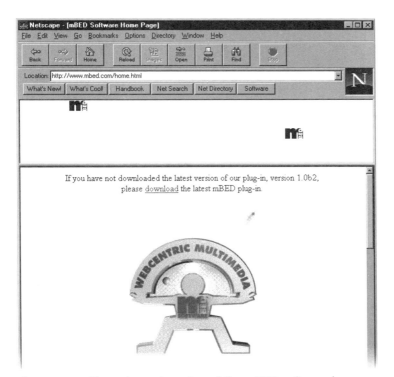

Figure 3-14: The animated version of the mBED software home page.

There's no formal directory of mbedlet-enhanced sites; but according to company officials, some of the most exemplary sites include

✦ **SilkPresence** (http://www.silkpresence.com/silkpresence/). At SilkPresence, you'll find an mbedlet that shows a *2001*-like monolith with a shadow that revolves around it and buttons that change their textures as your mouse pointer passes over them. The site — an advertisement and demonstration for an Internet consultant — also boasts some nifty information about cutting-edge Web technologies and links to some top-notch sites. The SilkPresence welcome page, with the monolith-and-shadow mbedlet, appears in Figure 3-15.

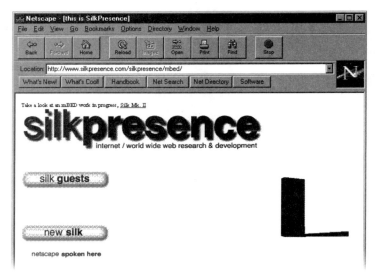

Figure 3-15: SilkPresence (http://www.silkpresence.com/silkpresence/).

✦ **Fingerstyle Guitar Online** (http://www.cstone.net/~crispy/acoustic.html). This site provides an excellent demonstration of how you can use mbedlets to enhance interface design. A guitar-tutorial site that instructs novices in the intricacies of fingering and picking an acoustic guitar, Fingerstyle features buttons that change shape as your mouse pointer passes over them, animated maps of the site, and pop-up messages that help site visitors determine the functions of various interface elements. Though the site falls down occasionally — not all the mbedlets do what the site manager claims, and the site's frames don't always work right — Fingerstyle Guitar Online is a great example of how plug-ins can enhance a site's user interface. The site's welcome page, with animated buttons, appears in Figure 3-16.

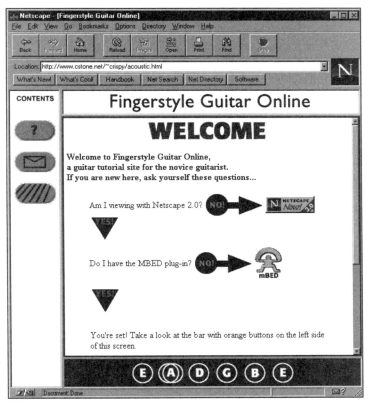

Figure 3-16: Fingerstyle Guitar Online (http://www.cstone.net/~crispy/acoustic.html).

Authoring for mBED

To create an mbedlet, you use an mbedlet. This self-referential, almost Zenlike statement testifies to the versatility and usefulness of the mBED plug-in. The mbedlet you use for designing Web animation is the Incredible Mbedable Machine, which you'll find on the mBED Software site at http://www.mbed.com/machine.html. The Machine appears in Figure 3-17.

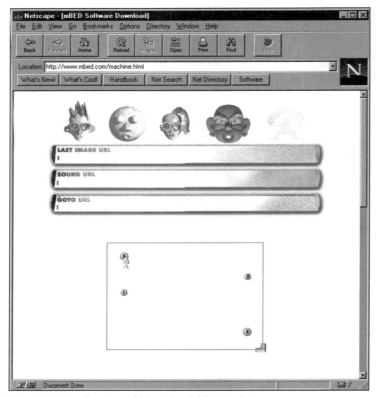

Figure 3-17: The Incredible Mbedable Machine.

The Machine holds you to creating mbedlets in a pretty narrow range of styles — basically, you build an animation in which one of five images moves from one point to another. You get to define whether the graphic spins and whether it moves in a straight path or a curvy one. You also get to say whether the moving object reacts to mouse clicks at all. When you're happy with the behavior of the demonstration plug-in you've created, click on the Make Mbedlet button, and a new browser window will appear. The new window will contain a link that, when clicked on, downloads your new mbedlet to your computer. There are other links in the new window that allow you to download the image files, sound files, and other elements that make up your mbedlet. You must store all these files on your Web server if you want the mbedlet to be accessible to Web surfers who visit your site. One of these pages appears in Figure 3-18.

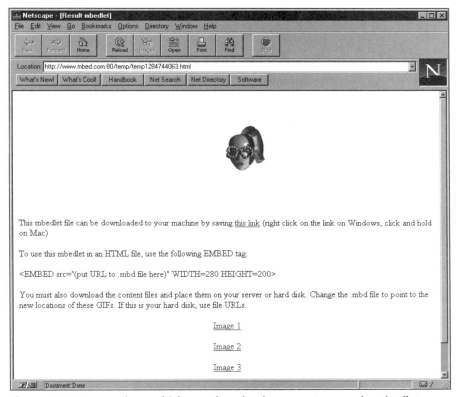

Figure 3-18: A page from which you download your custom-made mbedlet.

Embedding mbedlets in your Web pages is, as usual, handled with the <EMBED> tag. The Incredible Mbedable Machine, though, makes HTML coding for mbedlets very easy, since the browser window that contains the links for downloading your multimedia files also contains the needed snippet of HTML code. A typical <EMBED> tag for an mbedlet looks like this:

```
<EMBED SRC="http://www.foo.com/mbedlets/FOOTBALL.MBD" WIDTH=280
       HEIGHT=200>
```

That code puts an mbedlet called FOOTBALL.MBD in a 280-pixel-by-200-pixel box on your Web page.

Mbedlets are, in fact, miniature computer programs. You may want to examine the guts of an mbedlet at some time by looking at the source code that makes an mbedlet run, as you would with any other computer program.

To view source code, call up the page that contains the mbedlet whose source code you want to see. Then, use your browser's command for viewing the source code of the Web page. In Netscape Navigator, choose View, Document Source from the menu bar. You'll see the HTML code for the Web page.

In the HTML code, look for the `<EMBED>` tag of the mbedlet that interests you. Note the filename of the mbedlet. The filename will follow the `SRC` attribute in the `<EMBED>` tag and will have an .MBD extension.

Enter mbedlet's URL in your browser's location box. For example, if you saw an mbedlet at `http://www.davewall.com/home.htm`, and you discovered that the mbedlet's filename was JUGGLER.MBD, you'd enter `http://www.davewall.com/JUGGLER.MBD` in your browser's location box.

Press the Enter key. Your browser will then display the mBED placeholder icon. Choose View, Document Source from the menu bar again. You'll see the mbedlet's source code, free for the copying and pasting. Be sure, though, that the mbedlet's author has given permission if you intend to modify or redistribute the mbedlet code.

MovieStar

Creator: Intelligence at Large

Function: Displays QuickTime movies

Home Site: `http://www.beingthere.com/`

Supported Platforms: All Macintosh and Windows systems

Authoring Tool: MovieStar Maker

Good Examples: A QuickTime archive at `http://www.beingthere.com/moviestar/movies/`; MTC Movies at `http://www.itp.tsoa.nyu.edu/~boom/mtcmovies2.html`

One of the first plug-ins for playing QuickTime movies, MovieStar is excellently robust and versatile. Though it doesn't stream video — meaning you have to wait until an entire movie downloads before you can see any of it — MovieStar offers simple, intuitive controls and high-quality reproduction of video footage (see Figure 3-19).

Plug-in Power Rating: ★★★

Figure 3-19: MovieStar showing a QuickTime movie.

Installing MovieStar

To install MovieStar:

1. Make sure your browser is equipped with QuickTime version 2.1 or later. If you need QuickTime, download it from `http://quicktime.apple.com/qt/sw/licensew.html`.

2. Point your browser at `http://www.beingthere.com/moviestar/plugins/getmstar.html/`.

3. Click on the link that corresponds to your operating environment.

4. Scroll to the bottom of the page and fill in the registration form. Click on the CONTINUE button.

5. Click on one of the download links that corresponds to your operating environment.

6. Save the downloaded file by itself in a temporary directory.

7. Shut down your browser.

8. Windows users will have to decompress the downloaded file with WinZip. Macintosh users should use StuffIt to decompress their downloaded file.

9. Windows 95 users should run the file they unzipped — it's an automatic installation routine that will install MovieStar automatically. Macintosh and Windows 3.*x* users should move the plug-in file to their PLUGINS directories.

10. Restart your browser. MovieStar will be ready to go.

Using MovieStar

Using MovieStar is like using a VCR. At the bottom of a MovieStar frame, you'll find several controls, all of which are labeled in Figure 3-20. The main controls are

✦ **Volume.** Click on the Volume button to reveal a vertical slider that allows you to control the volume.

✦ **Play/Pause.** If the movie isn't playing, this button makes it start. Otherwise, it pauses the playback.

✦ **Position slider.** Find a specific frame of a movie by dragging the position slider back and forth.

✦ **Rewind**. Quickly move backward through a movie.

✦ **Fast-forward.** Quickly move forward through a movie.

Plugged-in sites

Want to see what MovieStar can do? Point your browser at any QuickTime archive (Yahoo! keeps a listing) or at one of these movies:

✦ **Snake Hunt** (http://www.tsoa.nyu.edu/itp/mtc/mov/snakehunt.mov). Marvel as grown-ups flail in the grass in search of a snake. What would Milton say? Snake Hunt appears in Figures 3-19 and 3-21.

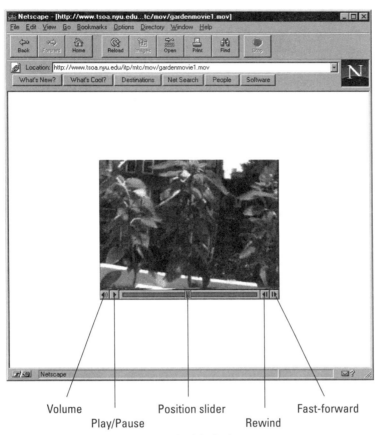

Volume   Position slider   Fast-forward
      Play/Pause   Rewind

Figure 3-20. MovieStar's controls, labeled.

Figure 3-21: MovieStar on a Snake Hunt.

✦ **The Gnarlier the Better** (`http://www.tsoa.nyu.edu/itp/mtc/mov/gardenmovie1.mov`). A product, like Snake Hunt, of urban gardener ***, The Gnarlier the Better illustrates how ruined urban land can become beautiful and useful garden space. The movie appears in Figure 3-22.

Authoring for MovieStar

You can create QuickTime movies — the kind MovieStar can play — with practically any video-authoring package, since most such programs support QuickTime. Adobe Premiere is but one popular example.

After generating a QuickTime movie, you should prepare it for the Web with MovieStar Maker, a demonstration version of which you can download free of charge from the Intelligence at Large site.

Figure 3-22: The Gnarlier the Better.

When you're ready to attach MovieStar content to a Web page, use the ⟨EMBED⟩ tag. In addition to the basic SRC, WIDTH, and HEIGHT attributes, MovieStar supports many optional attributes. They are

- ✦ LOOP. Set to TRUE, the clip repeats infinitely. Set to FALSE, it plays only one time. Set to PALINDROME, the clip plays forward, then backward, infinitely. If you set LOOP equal to an integer, the clip repeats that many times.

- ✦ AUTOSTART. Set to TRUE, the movie plays automatically when loaded. Set to FALSE, the user must click on the Play button.

- ✦ AUTOPLAY. Equivalent of AUTOSTART.

- ✦ HREF. Set equal to a partial (relative) URL, HREF lets you treat your movie like a linked image.

- ✦ HREFABS. Set equal to a full (absolute) URL, HREFABS is similar to HREF.

- ✦ HREFTARGET. Specifies the wanted frame or window of a URL specified in HREF or HREFABS.

- ✦ ISMAP. Designates the video frame as a clickable map.

◆ CONTROLLER. Set equal to TRUE, FALSE or BADGE, CONTROLLER specifies how the video controls appear. The BADGE value puts a small filmstrip icon in the video frame, which you can click on to bring up the entire control panel.

◆ MCWITHBADGE. MCWITHBADGE=TRUE is the same as CONTROLLER=BADGE.

◆ MCNOTVISIBLE. MCNOTVISIBLE=TRUE is the same as CONTROLLER=FALSE, while MCNOTVISIBLE=FALSE is the same as CONTROLLER=TRUE.

◆ NOPICTURE. When present, NOPICTURE hides the MovieStar logo, which usually appears before the video.

◆ VOLUME. Set to an integer between 0 and 100, inclusive, VOLUME specifies how loud the plug-in should play the clip's sound track.

◆ PLAYRATE. Set to an integer that represents a percentage of the normal QuickTime playback rate, PLAYRATE defines how fast a clip plays.

◆ MCWITHFRAME. When set equal to TRUE, MCWITHFRAME puts a thin black border around the video frame.

◆ MCSCALEMOVIETOFIT. Set to TRUE, MCSCALEMOVIETOFIT makes the movie larger, to fit the frame defined by WIDTH and HEIGHT. Left equal to FALSE, the default, MCSCALEMOVIETOFIT centers the video.

◆ MCTOPLEFTMOVIE. Set to TRUE, MCTOPLEFTMOVIE moves the video frame to the top-left corner of the frame defined by WIDTH and HEIGHT. Left equal to FALSE, the default, MCTOPLEFTMOVIE centers the video.

PreVU

Creator: InterVU

Function: Enables you to view embedded MPEG video clips with audio tracks

Home Site: http://www.intervu.com/prevu.html

Supported Platforms: All Macintosh and Windows 95 systems

Authoring Tool: Any video editor, such as Adobe Premiere, that can output MPEG files

Good Examples: A video tour of Todos Santos Island (http://www.intervu.com/devzone/demolib/todos/todosmain.html); a clip of the Navy's Blue Angels precision flying team (http://www.intervu.com/prevu.html)

As little tolerance as I have for them, I feel like invoking the presence of MTV animated vidiots Beavis and Butt-Head to properly laud PreVU. That's how cool this plug-in is — it requires a couple of professional screen-watchers to properly sing its praises. But, in the interest of space (and copyright), this book will stick to plain, old descriptive prose.

PreVU lets Web site designers embed MPEG video clips, complete with audio tracks, in Web pages almost as easily as they can embed still GIF or JPEG graphics. That means PreVU heralds an era when, instead of pages populated with boring stills, the Web will be full of pages loaded with sound and video. PreVU streams video data — that is, it will start playing a video before the video has been entirely downloaded — and the plug-in will automatically start playing a video when someone downloads the page on which it appears.

PreVU's main shortcoming is its lack of controls. There's no way to rewind a video partially — you must start watching it from the beginning. Also, there's no playback speed control, and there's no way to shut off the audio portion of a clip in order to cut down on distraction or reduce download time. Still, PreVU is an excellent player for the very common MPEG video file format.

Plug-in Power Rating: ★★★★

Installing PreVU

To install PreVU on a Windows 95 system:

1. Point your browser at `http://www.intervu.com/prevu.html` and download the file IV0_952.EXE. (The filename may have changed by the time you read this). Save the file alone in a temporary directory.

2. After the file downloads completely, shut down your browser.

3. Run IV0_952.EXE, or whichever file you downloaded. It's PreVU's setup program.

4. Step through the dialog boxes in the installation program. You'll probably want to install PreVU in the default location specified by the installation routine, but you can alter the target directory if you want.

5. At the end of the installation process, click on Yes when asked if you want to see a demonstration and help page. Your browser will restart, and you'll immediately get an idea of what PreVU can do for you (although you may have to scroll down a bit to see the video example).

To install PreVU on a Macintosh computer:

1. Point your browser at `http://www.intervu.com/prevu.html` and download the file MACPVOp92.HQX. (The filename may have changed by the time you read this.) Save the file alone in a temporary directory.

2. After the file downloads completely, shut down your browser. Decompress the file with StuffIt Expander.

3. Run MacPVOp92, or whichever executable came from the file you downloaded. It's PreVU's setup program.

4. Step through the dialog boxes in the installation program. You'll probably want to install PreVU in the default location specified by the installation routine, but you can alter the target directory if you want.

5. At the end of the installation process, click on Yes when asked if you want to see a demonstration and help page. Your browser will restart, and you'll immediately get an idea of what PreVU can do for you (although you may have to scroll down a bit to see the video example).

Using PreVU

The slickest function of PreVU is as a player of embedded video (video that's been integrated into a Web page with text and traditional graphical elements). When playing embedded MPEG files (you'll learn how to embed such files in your own pages later in this section), PreVU runs the video in a frame amid other parts of a larger Web page.

Using PreVU to play embedded files isn't hard. When your browser loads a page containing an embedded MPEG, PreVU will occupy a frame within the page (not a free-floating window). Before you click on the Play button (the green triangle in the lower-left corner of the PreVU frame), the plug-in will display the first frame of the video it's downloading. Figure 3-23 shows a video ready to play.

If you want to play the video, click on the Play button or click on the frame of video itself. Though PreVU does use streaming, videos play best when they've downloaded completely. So unless you're on an intranet or a very-high-speed Internet connection, you may want to wait a bit while the whole video descends from the Web into your computer. You can stop a video as it's playing by clicking on the Stop button (the red square that replaces the Play button while the video is in progress) or clicking on the video frame itself. Figure 3-24 shows PreVU actually playing a video.

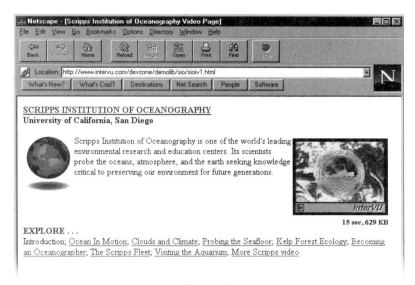

Figure 3-23: PreVU waiting to play a video.

You can also use PreVU as a player for MPEG videos that reside locally on your own computer's hard disk. Double-click on an MPEG file to open it with your browser and play it with PreVU, or drag the file's icon to your browser's window. If you follow this route, your videos will play in the center of a blank browser window — not as attractive as embedded video, but completely functional.

After PreVU finishes playing a video, a button with a picture of a floppy disk on it will appear next to the Play button. That's the Save As button. Click on the Save As button to save the file to a local disk.

Note that if the speaker icon in the lower-right corner of the PreVU frame is crossed out, the video has no accompanying audio. Also be aware that if you click on the PreVU logo next to the speaker, and you're connected to the Web, your browser will call up the InterVU home page.

Figure 3-24: PreVU in action.

Plugged-in sites

Lots of Web sites have archives of MPEG video clips, but relatively few sites take advantage of the really appealing multimedia capabilities of PreVU by embedding videos among other Web content. Here are a few sites that do embed videos. Be sure to check them out:

✦ A video tour of Todos Santos island, off the coast of California (`http://www.intervu.com/devzone/demolib/todos/todosmain.html`). This example appears in Figure 3-25.

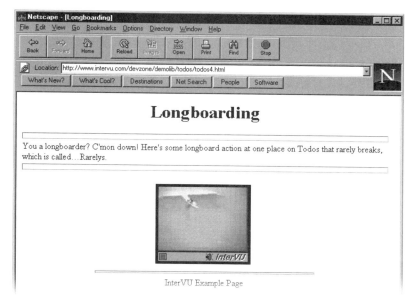

InterVU Example Page

Figure 3-25: Video surfing at Todos Santos.

✦ A brief demo clip on the InterVU site (`http://www.intervu.com/prevu.html`). At this writing, the demo features footage of the Navy's Blue Angels precision-flying team. This demo appears in Figures 3-23 and 3-24.

Authoring for PreVU

You can create MPEG videos with any of several video-editing tools, including Adobe Premiere. Explaining elaborate video software is beyond the scope of this book.

How do you embed your MPEG videos in your Web pages? Again, it's a function of the `<EMBED>` tag. The basic syntax for the `<EMBED>` tag is

```
<EMBED SRC="BIKE.MPG" WIDTH=200 height=150>
```

In this example, the embedded video clip is called BIKE.MPG (it's in the same directory as the Web page on which you see it), and it will appear in a frame 200 pixels wide and 150 pixels high.

Remember, when setting `HEIGHT` and `WIDTH` for embedded MPEG videos meant to be viewed with PreVU, you have to add 29 pixels to the height of your video frames to allow space for the control bar at the bottom of the video window. (If you use the `CONBAR=NO` attribute, which you'll learn about soon, you need to add only 10 pixels to the vertical size of your frame.) Likewise, you need to add 10 pixels to the width of your video frames to allow for left and right borders. You can determine the size of your video frames in your video-editing program.

SRC, WIDTH, and HEIGHT are the only attributes you absolutely *must* include in your <EMBED> statements. There are some other attributes that may prove useful to you, though:

- ✦ AUTOPLAY. Including the attribute AUTOPLAY=YES in your <EMBED> tag causes the video to start playing without any action from the person viewing the page on which the tag appears. Leaving the AUTOPLAY attribute out, or specifying AUTOPLAY=NO, causes the first frame of the video to display automatically; but the video won't run without a mouse click.

- ✦ FRAMERATE (Windows systems only). Lets you define the number of frames PreVU plays each second, from 1 to 20. If you wanted your video to play at 15 frames per second, for example, you'd add FRAMERATE=15 to your <EMBED> tag. Don't diddle with the FRAMERATE attribute if you can help it, because if you specify a framerate, you'll lose the sound from your video clip.

- ✦ LOOP. Lets you specify how many times you want a video to repeat each time it starts. There's no way to tell the video to play infinitely, but you can specify something like LOOP=150, which has the same practical result.

- ✦ DOUBLESIZE (Windows systems only). Doubles the height and width of the frames in your video. If you use this attribute (syntax is DOUBLESIZE=YES), make sure you double your WIDTH and HEIGHT attributes, too.

- ✦ HALFSIZE (Windows systems only). Halves the height and width of the frames in your video. If you use this attribute (syntax is HALFSIZE=YES), make sure you halve your WIDTH and HEIGHT attributes, too.

- ✦ CONBAR. When the CONBAR=NO attribute appears in the <EMBED> tag, the control bar doesn't appear at the bottom of your PreVU pane. Be sure to adjust your HEIGHT attribute to allow for the reduced space demand.

- ✦ FRAMES. You must add the attribute FRAMES=YES if the page in which you're embedding an MPEG clip uses Netscape frames. This attribute also has the same effect as AUTOPLAY=YES in Macintosh browsers.

QuickTime

Creator: Apple Computer

Function: Displays QuickTime movies

Home Site: http://quicktime.apple.com/

Supported Platforms: All Windows and Macintosh systems

Authoring Tool: Any video package that complies with the QuickTime standard

Good Examples: An archive at `http://www.mediacity.com/~erweb`

Long-awaited by the browser crowd, Apple demonstrates with its QuickTime plug-in how video should be done on the Web. Offering streaming video and an extremely intuitive interface on top of excellent image quality, Apple raises the ante by making this plug-in useful not only for QuickTime video, but also for MPEG sound, QuickTime VR and QuickTime animations (see Figure 3-26).

You need to install QuickTime on your browser — as quickly as possible!

Plug-in Power Rating: ★★★★

Installing QuickTime

To install QuickTime

1. Point your browser at `http://quicktime.apple.com/qt/sw/licensep.html`.

2. Read the license agreement. If you agree to its terms, click on the Yes, I agree to these terms link at the bottom of the page.

3. Click on the link that corresponds to your operating environment.

4. Windows users should use WinZip to decompress the file they downloaded; Macintosh users should use StuffIt.

5. Shut down your browser.

6. Move the plug-in file to your PLUGINS directory. For Windows users, the plug-in file is a .DLL file. Macintosh users can recognize the characteristic plug-in puzzle-piece icon.

7. Restart your browser. QuickTime is ready for use.

Figure 3-26: QuickTime playing a BMW ad.

Using QuickTime

When you first download a page that contains an embedded QuickTime movie, you'll see the QuickTime logo and, most likely, the QuickTime control bar. When you see the logo, know that QuickTime is downloading information about the clip it is to play — it'll start playing it as soon as it has about 10 percent of the file downloaded.

If the controls are on the screen, take a look at the position slider (labeled in Figure 3-27). See how the left part of it is turning black, while the rest of it remains gray? The black portion of the bar indicates how much has been downloaded into your machine.

The other controls mimic those of a VCR or CD player. They are

✦ **Volume.** Click on the volume button to reveal a vertical slider with which you can adjust the sound volume.

✦ **Play/Pause.** When the clip is not playing, a click on the Play/Pause button with start it. When it's already playing, clicking on the button will halt playback.

✦ **Position slider.** Use the position slider to move back and forth through the movie.

✦ **Rewind.** Click on the rewind button to move back about 10 frames.

✦ **Fast-forward.** Click on the fast forward button to move ahead about 10 frames.

One of the coolest things about QuickTime is that it does much more than play movies. You can use QuickTime to play animations, MPEG sounds, and QuickTime VR virtual reality scenes.

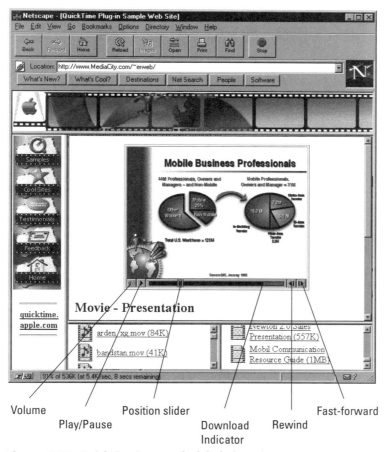

Figure 3-27: QuickTime's controls, labeled.

Plugged-In Sites

The best way to see what QuickTime can do is to point your browser at `http://www.mediacity.com/~erweb`, where Apple has assembled all kinds of demonstration clips highlighting the capabilities of QuickTime on the Web. All the illustrations in this section came from the Mediacity archive.

A couple of animation examples:

✦ **Learning to count** (`http://www.MediaCity.com/~erweb/frame/QuickTimeDemo/animation/number.html`). Here, QuickTime — without its control panel — plays an animated sequence of numbers under a corresponding number of cartoon worms (see Figure 3-28).

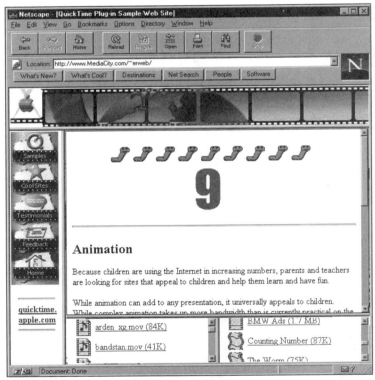

Figure 3-28: QuickTime playing an educational animation.

✦ **Clock** (`http://www.MediaCity.com/~erweb/frame/QuickTimeDemo/animation/clockgraphic.html`). Don't let this animation run too long in the background — the music that accompanies the surreal animation surely will drive you crazy (see Figure 3-29).

Figure 3-29: QuickTime and a wild animated clock.

Authoring for QuickTime

You can create QuickTime movies with practically any video-editing software, since nearly all of them support the QuickTime file standard. Most animation packages support QuickTime, too, and you can use Apple's QuickTime VR software to create virtual — reality scenes for QuickTime. You'll probably want to use Apple's Internet Movie Tool to optimize QuickTime files for streaming.

One especially attractive feature of QuickTime is the simplicity of its <EMBED> statement. In addition to the required SRC, WIDTH and HEIGHT attributes, QuickTime has only a few easy-to-understand optional attributes. They are

◆ CONTROLLER. Set to either TRUE or FALSE, CONTROLLER determines whether the controls appear at the bottom of the QuickTime frame.

◆ LOOP. Set to TRUE, the clip repeats over and over. Set to FALSE, the clip plays only once. Set to PALINDROME, the clip plays forward, then backward, over and over.

◆ AUTOPLAY. Set to TRUE, the clip starts playing automatically as soon as it's loaded. Set to FALSE, the clip waits for a click on the Play button.

Shockwave for Director

Creator: Macromedia

Function: Lets you view animations (complete with sound and interactivity) on the Web

Home Site: http://www.macromedia.com/Tools/Shockwave/index.html

Supported Platforms: All Macintosh and Windows systems

Authoring Tool: Macromedia Director

Good Examples: A shoot-em-up game at http://www.ezone.com/littlealien; an opportunity to rearrange Bob Dole's face at http://zoetek.com/entrance/doledir/Dole15.html; animated cartoons at http://www.bigtop.com/theater/sh_today.html; and a version of the Yahoo! subject tree with an animated banner at http://shock.yahoo.com/shock/

The granddaddy of the plug-in movement, Shockwave for Director is the best-known browser plug-in out there. It lets you view animations with sound that were created with the Macromedia Director authoring suite. Shockwave for Director made the Essential list because so many sites use Director files to bring their information to life — you don't want to browse without this plug-in.

Despite its popularity, Shockwave for Director has one serious shortcoming: It doesn't employ streaming. When you load a page that contains Shockwave for Director animations (Macromedia calls such pages "shocked" pages), you have to wait for the entire animation file to download. This can take a long time on a slow modem connection, and you should consider this delay if you're planning to include Director material in your site.

Plug-in Power Rating: ★★★★

Installing Shockwave for Director

Macromedia has three plug-ins, all with the Shockwave name. There's Shockwave for Director, the subject of this section. There's Shockwave for Freehand, which displays interactive graphics created with Macromedia FreeHand. And there's Shockwave for Authorware, which lets you create multimedia presentations optimized for CD-ROMs and intranets. You'll learn more about Shockwave for FreeHand and Shockwave for Authorware in Chapter 5 of this book. For now, the important thing to note is that Macromedia would like you to download all three at one time.

For the purposes of this book, I'll assume that you want to download and install only the Shockwave for Director plug-in here. You'll learn how to download and install the other two Macromedia plug-ins when you come to Chapter 5.

To install Shockwave for Director on a Windows 95 system:

1. Point your browser at `http://www-1.macromedia.com/Tools/Shockwave/Plugin/plugin.cgi`, and scroll down to the Custom Download area. Select Director from the list of options that follows the question, "Which applications do you need Shockwave for?" and select Windows 95 or Windows 3.1 from the box next to the question, "Which platform do you use?" Click on the Find Plug-ins button.

2. You'll have to read through Macromedia's license agreement and click on Accept if you agree with the terms it outlines.

3. Click on a server (i.e., `ftp1.macromedia.com`) from which to download the plug-in. Save the file N32D40.EXE (for Windows 95) or N16F50B2.exe (for Windows 3.1) to a temporary directory, by itself (remember, the files may have different names by the time you read this). The file is a self-extracting archive that contains the plug-in files.

4. When the file has finished downloading, shut down your browser.

5. Open the folder that contains the file you downloaded or find it with the File Manager in Windows 3.1. Double-click on its icon. A DOS window will open as the file decompresses itself. When the word Finished appears in the title bar, close the DOS window.

6. Look in the folder that contains the file you downloaded and its expanded contents. Double-click on the file called SETUP.EXE.

7. Step through the setup program. Accept the defaults, unless you installed your browser in non-standard directories.

8. Restart your browser. Shockwave for Director will be ready to go.

To install Shockwave for Director on a Macintosh or Power Macintosh:

1. Point your browser at `http://www-1.macromedia.com/Tools/Shockwave/Plugin/plugin.cgi`, and scroll down to the Custom Download area. Select Director from the list of options that follows the question, "Which applications do you need Shockwave for?" and select 68K Macintosh or Power Macintosh from the box next to the question, "Which platform do you use?" Click on the Find Plug-ins button.

2. You'll have to read through Macromedia's license agreement and click on Accept if you agree with the terms it outlines.

3. Click on a server (i.e., `ftp1.macromedia.com`) from which to download the plug-in. Save the file NPPD40.SEA.HQX (for Power Macintosh) or N68D40.SEA.HQX (for Macintosh) to a temporary folder, by itself (remember, the files may have different names by the time you read this). The file is an archive that contains the plug-in files.

4. After the file downloads completely, shut down your browser.

5. Double-click on the downloaded file. It will start StuffIt Lite, which will extract the plug-in files from the archive file.

6. In the folder into which StuffIt Lite decompressed the archive, you'll find a file called NP-MacPPC-Dir-Shockwave (on Power Macs) or NP-Mac68K-Dir-Shockwave (on standard Macs). Drag that file to your Plugins folder.

7. Restart your browser.

Using Shockwave for Director

This is another real zero-brainer. If you've installed Shockwave for Director properly, it will go to work displaying animations and interactive graphics as soon as you open the pages on which they appear. There aren't any adjustments to be made, options to be chosen, or dialog boxes to be negotiated.

In order for Shockwave for Director to work, you must be sure your browser's disk cache is 10,000 kilobytes, or larger, in size. In Netscape Navigator, you adjust the size of your disk cache by choosing Options, Network Preferences from the menu bar, then clicking on the Cache tab. Enter **10000** in the Disk Cache box and click on OK.

Plugged-in sites

Macromedia has established an excellent clearinghouse of links to Shocked sites from which you can find Shockwave for Director-based games, presentations, and entertainment sites. It's at `http://www.macromedia.com/Tools/Shockwave/Gallery/Epicenter/index.html`. You'll find links to sites tailored to Shockwave for Freehand and Shockwave for Authorware in this directory, too.

On the directory page, there's also a link to the Shocked Site of the Day, a featured site that gets prominent play on the Macromedia directory for 24 hours.

A few notable sites in the directory include

✦ **Shock Yahoo** (`http://shock.yahoo.com/shock/`). Functionally almost identical to the traditional, static Yahoo, Shock Yahoo adorns the venerable subject tree with an animated banner. The letters in the word Yahoo! spin and jiggle, and a tinny tune plays as you browse the subject headings. This site is good mainly for its novelty, since the Shockwave animation adds nothing to the usefulness of Yahoo, and the toy-piano tune gets really annoying in short order. Figure 3-30 shows the Shock Yahoo site.

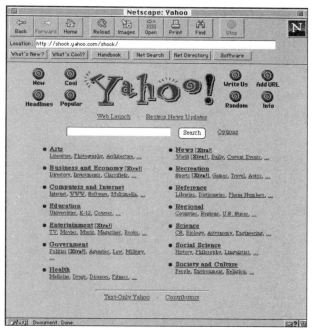

Figure 3-30: Shock Yahoo.

✦ **Shockwave Blackjack** (`http://www.onramp.net/joker/blackjack.html`). Whatever it is about computer card games that appeals to the deepest corners of computer users' souls, this site has it. A fully animated version of the popular casino game Blackjack put together by Onramp, an Internet Service Provider, this site makes the Web the dealer and keeps score as you try your luck. Shockwave Blackjack appears in Figure 3-31.

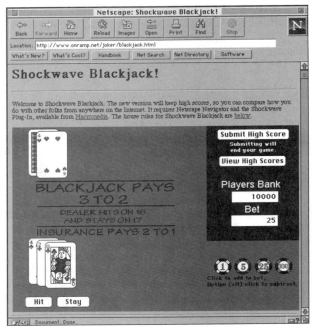

Figure 3-31: Shockwave Blackjack (http://www.
onramp.net/joker/blackjack.html).

✦ **Home Repair Encyclopedia Tips** (http://www.btw.com/tips/home/
swhre/tips.htm). A series of animated tutorials on several fix-it-yourself
household projects. Offering guidance in such areas as "Relighting a Pilot
Light" and (ahem) "Searching for Studs," Home Repair Encyclopedia Tips
illustrates the potential of Shockwave for Director as a teaching tool. Home
Repair Encyclopedia Tips appears in Figure 3-32.

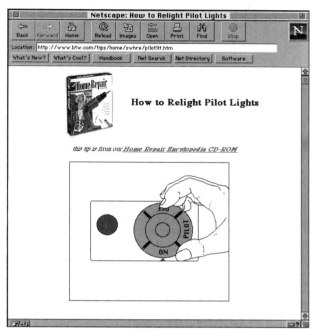

Figure 3-32: Home Repair Encyclopedia Tips (http://
www.btw.com/tips/home/swhre/tips.htm).

✦ **The Animagic Interactive Design pages** (http://www2.AniMagic-media.
com/AniMagic/). These pages illustrate how you can use Shockwave for
Director to enhance your pages' navigability and graphic appeal. The
Animagic welcome page, with Shocked navigation aids, appears in Figure 3-33.

Figure 3-33: The Animagic Interactive Design pages
(`http://www2.AniMagic-media.com/AniMagic/`).

Authoring for Shockwave for Director

Creating files to be played with Shockwave for Director requires Macromedia Director, a serious multimedia-creation tool you'll have to buy for several hundred dollars. Director is a powerful, complex program that has several complete books devoted to its minutiae, and it cannot be covered in even the most cursory way in these pages.

Once you've created a Director presentation, you should use a free tool called Afterburner to prepare it for efficient transmission over the Web. Afterburner, available on the Web at `http://www.macromedia.com/Tools/Shockwave/Director/aftrbrnr.html`, compresses Director files and makes them easier to stream without degrading their appearance.

To attach a Director presentation to a Web page, you use — surprise — the `<EMBED>` tag. There are no unusual attributes in an `<EMBED>` tag that attaches a Director file to a Web page — just the required `SRC`, `WIDTH`, and `HEIGHT` attributes.

Sizzler

Creator: Totally Hip Software

Function: Views QuickTime movies and Sizzler files that include sound and animation

Home Site: `http://www.totallyhip.com/`

Supported Platforms: All Macintosh and Windows systems

Authoring Tool: Any animation- or video-editing tool that can generate .AVI or .DIB files — and that's most of them. You also need Sizzler Converter to prepare the unadorned multimedia files for streaming across the Web into the Sizzler plug-in.

Good Examples: The Circle of Dust home page (`http://virtu.sar.usf.edu/ ~wilder/dust/`); The Speared Peanut Design Studio (`http://web.wt.net/ ~sprdpnut/sizzlerpeanut.html`); The first fly ever caught in the Web (`http://www.cibernet.it/thebox/english/first_fly.html`)

Sizzler represents excellent network engineering work. Animations created with the Sizzler authoring tools (Sizzler Editor and Sizzler Converter) meet the two most important criteria for successful Web technologies: They're of high quality and they're fast. By employing a slick streaming arrangement, Sizzler files download to your computer like JPEG images in your unplugged browser — blurry at first, but progressively and quickly clearer.

Sizzler, a product of Totally Hip Software, offers a great combination of high-quality output and simple authoring. Whether you're looking to add animation to your Web site, or simply want to explore some of the best pages on the Web, Sizzler is the plug-in you'll need on your browser.

Plug-in Power Rating: ★★★

Installing Sizzler

To install Sizzler on your computer, open `http://www.totallyhip.com/ sizzler/6b_sizz.html` with your browser and click on either the Windows link (for both Windows 3.1 and Windows 95) or the Macintosh link (for both Macs and Power Macs).

If you're installing Sizzler on a Windows 3.1 or Windows 95 system:

1. Click on the link for the plug-in you want, either Windows 3.1 or Windows 95. You'll move to a point farther down the page where you can download the

file you need. At this writing, the files are S32P10B2.EXE for Windows 95 and S16P10B2.EXE for Windows 3.1. The filenames surely will have changed by the time you check out the Totally Hip site. Click on the link to download the file you need.

2. Save the downloaded file by itself in a temporary directory. The file is the installation program.

3. After the file downloads completely, shut down your browser.

4. Run the file you downloaded. Step through the installation program, accepting the defaults unless your browser resides in an unusual corner of your hard drive.

5. Restart your browser. Sizzler will be ready to use.

If you're installing Sizzler on a Macintosh or Power Macintosh, you need a copy of StuffIt Lite or StuffIt Expander. You can get StuffIt Expander from the Aladdin Systems site at http://www.aladdinsys.com/. To install Sizzler on a Macintosh or Power Macintosh:

1. Click on the Download link under Sizzler Plug-in for Macintosh.

2. Save the file SIZZLERPLUGIN.SIT.HQX to a temporary folder by itself.

3. When the file has downloaded completely, shut down your browser.

4. Find the icon labeled Sizzler Installer. Double-click on it.

5. The rest of the installation routine runs automatically. Restart your browser when the installation program finishes its work.

Using Sizzler

There's nothing special you need to know to "use" Sizzler. When you come across a Sizzling site, and your browser has Sizzler properly installed, the plug-in takes care of displaying the Sizzler files with no special attention or instructions from you.

Plugged-in sites

There aren't yet a lot of Sizzler-enhanced sites, but the ones that do exist are quite cool and bode well for the future of Totally Hip's technology. When you're surfing around with your newly installed Sizzler plug-in, be sure to visit the Sizzling Sites directory at http://www.totallyhip.com/sizzler/sites/siz_sites.html. In the directory (and be sure to check out the spinning logo at the top of the table while you're there), you'll find links to all the best Sizzler sites — including these fun ones:

◆ **The Circle of Dust home page** (http://virtu.sar.usf.edu/~wilder/dust/). On this site, the official Web home of the industrial band Circle of

Dust, you'll find some nifty pulsating navigation aids. Though the Sizzler animations aren't hyperlinked at this writing, they do add to the tone of the page. Check it out in Figure 3-34.

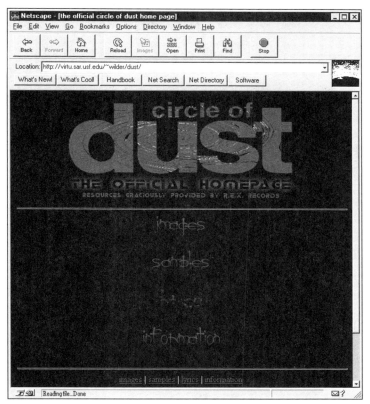

Figure 3-34: The Circle of Dust home page (`http://virtu.sar.usf.edu/~wilder/dust/`).

✦ **The Speared Peanut Design Studio** (`http://web.wt.net/~sprdpnut/sizzlerpeanut.html`). Break out your cardboard-and-cellophane 3-D glasses for this Sizzler animation! The people at Speared Peanut, a graphic design outfit, built this rotating legume to pop out at you when you look at it with one red lens and one blue lens. Remember those cheesy monster flicks? This is *Attack of the Rotating Peanut.* The site appears in Figure 3-35.

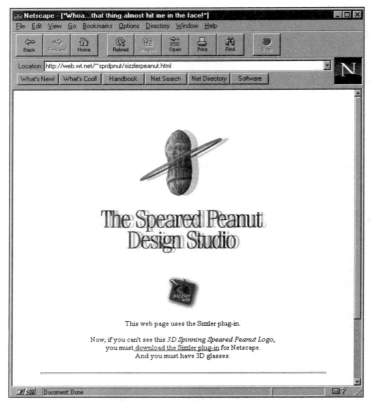

Figure 3-35: The Speared Peanut Design Studio (`http://web.`
`wt.net/~sprdpnut/sizzlerpeanut.html`).

✦ **The first fly ever caught in the Web** (`http://www.cibernet.it/thebox/`
`english/first_fly.html`). Gloriously deadpan, this site shows an animated fly struggling to free itself from the Web. Sizzler's ability to download high-resolution images in a hurry is clear on this page. Take a look at Figure 3-36.

Authoring for Sizzler

The easiest way to create files for the Sizzler plug-in is to use a video- or animation-editing program such as Adobe Premiere or Macromedia Director to build an .AVI or .DIB file, then use Sizzler Converter (available at the Totally Hip site) to make the file into a sprite file (with an .SPR extension) that the Sizzler plug-in can handle. Alternately, you can use the Sizzler Editor (also at Totally Hip) to assemble still graphics into a coherent sequence, then prepare them for streaming with Sizzler Converter.

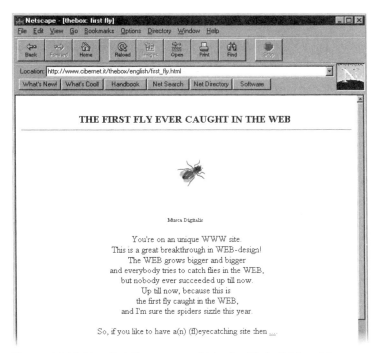

Figure 3-36: The first fly ever caught in the Web (`http://www.`
`cibernet.it/thebox/english/first_fly.html`).

Once you've built a sprite file (the name comes from a generic computer term for a graphic that moves around on a video screen — in a sprightly fashion, one might say), you have to attach it to a Web page. This is done with the `<EMBED>` tag. A typical use looks like this:

```
<EMBED SRC="SEAGULL.SPR" HEIGHT=200 WIDTH=300>
```

In this example, the sprite file is called SEAGULL.SPR, and it occupies a box on the Web page that is 200 pixels tall and 300 pixels wide. There are no other attributes available for use with Sizzler.

VDOLive

Creator: VDOnet

Function: Plays streaming video encoded in a special VDOLive
.VDO extension) that's compatible with Video for Windows

Home Site: `http://www.vdolive.com/`

Supported Platforms: All Windows systems

Authoring Tool: You can create Video for Widows files with any video-editing program such as Adobe Photoshop. You must then convert those files to .VDO format with tools that come with the VDOLive server. You can get the server and the tools by registering as a beta tester at `http://www.VDOLive.com/betareg.htm`.

Good Examples: CBS News at `http://uttm.com/`; highlights from San Francisco's KPIX-TV at `http://www.kpix.com/video/`; Bill Nye, the science guy, at `http://nyelabs.kcts.org/video/billnye.html`

The first plug-in to support streaming video, VDOLive was also the first to give the Web community a taste of video-on-demand. Though in practice the technology suffers greatly under the bandwidth constraints of slow connections, VDOLive works passably well on dialup connections and is handy on speedy local — area networks and intranets. It's an excellent plug-in for serving video across a corporate network or other high-speed system of clients and servers.

Unfortunately, there's no VDOLive plug-in for any Macintosh machine at this writing, though there is a handy helper application that plays .VDO files. You can get that helper app from the VDOnet site, too.

Plug-in Power Rating: ★★★★

Installing VDOLive

To install VDOLive on a Windows 95, Windows NT, or Windows 3.1 system:

1. Open `http://www.VDOLive.com/download/`, select The VDOLive Player from the box labeled Product, and choose Windows 95 or Windows 3.1 from the box labeled Operating System. Click on the Click on to display download sites button.

2. Choose one of the FTP servers near your physical location and save the file (either PLGPLY32.EXE for Windows 95 or PLGPLY16.EXE for Windows 3.1) to a temporary directory by itself.

3. PLGPLY32.EXE and PLGPLY16.EXE are the setup programs for VDOLive under Windows 95 and Windows 3.1, respectively. After the file has downloaded completely, double-click on its icon. The Setup program will start.

4. Step through the Setup program, accepting the defaults unless you installed your browser in a non-standard directory.

5. Shut down and restart your Web browser. The VDOLive plug-in will be ready to go.

Using VDOLive

When you call up a page with embedded .VDO content, you'll see a black field containing two spinning deltas and a pair of dots. That's the VDONet logo, and it indicates that VDOLive is filling its buffer — downloading enough video data to keep you occupied until streaming can catch up and keep the video frames coming. Once the picture comes in, you can right-click on (for Windows users) or long-click on the image, and a pop-up control menu will appear. With the pop-up menu, you can adjust a few options, including whether VDOLive works as part of your browser or as a helper application when you encounter a non-embedded video clip. You can also stop and start the video playback via the pop-up menu.

If you operate on a corporate network that's protected by a firewall (a special computer that provides security from Internet intruders for a local area network), VDOLive won't work for you. You'll have to figure out a way to bypass the firewall — or wait for a future edition of the VDOLive plug-in.

Plugged-in sites

The Web is loaded with cool stuff to view with the VDOLive plug-in, thanks mainly to the fact that VDOLive was the first streaming video solution on the market for Windows machines.

The following sites show you what can happen when television experts get involved in the Web. Not only do these sites serve as libraries of video, letting you have access to video segments when you want or need them, but they also give Web surfers a taste of things to come:

✦ **Highlights from San Francisco's KPIX-TV** (http://www.kpix.com/video/). San Francisco television station KPIX-TV has encoded some of its best news and features segments as streaming VDOLive video. You can go to the KPIX-TV site, click on the link for whichever story you want (topics range from earthquake preparedness to Internet political activism), and enjoy the show on your monitor. You can refer back to favorite segments anytime you want, or skip links to videos that don't interest you. A frame from the earthquake feature appears in Figure 3-37.

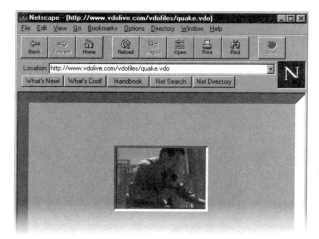

Figure 3-37: VDOLive at the KPIX-TV site (`http://www.kpix.com/video/`).

✦ **UTTMlink** (`http://uttm.com/`). UTTMlink, CBS News' "Up to the Minute" Web site, serves more as an advertisement for CBS News than as a news source; but the video's good, nonetheless. At UTTM, you'll find such things as excerpts from an upcoming Walter Cronkite special and teasers for what's going to be on CBS News that evening. A shot of a clip from UTTM appears in Figure 3-38.

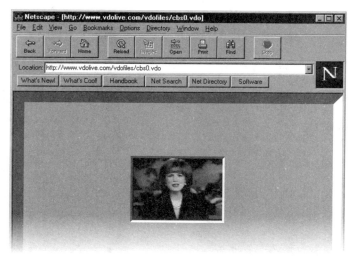

Figure 3-38: CBS News meets VDOLive (`http://uttm.com/`).

Authoring for VDOLive

Authoring movies for VDOLive requires any video-editing program that will output movies in Video for Windows (.AVI) format. Many programs, including the popular Adobe Premiere, can generate Video for Windows footage. Making .AVI files into .VDO files requires a converter program from the VDOnet Web site. You also need the VDOLive Server, which costs $120, U.S., for each outgoing stream of video you plan to serve.

To attach VDOLive content to your Web pages, use the `<EMBED>` tag and the three standard attributes: `SRC`, which specifies the URL of the .VDO file; `HEIGHT`, which specifies the height of the frame in pixels; and `WIDTH`, which specifies the width of the frame in pixels. A typical VDOLive `<EMBED>` statement looks like this:

```
<EMBED SRC="GOOSE.VDO" HEIGHT=250 WIDTH=400>
```

ViewMovie

Creator: Ivan Cavero Belaunde

Function: Plays QuickTime movies

Home Site: `http://www.well.com/user/ivanski/download.html`

Supported Platforms: All Macintosh systems

Authoring Tool: Adobe Premiere or any other video editor that can output QuickTime files

Good Examples: A trip to Ben's office at `http://www.rollanet.org/~ben/gooff.html`; skydiving at `http://www.cybert8t.com:80/corchard/skydiving.html`

ViewMovie represents a triumph of the Internet community. Though this plug-in was largely designed and completely coded by Ivan Cavero Belaunde (frequently on a boat off the coast of Peru), Belaunde received suggestions and guidance from the Web community at large. As a result, ViewMovie is one of the most useful, reliable, and fun plug-ins available.

Used to play QuickTime movies embedded in Web pages, ViewMovie has simple, intuitive controls and an attractive appearance on Web pages. It's also a Web publisher's dream, since practically every video- and animation-editing program (especially those for the Macintosh) can generate QuickTime movies, and Belaunde has built dozens of control attributes into the `<EMBED>` tag for ViewMovie. The plug-in's one serious shortcoming is that it doesn't support streaming — you'll have to wait for a movie to download completely before you can view it. Regardless, ViewMovie should have a place in your plug-ins folder.

Plug-in Power Rating: ★★★★

Installing ViewMovie

To install ViewMovie on a Macintosh:

1. Point your browser at `http://www.well.com/user/ivanski/download.html`.

2. Click on the download link.

3. When the file downloads completely, use StuffIt Expander to decompress it. You may have already configured your browser to decompress stuffed files automatically.

4. Shut down your browser.

5. Drag the file VIEWMOVIE from the folder into which it decompressed to the PLUGINS folder.

6. Restart your browser. Point your browser at one of the example sites to test ViewMovie.

Using ViewMovie

As is true with all good plug-ins, there's not much involved in using ViewMovie. Double-clicking on the frame starts the motion; single-clicking on the frame stops it. In most cases, there's also a control bar at the bottom of the frame that lets you shuttle back and forth in the movie and a start/stop button. You can see the controls in Figures 3-39 and 3-40.

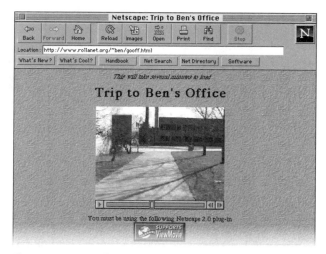

Figure 3-39: A Trip to Ben's Office (`http://www.rollanet.org/~ben/gooff.html`).

Plugged-in sites

ViewMovie's origins in collaboration seem to have spawned some playful sites that use it. Many of the ViewMovie sites make you feel as though you've been invited into a fellow hobbyist's home to explore the latest developments in an interest you share. Visit these sites, both created by individuals for personal reasons, and you'll see what I mean

- ✦ **A Trip to Ben's Office** (`http://www.rollanet.org/~ben/gooff.html`). Here, Ben Strehlman has posted a QuickTime movie showing his path to work. He seems to have held a video camera in his hand as he drove to work, then as he walked to his building and, finally, to his chair. It sounds silly, but it gives you a little insight into Ben's life — and the video might be useful if you had to find Ben's office, too. This site appears in Figure 3-39.

- ✦ **Charlie Orchard's Skydiving Page** (`http://www.cyberg8t.com:80/corchard/skydiving.html`). Charlie Orchard likes to jump out of airplanes, and he proves it with this page. An embedded QuickTime movie of Charlie free-falling through a hula hoop shows you what kind of person he is. ViewMovie has added life to this otherwise potentially dull page. Check it out in Figure 3-40.

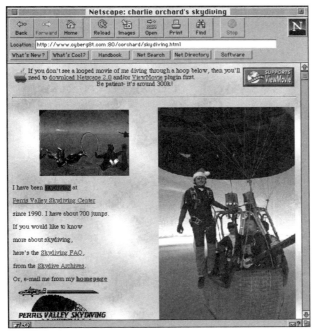

Figure 3-40: Charlie Orchard's Skydiving Page (`http://www.cyberg8t.com:80/corchard/skydiving.html`).

Authoring for ViewMovie

You can create QuickTime movies with almost any video- or animation-editing software package. The interesting part of authoring with ViewMovie comes when you code the HTML to attach your movies to a Web page.

Again, the <EMBED> tag takes center stage. Bellaunde has, however, decked the tag out with lots of attributes that enable you to customize the appearance of your clip on the page. You'll find a complete guide to them at http://www.well.com/ user/ivanski/viewmovie/docs.html. In summary, the mandatory attributes are

- ◆ SRC. Defines the QuickTime movie to be embedded. A typical use is SRC="DUCK.QT".
- ◆ WIDTH. The width, in pixels, of the box allocated to the embedded movie.
- ◆ HEIGHT. The height, in pixels, of the box allocated to the embedded movie. You must add 16 to the actual height of your movie's frames to allow for the ViewMovie controls, unless you specify CONTROLLER=FALSE. You'll learn more about the optional CONTROLLER attribute later in this section.

The optional attributes are

- ◆ LOOP. Specifies what the movie does when it gets to the last frame. LOOP=FALSE causes the movie to play once and stop; LOOP=TRUE causes the movie to start over again; LOOP=PALINDROME causes the movie to play forward, then backward, over and over. Unless you specify otherwise, ViewMovie assumes LOOP=FALSE.
- ◆ AUTOPLAY or AUTOSTART. If you set AUTOPLAY (or the equivalent AUTOSTART) equal to TRUE, the movie will start playing as soon as the page loads. Otherwise, it will wait for a click.
- ◆ CONTROLLER. Defines whether or not the ViewMovie controls appear. If you set CONTROLLER=FALSE, you don't have to add 16 pixels to the HEIGHT attribute.
- ◆ KEEPASPECTRATIO. Determines what happens if the box you define with WIDTH and HEIGHT doesn't match the proportions of the video frames. If you set KEEPASPECTRATIO=TRUE (which is the default), ViewMovie will truncate your frames rather than distort them. If you specify KEEPASPECTRATIO=FALSE, ViewMovie will distort your frames.
- ◆ HREFABS. Lets you make the movie a hyperlink. By adding the attribute HREFABS="http://www.foo.com/donuts/tyler.html" you would make the movie frame a hyperlink that would call up http://www.foo.com/ donuts/tyler.html when clicked on.

Note that using the HREFABS attribute renders the video controls useless and that the URL you specify must be an absolute, not partial, one.

✦ ISMAP. An attribute that takes no value, ISMAP works with HREFABS to make a video into an imagemap — a graphic with clickable regions that perform different functions. A typical use of ISMAP is

```
<EMBED SRC="DUCK.QT" HEIGHT=256 WIDTH=300 ISMAP
       HREFABS="http://www.foo.com/cgi/duckmap.cgi">
```

✦ PLAYRATE. Determines the length of the delay between when the movie finishes downloading and when it starts playing. Takes values from 0 to 100.

✦ VOLUME. Sets the volume at which the audio portion of the movie plays as a percentage of the volume set in the movie itself. Set VOLUME to an integer value.

✦ PLAYEVERYFRAME. If you set PLAYEVERYFRAME=TRUE, ViewMovie will skip no frames, regardless of the sluggishness of your system. The default is PLAYEVERYFRAME=FALSE, which allows the plug-in to skip frames as needed to keep up with the audio track.

✦ QUALITY. If you set QUALITY=HIGH, ViewMovie will reduce the movie's playback frame rate to provide excellent color and dithering. If you don't add the QUALITY attribute, or set it to DRAFT, ViewMovie will play the movie with poorer image quality but higher frame rate.

CHAPTER 4

VRML and Three-Dimensional Imaging

Take a second and try to visualize the Web.

You're probably picturing something along the lines of a spider's web, with little nodes of information connected by gossamer strands of network data paths. That's the picture that most people seem to come up with, and it's an apt depiction of a hypermedia information-retrieval system that's based on moving from one chunk of data to another to another via hyperlinks embedded in the information. Maybe you can use a search engine or subject tree such as Alta Vista or Yahoo!, to find your way to a good starting point on the Web; but you're essentially limited to moving in a linear sequence, from one page to the next and from one site to the next.

The trouble with that arrangement is it has absolutely no resemblance to the way information is organized in real life. Take for example a library, which is a suitable parallel to the Web because a library, too, is a repository of information. Libraries aren't organized in two dimensions. You do not (usually) have to page through the kids' books to get to the cookbooks or the French history books to reach the law encyclopedias. You can go directly to the librarian or catalog and find out the location of the materials that interest you, then proceed there directly.

What is more, libraries are organized in three dimensions. The card catalog and library map may tell you that the bird-identification guides are on the second floor near the front window, or that the job-search manuals can be found in the basement across from the water fountain. As human beings, we readily understand those locations and can intuitively figure out how to get there. We're programmed to operate in three-dimensional space. Therefore, "next door to the courthouse" makes much more sense to us than "http://www.cybercorp.com/," which is how we have histori-cally described the location of information on the Web.

Which brings us to the appeal of Virtual Reality Modeling Language (VRML) and other kinds of three-dimensional computer imaging. These systems — the subject of this chapter — facilitate the encoding of computer information as objects in three-dimensional space that computer users can navigate through in more or less the same way they would navigate through a real-life room, canyon, airplane cock-pit, or whatever. Three-dimensional rendering systems — particularly VRML, which is the most general-purpose of the network-aware rendering systems covered in this chapter — provide a means of bringing computerized information into a realm of representation that human beings readily understand. Prior to the advent of VRML, humans had to adapt to the machines' way of representing data — an unnat-ural and efficiency-reducing nod to the imperfection of computer technology.

Mark Pesce, one of the creators of the original VRML specification, has said that he envisions VRML as a step toward the ultimate interface with the physical world — one in which a wealth of computer information is superimposed upon a graphical representation of the world itself. With the system he imagines, you could, for example, walk around a computer representation of your hometown. When you looked at a large manufacturing plant down the street from your house, you could have immediate access to the plant's environmental record, which might reside on a distant government computer. If you were lost in a strange city, you might be able to pinpoint your location in a VRML model of the city with the help of a global-positioning attachment for your portable computer, then have the com-puter show you the way to your destination, using the VRML city model as a guide.

This is not to say that VRML is The Answer to the problem of un-intuitive inter-faces and obscure, computer-generated representations of data. VRML is still deep in the development stages. You're much more likely to use the plug-ins in this chapter to display three-dimensional helicopters and space shuttles — which, despite being cool, are more "gee-whiz" phenomena than useful tools — than to help you explore the virtual surfaces of distant planets. Some of these plug-ins aren't too stable (they're more likely than, say, the document-viewer plug-ins to make your browser crash), and they'll certainly tax the capabilities of your system more than plug-ins that are farther from the cutting edge of network technology. Be prepared to wait longer than usual for VRML files to download.

The point is that VRML and the other rendering languages covered in this chapter are on the edge. They may represent the next stage of networked data representa-tion and navigation. They may be harbingers of Web interfaces to come. They may seem to be slow, fragile toys today; but many of the Web's top visionaries — such as Tim Berners-Lee, the physicist who originally proposed the Web — see virtual reality as a likely replacement for the text-based information system we have today.

For more information about VRML, including a guide to building sites with it and some thoughts on its potential applications, read Mark Pesce's book, *VRML: Browsing and Building Cyberspace.*

In this chapter, you'll read a fair amount about VRML 1.0 and several different variations on VRML 2.0. The basic distinction between the two versions of the modeling language is interactivity: VRML 1.0 displays static, three-dimensional objects that just sit there; while the various VRML 2.0 "standards" add behaviors (such as animation, sound, and click-on responses) to the basic objects.

There are several different kinds of VRML 2.0 — it's not really a standard at all. Moving Worlds is one popular variation, while Virtual Reality Behavior Language (VRBL) is another. If a site tells you that you need a particular plug-in to view its worlds, get that plug-in and install it. VRML 2.0 is so irregular that you can't expect a single plug-in to handle all its variations.

All of the VRML plug-ins in this chapter respond to the same data types; so you're likely to cause your browser to crash if you have two or more VRML plug-ins installed at once, and you try to load a VRML world. When you install a new VRML plug-in, remove any old ones you have in your PLUGINS folder (you can look at the property sheet for each plug-in).

Chemscape Chime

Creator: MDL Information Systems

Function: Allows you to view and manipulate 3-D images of molecules in Molfile (.MOL), Brookhaven Protein Databank (.PDB) and other popular formats

Home Site: http://www.mdli.com/chemscape/chime/chime.html

Supported Platforms: All Windows and Macintosh systems

Authoring Tool: Molfile; any of several other molecule-rendering packages

Good Examples: A demonstration page at http://www.mdli.com/chemscape/chime/example/sample/sample.html; DNA at http://www.mdli.com/chemscape/chime/example/rotdna/dna_rot.html

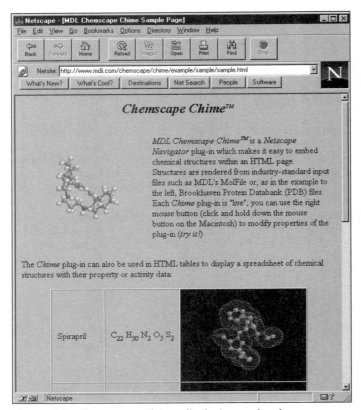

Figure 4-1: Chemscape Chime displaying molecules.

You've probably had the experience of watching an expert practicing his or her craft and realizing that even though you have no training or experience on which to base your opinion, you think the expert is doing excellent work. Everything seems to happen perfectly.

If you are not a chemist, biologist, or other professional knowledgeable about molecular structure, that is the feeling you'll have when you install Chemscape Chime (see Figure 4-1). If you are such a professional, you'll realize that you have a powerful tool for rendering complicated models of chemical structures at your disposal. Chemscape Chime does for the molecule set what Harvard Graphics did for accountants — it gives them a powerful, attractive way to communicate complex ideas to colleagues, students, and other audiences. Perhaps by limiting its purpose — Chemscape Chime needs only to display molecules, not molecules, AND houses, AND airplanes, AND horses, as the VRML plug-ins attempt to do — Chemscape Chime guarantees that it can do a good job at its assumed task.

If you're a plug-in developer, install Chemscape Chime and examine it carefully. Every plug-in should be as robust, feature-rich and aesthetically attractive as this one.

Plug-in Power Rating: ★★★★

Installing Chemscape Chime

To install Chemscape Chime on a Windows system:

1. Point your browser at `http://www.mdli.com/chemscape/chime/chime.html`.

2. Click on the link that says Download Chime.

3. Scroll about halfway down the page that appears next and click on the link that says Download Chime for Windows 95 and Windows NT, or scroll farther down and click on the link that says Download Chime for Windows 3.1.

4. Click on the link that says Download Chime without the Installer. At this writing, neither of the Windows versions has installers, though MDL says they're on the way.

5. Save the file by itself in a temporary directory.

6. When the file has downloaded completely, shut down your browser.

7. Double-click on the file you downloaded. It's a self-extracting .ZIP archive and will unpack several files from itself. Close the .ZIP window when the decompression process is complete.

8. Move the file NPCHIME.DLL to your PLUGINS directory.

9. Restart your browser. Chemscape Chime is ready for use.

To install Chemscape Chime on a Macintosh system:

1. Point your browser at `http://www.mdli.com/chemscape/chime/chime.html`.

2. Click on the Download link.

3. Scroll about halfway down the page that appears next and click on the link that says Download Chime for the Macintosh (PowerPC and 68K).

4. When the file has downloaded completely, shut down your browser.

5. The file you downloaded is encoded in BinHex format. You'll need to run it through the Macintosh's BinHex program to prepare it for use. Your browser may be configured to handle this process automatically.

6. Run the Chemscape Chime Installer program. Respond to the prompts as needed.

7. Restart your browser. Chemscape Chime will be ready for use.

 The Macintosh version of Chemscape Chime doesn't work well (if at all) with Netscape Navigator 2.0. If you're having trouble with Chemscape Chime on your Macintosh, make sure you have installed the latest version of Netscape Navigator — version 3.0 or later.

Using Chemscape Chime

The cool thing about Chemscape Chime is that it can be extremely simple — you can just load a page that contains an embedded molecule image and let Chemscape Chime display it automatically — or you can use Chemscape Chime's pop-up menu (pictured in Figure 4-2) to adjust the image to your liking.

The pop-up menu lets you do everything you could want with the displayed molecule, from saving it on your hard disk, to altering its color, to changing the speed and axis of its rotation. One of the most useful options on the pop-up menu is the Display item, which you can use to alter the appearance of the molecule on your screen. Your options include the following:

✦ **Wireframe.** Renders the molecule as a solid structure represented by a gridded surface.

✦ **Sticks.** Renders the molecule's atomic bonds as colored bars.

✦ **Ball & Stick.** Remember your eighth-grade science project, when you linked Styrofoam balls with colored dowels to represent a molecule? That's what this option does.

✦ **Spacefill.** Shows the volume occupied by each atom's electron cloud.

✦ **Dot Surface.** A lot like Wireframe, but with dots instead of a grid.

✦ **Backbone, Ribbon, Strand, and Cartoon.** Four ways to show the general structure of molecules without rendering individual atoms.

Plugged-in sites

Chances are, if you're a scientist who's excited about the existence of Chemscape Chime, you probably know where there are some molecule files you can view with it — you probably have a collection on your own computer. If you're just along for the ride, you'll find a directory of Chime-compatible sites at `http://www.mdli.com/chemscape/chime/sampidx.html`.

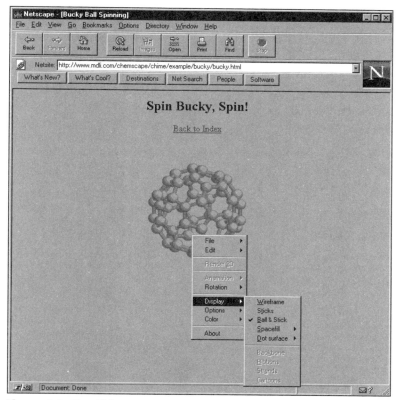

Figure 4-2: The Chime pop-up menu.

Here are a couple of especially cool examples:

✦ **A copy of Peter Nixon's paper, "The Photosynthetic Reaction Centre From the Purple Bacterium *Rhodopseudomonas viridis*"** (`http://www.mdli.com/chemscape/chime/example/hyperact/1prc.html`). (See Figure 4-3.) If you know what this thing is, you obviously know more about purple bacteria than I. In any case, this is an excellent example of Chemscape Chime's proficiency at displaying extremely complex molecules quickly and attractively. This page also demonstrates the Web's appeal as a publishing medium — the printed version of this paper doesn't feature an animated molecule that scientists can examine from any angle they wish.

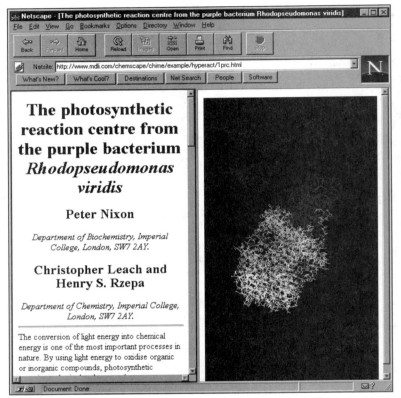

Figure 4-3: A very complex molecule in .PDB format, displayed with Chime.

✦ **DNA (**http://www.mdli.com/chemscape/chime/example/rotdna/
dna_rot.html**).** Figure 4-4 shows a Chemscape Chime depiction of the one complex molecule that everyone knows. Try displaying this DNA in Backbone mode — then the double-helix structure Watson and Crick discovered will become more clear. This page also demonstrates the educational value of Chemscape Chime.

Authoring for Chemscape Chime

If you have a real use for Chime, you're probably familiar with a program used to create three-dimensional images of molecules on a computer. Any program that outputs molecule images in .PDB, .MOL, .EMB, .EMBL, .XYZ, .GAU, .SPT, .MOP, .CSM, .CSML, .TGF or .RSML is compatible with Chime. Molfile seems to be a popular program for modeling molecules.

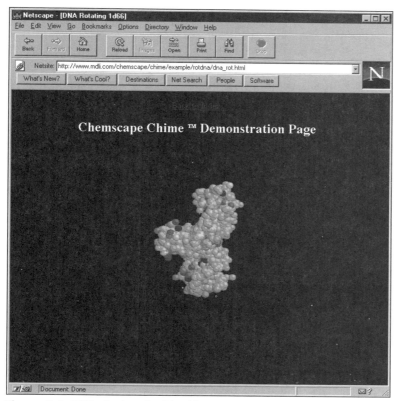

Figure 4-4: DNA displayed with Chime.

Like all plug-ins, Chemscape Chime uses the `<EMBED>` tag to attach its files to Web pages. A basic Chemscape Chime `<EMBED>` statement looks like this:

```
<EMBED SRC="BENZENE.PDB" HEIGHT=100 WIDTH=50>
```

That statement, which contains all the mandatory attributes, causes the file BEN-ZENE.PDB to be displayed in a box 100 pixels high by 50 pixels wide.

Chemscape Chime also supports a lot of optional attributes:

✦ STARTSPIN. Set to YES or NO (or the equivalent TRUE or FALSE), STARTSPIN determines whether the molecule starts to rotate as soon as it's loaded into a Web page.

✦ SPINX. Set to an integer, SPINX determines the rate of spin along the X axis. For example, SPINX=90 would cause the molecule to rotate a quarter turn every second.

- ◆ SPINY. Same as SPINX, except SPINY determines the rate of spin around the Y axis.

- ◆ SPINZ. Same as SPINX and SPINY, except SPINZ determines the rate of spin around the Z axis.

- ◆ SPINFPS. Set to an integer, SPINFPS defines the number of frames displayed each second as the molecule spins. Try values between 10 and 20.

- ◆ STARTANIM. Set to YES or NO (or the equivalent TRUE or FALSE), STARTAN-IM is the equivalent of STARTSPIN for an .XYZ file.

- ◆ ANIMFPS. The equivalent of SPINFPS for an .XYZ file.

- ◆ DISPLAY3D. Set to WIREFRAME, BACKBONE, STICKS, SPACEFILL, BALL&STICK, RIBBONS, STRANDS, or CARTOONS, DISPLAY3D determines the default display mode for a molecule.

- ◆ COLOR3D. Set to MONOCHROME, CPK, SHAPELY, GROUP, CHAIN, TEMPERA-TURE, STRUCTURE, or USER, COLOR3D sets the default color scheme.

- ◆ OPTIONS3D. Set to SLAB, HYDROGEN, HETERO, SPECULAR, SHADOWS, STEREO, LABELS, or DOTS, OPTIONS3D shows which options are in effect. You can use OPTIONS3D more than once in a single <EMBED> statement to engage more than one option.

- ◆ PALETTE. Set to FOREGROUND or BACKGROUND, PALETTE determines what colors Chemscape Chime can use; FOREGROUND gives it the right to use any colors it needs.

- ◆ HBONDS. Set to ON, OFF, or an integer, HBONDS determines how hydrogen bonds are displayed. ON makes them dashed lines, OFF makes them go away, and an integer causes them to appear as solid lines of a specific thickness.

- ◆ SSBONDS. Same as HBONDS, except for disulfide bonds.

- ◆ SCRIPT. Set to any Rasmol script command, SCRIPT gives you another way to animate your molecule. You can attach more than one script command to a single SCRIPT attribute if you separate them with "|" or ";."

- ◆ CSML. Same as SCRIPT, except for CSML commands.

If you're going to publish files on the Web for Chemscape Chime, you'll need to configure your server to handle some unusual MIME types. Some MIME types for chemical models include

- ◆ chemical/x-mdl-molfile, with extension .MOL

- ◆ chemical/x-mdl-tgf, with extension .TGF

- ◆ chemical/x-mdl-rxnfile, with extension .RXNFILE

✦ chemical/x-pdb, with extension .PDB

✦ chemical/x-gaussian-input, with extension .GAU

✦ chemical/x-xyz, with extension .XYZ

✦ chemical/x-mopac-input, with extension .MOP

✦ chemical/x-embl-dl-nucleotide, with extensions .EMB and .EMBL

✦ chemical/x-csml, with extensions .CSM and .CSML

✦ application/x-spt, with extension .SPT

Cosmo Player

Creator: Silicon Graphics

Function: Lets you explore VRML 2.0 (and VRML 1.0) worlds

Home Site: `http://webspace.sgi.com/cosmoplayer/`

Supported Platforms: Windows 95 and Windows NT

Authoring Tool: Any of several tools that generate VRML 2.0 worlds. SGI lists some handy tools at `http://webspace.sgi.com/tools/`.

Good Examples: Boink! at `http://webspace.sgi.com/worlds/vrml2/boink/boink.wrl`; a directory at `http://webspace.sgi.com/worlds/vrml2.html`

The first plug-in to support any of the VRML 2.0 standards, Cosmo Player lets you explore three-dimensional worlds that their creators have enhanced with motion, sound, and interactivity under the Moving Worlds scheme (see Figure 4-5). Cosmo Player also automatically translates VRML 1.0 worlds into VRML 2.0 on-the-fly so you can use a single plug-in for almost all your Web-based virtual reality applications.

Plug-in Power Rating: ★★★

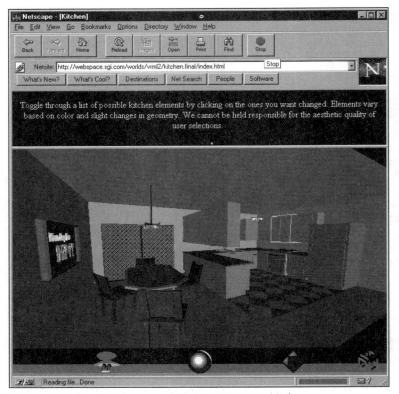

Figure 4-5: Cosmo Player exploring a VRML 2.0 kitchen.

Installing Cosmo Player

To install Cosmo Player on a Windows machine:

1. Point your browser at `http://webspace.sgi.com/cosmoplayer/download.html`.
2. Scroll about halfway down the page, and click on one of the Download Now! buttons.
3. Save the downloaded file by itself in a temporary directory.
4. When the file has downloaded completely, shut down your browser.

5. Run CPSETUP.EXE, the file you downloaded. CPSETUP.EXE is an automated installation routine that takes care of the details of installation for you. Step through the installation program, responding to the prompts as needed.

6. Re-start your browser. Cosmo Player will be ready for use.

Cosmo Player's sound features run better if you install Intel's RSX (Realistic Sound eXperience) software and Microsoft's DirectX, available at `http://www.intel.com/ial/rsx/install.htm`. You should visit that site, download RSX and DirectX, and install them at the same time you install Cosmo Player. Some of the other plug-ins in this chapter (several of those that work with Windows, anyway) work better with RSX and DirectX.

Using Cosmo Player

When you call up a VRML world to be interpreted by Cosmo Player, you'll probably have to wait a few seconds — exactly how long depends upon the speed of your connection to the Internet. While you wait for the world to load, you'll see a Cosmo Player graphic in the center of your browser window.

When the world appears, you have an important decision to make right away. Is this a world you want to walk through, or do you prefer to remain stationary and move the world so you can view it at different angles? Walking is better for such models as houses, cities, and castles; while you may want to use the latter option (called Examine mode) for models of molecules, cars, or animals. You can select your mode of exploration by right-clicking on the world and choosing a mode from the pop-up menu that appears.

You'll notice that the Cosmo Player controls don't always redraw properly when you're task-switching among several applications. To solve this problem, change the size of your browser window, then bring it back to its original size. This will force the window to redraw, and make the controls appear.

The easiest way to navigate through a world with Cosmo Player is to use the Page Up and Page Down buttons. These buttons move you from one predefined viewpoint to another — the builder of the world defined the viewpoints for you.

Alternately, you can use the controls on the "dashboard" — the strip on the bottom of the VRML window — to navigate (see Figure 4-6). The leftmost control moves you forward and back. The middle control turns you left, right, up, or down. The rightmost control tilts your viewpoint from side to side. With these controls, you can navigate around any scene you discover on the Web.

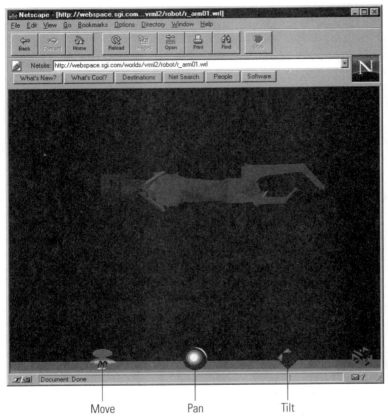

Move   Pan   Tilt

Figure 4-6: Cosmo Player's controls, labeled. The display shows an animated robot arm.

Plugged-in sites

You'll discover that all the VRML plug-ins in this chapter are designed to handle the same sort of files — VRML worlds. A world that's mentioned in the VRealm section can just as easily be visited with WIRL or VR Scout.

Cosmo Player, on the other hand, is a special case. Cosmo Player can interpret VRML 2.0 worlds. These worlds, endowed with sound and motion, are the next generation in VRML technology. You can explore VRML 1.0 worlds with Cosmo Player, but you can't explore VRML 2.0 worlds with a plug-in designed around the VRML 1.0 specification.

The sites in this section are VRML 2.0 worlds. If you want to see more, you'll find a directory of VRML 2.0 sites at `http://webspace.sgi.com/worlds/vrml2.html`.

Check out the Boink! site at `http://webspace.sgi.com/worlds/vrml2/boink/boink.wrl`. This world depicts the classic VRML 1.0 shapes: the cube, the cone, and the sphere. (See Figure 4-7.) When you load the page, they're just sitting there — but then click on the shapes. Make sure you have your speakers on, too.

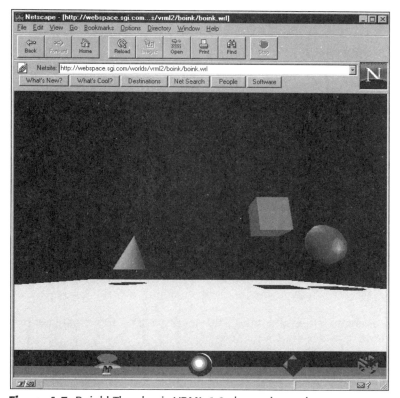

Figure 4-7: Boink! The classic VRML 1.0 shapes in motion.

Authoring for Cosmo Player

You have at least half a dozen options when you're looking for tools to create VRML 2.0/Moving Worlds scenes — including a tool that translates Doom scenes into VRML. SGI has a write-up on all the authoring tools at `http://webspace.sgi.com/tools/`.

Embedding content for Cosmo Player requires only the three basic `<EMBED>` attributes. Here's a typical usage:

```
<EMBED SRC="FACTORY.VRML WIDTH=200 HEIGHT=200>
```

That statement fits the file FACTORY.VRML into a box 200 pixels wide by 200 pixels high.

ExpressVR

Creator: Brad Anderson

Function: Navigates VRML worlds

Home Site: `http://www.cis.upenn.edu/~brada/VRML/ExpressVR.html`

Supported Platforms: All Macintosh systems

Authoring Tool: Any VRML 1.0 authoring tool, especially QuickDraw 3D

Good Examples: `http://vrml.arc.org/worlds`

Three of the plug-ins in this chapter — ExpressVR, VRML Equinox and Whurlplug — take advantage of Apple's QuickDraw 3D system extensions to create VRML browsers for the Macintosh. Apple's excellent three-dimensional rendering technology deserves much of the credit for the performance of these plug-ins, since it enabled the developers to create browsers without worrying about the details of how Macintoshes display three-dimensional worlds.

ExpressVR represents an excellent use of QuickDraw 3D, and probably is the best Macintosh VRML browser out there (see Figure 4-8).

Plug-in Power Rating: ★★★★

Installing ExpressVR

To install ExpressVR on a Macintosh:

1. Point your browser at `http://www.cis.upenn.edu/~brada/VRML/download.html`.

2. If you're running a Power Mac, you need to download QuickDraw 3D from Apple (`http://quickdraw3d.apple.com/`) before running ExpressVR. If you don't have QuickDraw 3D installed already, click on the link at the bottom of the page to get the latest version.

3. After installing QuickDraw 3D, click on one of the ExpressVR download links.

4. Use StuffIt or StuffIt Lite to unpack the downloaded file.

5. Shut down your browser. Run the file you downloaded. It's a self-extracting archive file that will extract the plug-in file. Make sure you specify that the plug-in file is extracted to your Plugins folder.

6. Restart your browser. ExpressVR will be ready to go.

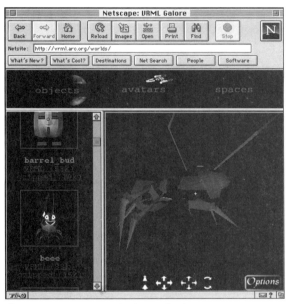

Figure 4-8: ExpressVR shows its bugs.

Using ExpressVR

The key to using ExpressVR lies at the bottom of the window in which it displays three-dimensional images. There, you'll find four controls and a button — the controls and button are labeled in Figure 4-9. The controls are

✦ **In and out.** Used to zoom in toward an object and back from it.

✦ **Fine movement.** Used to move up, down, and sideways slowly.

✦ **Coarse movement.** Used to move up, down, and sideways quickly.

✦ **Roll.** Used to spin your point of view along an axis perpendicular to your screen.

✦ **Options button.** Click on here to choose from points of view programmed into the scene, or to return to your starting point.

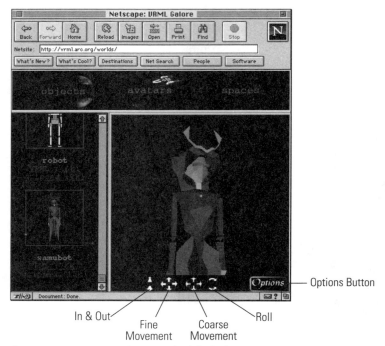

Figure 4-9: ExpressVR's controls, labeled.

Plugged-in sites

ExpressVR will work on any VRML 1.0 scene, so try it out on your favorites. If you don't know where to start, try the archive at http://vrml.arc.org/worlds. A couple of examples from that archive appear in Figures 4-10 and 4-11.

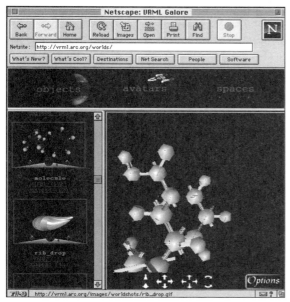

Figure 4-10: A molecule, viewed with ExpressVR.

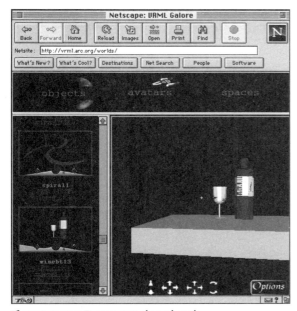

Figure 4-11: ExpressVR does lunch.

Authoring for ExpressVR

You can create worlds for exploration with ExpressVR with any VRML-authoring program, such as QuickDraw 3D for the Macintosh. You can get QuickDraw 3D at `http://quickdraw3d.apple.com/`

Attach your VRML files to Web pages with the `<EMBED>` tag and its mandatory attributes: `SRC`, `WIDTH` and `HEIGHT`.

Live3D

Creator: Netscape Communications

Function: Displays VRML and Moving Worlds environments

Home Site: `http://home.netscape.com/comprod/products/navigator/live3d/`

Supported Platforms: All Windows systems

Authoring Tool: Any VRML creation tool

Good Examples: The city of Siena at `http://www.construct.net/projects/planetitaly/Spazio/VRML/siena.wrl.gz`; a ballerina at `http://home.netscape.com/comprod/products/navigator/live3d/examples/woman/womballt.wrl.gz`

Supremely well-integrated with Netscape Navigator, Live3D (see Figure 4-12) is one of the most crash-resistant VRML plug-ins for that browser out there. If you're running Netscape Navigator, Live3D may be your best choice for viewing VRML scenes.

Though its interface isn't anything spectacular, Live3D supports some handy extensions to the VRML language. Top among these is its Spin transformation, which makes possible such displays as twirling ballerinas and helicopters with rotating blades.

Live 3D comes with Netscape Navigator 3.0 and later, so you need only download it if you have an earlier version of Navigator, a copy of Microsoft Internet Explorer, or a stripped-down version of Navigator 3.0.

Plug-in Power Rating: ★★★

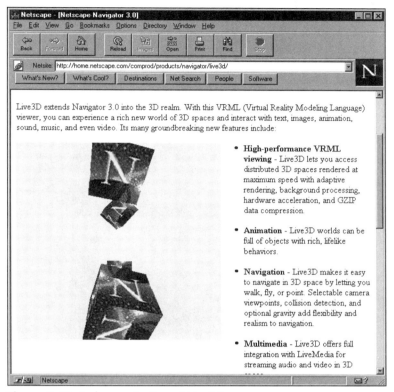

Figure 4-12: A demonstration of Live3D.

Installing Live3D

To install Live3D on a Windows machine:

1. Point your browser at `http://home.netscape.com/comprod/products/navigator/live3d/3dns_lic.html`, where the license agreement for Live3D resides. If you agree to abide by its terms, continue on to step 2.

2. Point your browser at `http://home.netscape.com/comprod/products/navigator/live3d/download_live3d.html`.

3. Click on one of the links under the heading for your operating environment.

4. Save the Live3D download file by itself in a temporary directory.

5. When the file has downloaded completely, shut down your browser.

6. Run the file you just downloaded. It's a self-extracting .ZIP file; and when the decompression routine is done, you'll have to close the window that it created.

7. Run SETUP.EXE. Respond to its prompts as needed, and it will handle the work involved in installing and configuring Live3D.

8. Re-start your browser. Live3D will be ready to go.

Using Live3D

Navigating through three-dimensional Web worlds with Live3D is simple — it's based mainly on moving the mouse. To move through a scene, place your mouse pointer on the scene, click, and drag. The world will move (if you're in Examine mode), or you will move (if you're in Walk mode). You can set your navigation mode via the pop-up menu, shown in Figure 4-13.

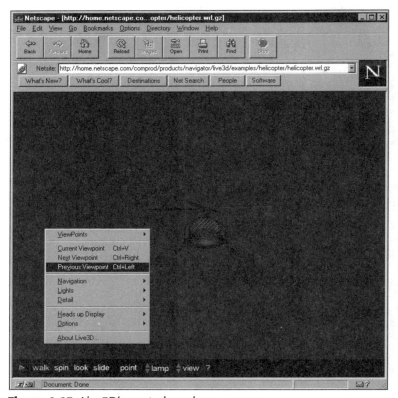

Figure 4-13: Live3D's controls and pop-up menu.

One of the cool features of Live3D may be mistaken for a problem because of a warning dialog box that it triggers. When you call up a world that's been compressed with the gzip UNIX compression utility, your browser will show a box that says, Warning: Unrecognized encoding: 'x-gzip'.

This is not a problem. What's happening? Live3D is equipped to decompress gzipped files on-the-fly — but your browser isn't. Therefore, your browser issues a warning, but when you click on the OK button, Live3D jumps in and takes over the task of interpreting the file.

Plugged-in sites

Netscape maintains a page that lists cool sites that work well with Live3D. You'll find the list at `http://home.netscape.com/comprod/products/navigator/live3d/cool_worlds.html`. Here are a couple of the best sites from that list:

✦ Check out the VRML ballerina at `http://home.netscape.com/comprod/products/navigator/live3d/examples/woman/womballt.wrl.gz`. She takes advantage of the animation extensions that are built into Netscape's Moving Worlds version of VRML. The ballerina appears in Figure 4-14.

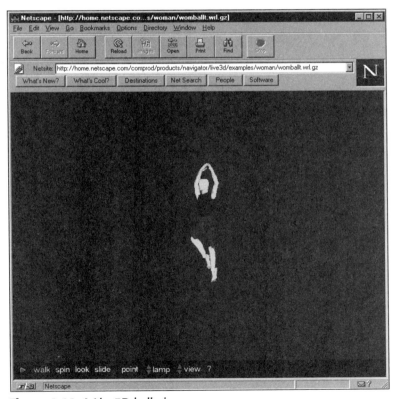

Figure 4-14: A Live3D ballerina.

✦ You can visit the Italian town of Siena at `http://www.construct.net/ projects/planetitaly/Spazio/VRML/siena.wrl.gz`. This site, known as Planet Italy, appears in Figure 4-15. You can maneuver around the town and, if you click on the right objects (the buildings on which text appears when your mouse pointer passes over them), you can call up pages that deal with Italian government, commerce, and culture.

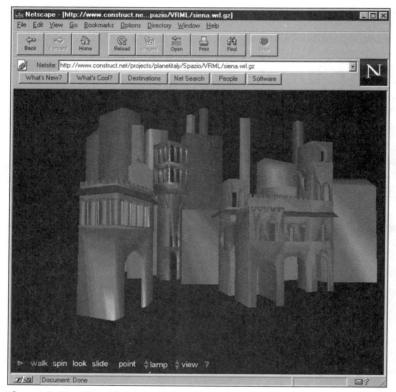

Figure 4-15: Siena, interpreted by Live3D.

Authoring for Live3D

You can use any of several authoring tools to create and edit your worlds and models, as you can with all the VRML plug-ins.

Attach VRML files to Web pages with the `<EMBED>` tag. In addition to the mandatory SRC, WIDTH and HEIGHT attributes, Live3D supports a couple of new ones:

✦ BORDER. Set to an integer, BORDER defines the width, in pixels, of the frame surrounding your embedded world. Setting BORDER=0 results in no border at all.

✦ ALIGN. Set to TOP, MIDDLE or BOTTOM, ALIGN determines how an embedded world aligns with the text on the line in which it is embedded.

Topper

Creator: Kinetix (A division of AutoDesk)

Function: Displays VRML and Virtual Reality Behavior Language (VRBL) worlds

Home Site: `http://www.ktx.com/`

Supported Platforms: Windows 95

Authoring Tool: Kinetix 3D Studio Max, among others

Good Examples: Some of the best demonstrations of Topper's unique features — special VRML behaviors — appear in the demonstration files that come with the package you download from Kinetix (see Figure 4-16).

Though you may be somewhat put off by the gigantic size of the Topper installation file, bear with it because Kinetix's VRML plug-in is one of the best. In addition to handling VRML 2.0/Moving Worlds files, Topper is able to interpret special Kinetix VRML commands. These commands include a nifty line-of-sight feature that can trigger certain behaviors whenever you see a certain object.

Plug-in Power Rating: ★★★

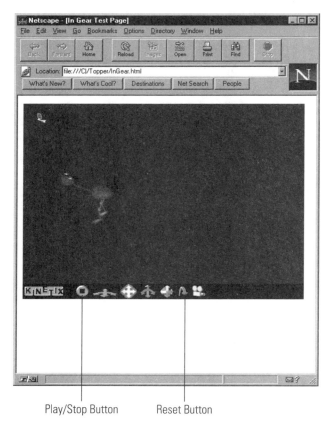

Play/Stop Button   Reset Button

Figure 4-16: One of the Topper demo files.

Installing Topper

To install Topper on a Windows machine:

1. Point your browser at `http://www.ktx.com/products/hyperwire/ download.htm`.

2. Click on the Download link under the Topper heading.

3. Save the file by itself in a temporary directory.

4. When the file has downloaded completely, shut down your browser.

5. Run the file you downloaded. It's an automated installation routine that installs Topper. Respond to the prompts as needed.

6. Re-start your browser. Topper will be ready for use.

Using Topper

One of the most novel features of Topper's interface is its Play/Stop button, which allows you to treat three-dimensional animations as you would a video clip, stopping and starting the action as it suits your whim. Labeled in Figure 4-17, the Play/Stop button looks exactly like the one on a CD player's control panel. It's a right-pointing triangle when the action is stopped, and it's a square when the animation is going on.

Otherwise, navigation is similar to most other VRML browsers. Each of the controls at the bottom of the display area is used to control motion in a particular plane, while the Reset control (also labeled in Figure 4-17) is used to return you to the original viewpoint.

Play/Stop Button   Reset Button

Figure 4-17: Topper's controls, with the Play/Stop and Reset buttons labeled.

Plugged-in sites

Topper can display any VRML 2.0/Moving Worlds scene available on the Web today. Additionally, special behaviors unique to a Kinetix version of VRML, Topper understands. To see those capabilities demonstrated, check out the files that the Topper installation routine put in your TOPPER directory.

The detailed teapot, part of the file CLICK_ME.HTM, appears in Figure 4-18.

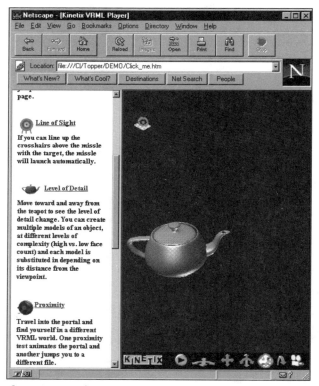

Figure 4-18: The Topper teapot.

Authoring for Topper

As is the case with all the VRML plug-ins, you can use any of several authoring tools to create and edit your worlds and models.

Embedding content for Topper in your Web pages is easy — the plug-in only supports the mandatory `<EMBED>` attributes. Here's a typical usage:

```
<EMBED SRC="SAILBOAT.VRML WIDTH=300 HEIGHT=200>
```

That statement fits the file SAILBOAT.VRML into a box 300 pixels wide by 200 pixels high.

Viscape

Creator: Superscape

Function: Displays VRML worlds

Home Site: `http://www.superscape.com/`

Supported Platforms: Windows 95

Authoring Tool: Any of several VRML 2.0 tools

Good Examples: Stonehenge at `http://www.superscape.com/Stonehenge.html`; Dancing Sailors at `http://www.intel.com/procs/pentium/nworldc.svr`; a virtual city at `http://www.superscape.com/Supacity.html`

You may think twice about the quality of a plug-in that not only re-starts your browser before it takes effect but requires you to reboot your machine, too. Viscape's installation routine seems to take a week — but that will be the end of your list of gripes. Once you've installed Viscape, you'll have a browser equipped with a fun, robust set of tools for exploring the Internet.

Just take a look at the dancing sailors in Figure 4-19. The dancing sailors, who can be found on the Intel site at `http://www.intel.com/procs/pentium/nworldc.svr`, say it all about the state of VRML — insanely cool, lots of fun, but of little practical use. I discovered the sailors late at night; and thanks to the CD in my computer's drive, they seemed to be dancing to Pink Floyd. Supremely surreal. I laughed for an hour.

Plug-in Power Rating: ★★★★

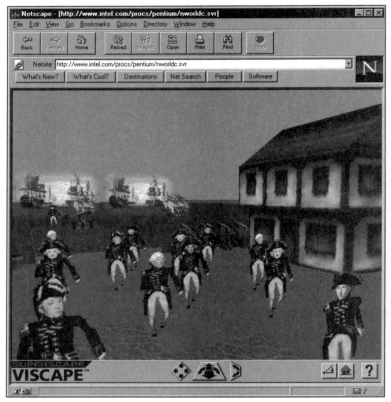

Figure 4-19: Viscape shows dancing sailors on the Intel site.

Installing Viscape

To install Viscape on a Windows machine:

1. Point your browser at http://www.superscape.com/.

2. Click on the Download link at the top of the page.

3. Click on one of the Download Site links about halfway down the page.

4. Save the file by itself in a temporary directory.

5. When the file has downloaded completely, shut down your browser. Also save everything you're doing in other programs and shut them down, too.

6. Run the file you downloaded. Respond to all the prompts. Sometimes the installation program will go a few seconds without apparently doing anything. Just wait — it's working.

7. At the end of the installation routine, the Viscape installer will ask you if it can re-start Windows. If you've saved all your files, click on Yes. Otherwise, click on No, save all your data, and restart Windows on your own.

8. Start your browser. Viscape will be ready to go.

Using Viscape

Navigating with Viscape is a matter of understanding the function of each of the three arrow controls arranged at the bottom of the display window (you can see the controls labeled with their respective functions in Figure 4-20):

✦ The leftmost arrow control moves your point of view up, down, left, and right in a vertical plane parallel to your monitor's screen.

✦ The middle arrow control moves your point of view forward (into the screen), back, and left and right in a horizontal plane.

✦ The rightmost arrow control tilts your point of view.

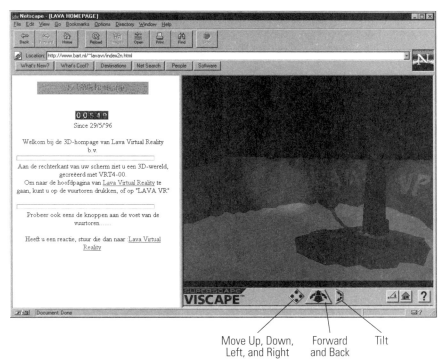

Figure 4-20: Viscape's controls, labeled.

Plugged-in sites

You can view lots of VRML 2.0-compliant sites with Viscape, but some of the best worlds seem to reside on Superscape's own machines. Here are a couple you must visit right away:

✦ **Stonehenge (**`http://www.superscape.com/Stonehenge.html`**).** The virtual Stonehenge site (see Figure 4-21) enables you to do things with this ancient monument you couldn't easily do otherwise — watch the sunrise, go back in time, watch it again, then fast-forward to the sunset and see how it affects the shadows of the monoliths. This site is an excellent application of VRML.

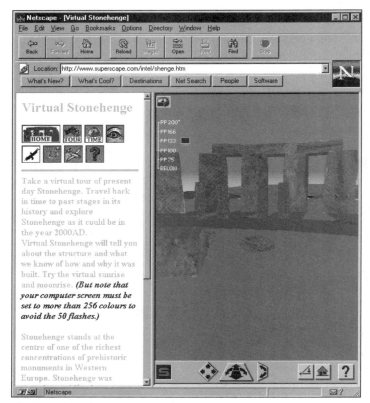

Figure 4-21: Viscape at Stonehenge.

✦ **Supercity II (**`http://www.superscape.com/Supacity.html`**).** Supercity II (see Figure 4-22) hearkens to Pesce's idea (see the introduction to this chapter) about using VRML to ease navigation through unfamiliar cities. You can navigate the streets of this futuristic, cartoonish city as you would in real life; or you can rise above the streets and fly directly to wherever you want to go. It's way-cool Web technology that may tell us something about the future.

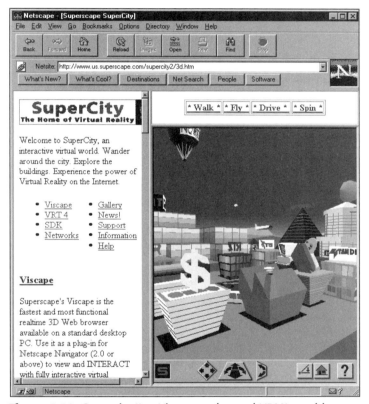

Figure 4-22: Supercity II, a Viscape-enhanced VRML world.

Authoring for Viscape

You can use any of several authoring tools to create and edit your worlds and models, as you can with all the VRML plug-ins. Superscape recommends its VRT suite of authoring applications. You can read about Superscape's line of tools at http://www.us.superscape.com/supercity2/vrt.htm.

Embedding content for Viscape in your Web pages is easy — the plug-in only supports the three basic <EMBED> attributes. Here's a typical usage:

```
<EMBED SRC="TIBURON.VRML WIDTH=300 HEIGHT=200>
```

That statement fits the file TIBURON.VRML into a box 300 pixels wide by 200 pixels high.

VR Scout

Creator: Chaco Communications

Function: Displays VRML worlds

Home Site: http://www.chaco.com/vrscout/

Supported Platforms: Windows 95

Authoring Tool: Any of several VRML authoring tools

Good Examples: A virtual art gallery at http://www.wishco.com/wish/3dgallery.wrl; an artsy coffeehouse at http://www.tristero.com/coffee/vrcoffee/coffee.wrl; the Brandenberger Tor at http://www.iion.com/travel/v_city/berlin/brand.wrl.gz

A yeoman-like VRML plug-in, VR Scout boasts plenty of useful features — such as a headlight that brightens up worlds that lack their own light sources — and very good stability. At this writing, VR Scout handles VRML 1.0 worlds only.

VR Scout works especially well on systems that lack special accelerator boards for three-dimensional graphics. This advantage derives from VR Scout's use of Microsoft Reality Lab, which doesn't require special hardware to accelerate the display of VRML and other three-dimensional objects.

Plug-in Power Rating: ★★★

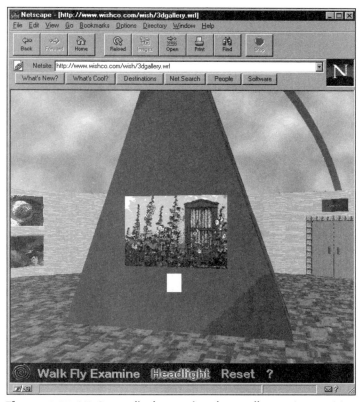

Figure 4-23: VR Scout displays a virtual art gallery at `http://www.wishco.com/wish/3dgallery.wrl`.

Installing VR Scout

To install VR Scout on a Windows machine:

1. Point your browser at `http://www.chaco.com/vrscout/`.

2. Click on Download VR Scout plugin Now!

3. On the page that appears, select VR Scout (plugin) from the upper drop-down list box. Choose your operating environment from the lower drop-down list box.

4. Click on the Click on to Display Download Sites button.

5. Click on the Download link at the top of the page that appears next (at this writing, there was only one download site available).

6. Save the file by itself in a temporary directory.

7. When the file has downloaded completely, shut down your browser.

8. Run the file you downloaded. It's an automated installation routine that installs VR Scout and the Microsoft Reality Lab files that VR Scout uses.

9. When the installation is complete, WordPad will open README.DOC automatically. Read this update file and close WordPad.

10. Re-start your browser. VR Scout will be ready for you to use.

Using VR Scout

Navigation with VR Scout is simpler than with other VRML plug-ins. Basically, you just put your mouse pointer somewhere on the displayed world, click, and drag the pointer in the direction you want to go. If you're in Walk or Fly mode, you'll move around the object. If you're in Examine mode, the object will move relative to you. Walk and Fly are best for structures, while Examine is ideal for viewing models such as molecular models that you don't actually want to go inside. You can select your mode from the pop-up menu or from the slate of controls at the bottom of the display. A special feature of VR Scout is the Headlight — a virtual miner's light that shines from your point of view in the direction you're facing. The headlight is handy for brightening dark corners of VRML worlds. Turn it on and off from the control bar or adjust its brightness on the pop-up menu.

The control bar and pop-up menu appear in Figure 4-24.

VR Scout, like Live3D, can handle VRML files that have been compressed with the gzip UNIX compression utility. This is good in that the compression yields shorter transmission times; but it causes an error in some browsers, notably Netscape Navigator.

When you call up a world that's been compressed with gzip, your browser will show a box that says, "Warning: Unrecognized encoding: 'x-gzip'."

This is not a problem. Just click on the OK button and VR Scout will get on with the show.

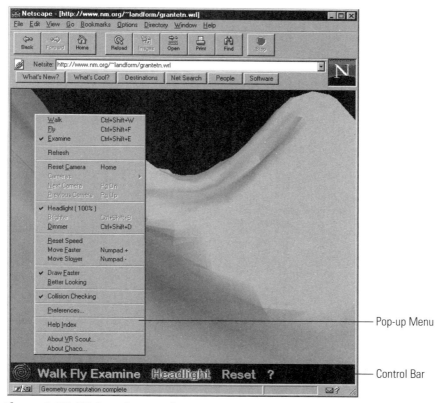

Figure 4-24: VR Scout's controls.

Plugged-in sites

Now that you have VR Scout installed, where should you go? Start scouting the Web for cool VRML. Here are some good places to check out:

✦ **The Coffee Gallery (**`http://www.tristero.com/coffee/vrcoffee/coffee.wrl`**).** A model of the real place in San Antonio, Texas. Shown in Figure 4-25, The Coffee Gallery features a bar, lots of tables and chairs, and artwork on the walls.

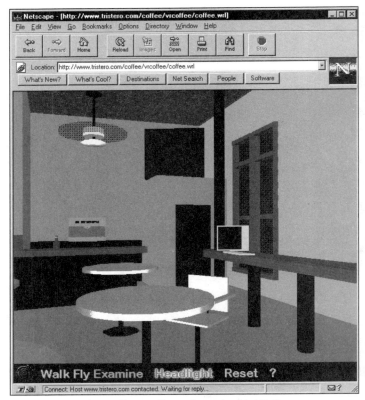

Figure 4-25: The Coffee Gallery, viewed with VR Scout.

✦ **The Brandenberger Tor (**http://www.iion.com/travel/v_city/berlin/
brand.wrl.gz**).** Standing for a long time at the center of Berlin, the
Brandenberger Tor has stood for both united and divided Germanies. Now
it's on the Web in three dimensions, and you're free to fly around and
through it. It appears in Figure 4-26.

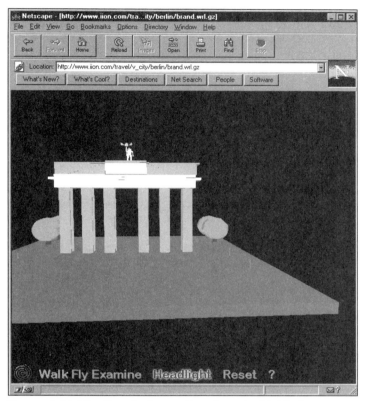

Figure 4-26: The Brandenberger Tor, viewed with VR Scout.

Authoring for VR Scout

As you can with all the VRML plug-ins, you can use any of several authoring tools to create and edit your worlds and models. Anything from a text editor (with which you can write straight VRML code) to an elaborate three-dimensional-modeling package may be used to author for VR Scout.

Embedding content for VR Scout in your Web pages is easy — the plug-in only supports the three basic <EMBED> attributes. Here's a typical usage:

```
<EMBED SRC="WASP.VRML WIDTH=300 HEIGHT=200>
```

That statement fits the file WASP.VRML into a box 300 pixels wide by 200 pixels high.

VRealm

Creator: Integrated Data Systems

Function: Displays VRML 1.0 worlds

Home Site: http://www.ids-net.com/

Supported Platforms: Windows 95

Authoring Tool: VRealm Builder, or any VRML authoring tool

Good Examples: A castle at http://www.ids-net.com/ids/vrml/worlds/castle.wrl; an art gallery at http://reality.sgi.com/employees/robinh/Models/robin1.wrl

Though the worlds it can handle are merely VRML 1.0 scenes, VRealm was one of the first plug-ins available; and its interface reflects refinement and robustness (see Figure 4-27). If you're planning to look only at static VRML worlds — and most three-dimensional material out there is still static — VRealm is worth considering.

Plug-in Power Rating: ★★

Installing VRealm

To install VRealm on a Windows machine:

1. Point your browser at http://www.ids-net.com/ids/plugin/downldpi.html.

2. Click on the Continue Download button at the bottom of the page.

3. Read the license agreement. If you agree to its terms, click on the Accept link at the bottom of the page.

4. Enter your name, e-mail address, Internet Service Provider, ZIP code, processor type, and modem speed in the registration form. Click on the Process button.

5. Click on one of the Download links — preferably the one for the location nearest yours.

6. Save the file by itself in a temporary directory.

7. When the file has downloaded completely, shut down your browser.

8. Run the file you downloaded. It's an automated installation routine that installs VRealm. Respond to the installation routine's prompts as needed.

9. Re-start your browser. VRealm will be ready for you to use.

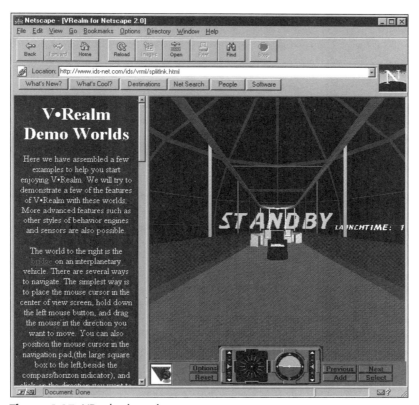

Figure 4-27: VRealm in action.

Using VRealm

To move around in a world you're viewing with VRealm, you can use your mouse by itself or use the mouse to manipulate the navigation controls at the bottom of your screen. To navigate with your mouse alone, place your pointer somewhere in the VRML window, click, and drag in the direction you want to go.

When you first open a VRML world with VRealm, you'll see a dialog box that says "Rendering VRML Scene" with a bar graph below it. This shows VRealm's progress in preparing the scene for display, and it's a handy feature that no other plug-in in the chapter offers.

To navigate with the Navigation Pad (labeled in Figure 4-28), click on the pad in the direction you want to go. Clicking the top of the pad results in forward movement, while clicking the bottom of the pad yields backward motion and clicking a side of the pad results in movement in that direction. Clicking near the center of the pad results in slow motion; clicking farther from the center results in faster motion.

Figure 4-28: VRealm's controls, labeled.

Plugged-in sites

You can use VRealm to display any VRML 1.0 world you like. Here are a couple of good examples for you to explore. You can reach both directly from the IDS site:

✦ **The Castle (**`http://www.ids-net.com/ids/vrml/worlds/castle.wrl`**).** This mist-shrouded castle may remind you of games you've played on your machine. Don't forget to go inside and try to climb the spiral staircase — an excellent test of your proficiency with the navigation controls. The castle appears in Figure 4-29.

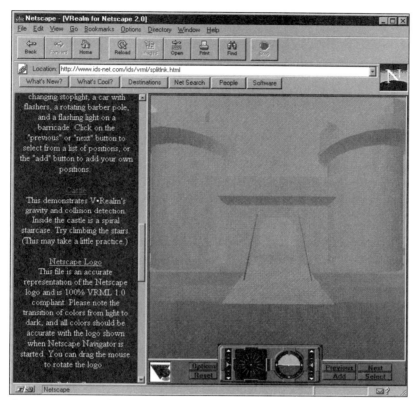

Figure 4-29: VRealm displaying a castle.

✦ **The Art Gallery** (`http://reality.sgi.com/employees/robinh/Models/robin1.wrl`). This online art gallery, shown in Figure 4-30, demonstrates the potential for a VRML-based navigation environment for the entire Web. Try clicking on the floating spheres — they're links to Web sites.

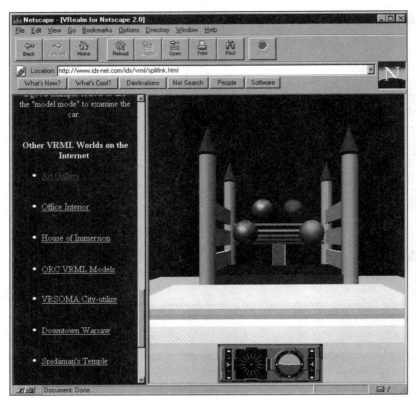

Figure 4-30: The Art Gallery, viewed by VRealm.

Authoring for VRealm

VRealm, like all the VRML plug-ins, lets you use any of several authoring tools to create and edit your worlds and models: anything from a text editor (with which you can write straight VRML code) to an elaborate three-dimensional-modeling package.

Here's a typical `<EMBED>` tag for VRealm:

```
<EMBED SRC="TRUCK.VRML WIDTH=150 HEIGHT=70>
```

That statement fits the file TRUCK.VRML into a box 150 pixels wide by 70 pixels high.

VRML Equinox

Creator: North Plains Systems

Function: Displays VRML 1.0 worlds

Home Site: http://www.northplains.com/EquiInfo.html

Supported Platforms: Power Macintosh

Authoring Tool: QuickDraw 3D

Good Examples: There's a collection of objects at http://www.northplains.com/EquiInfo.html

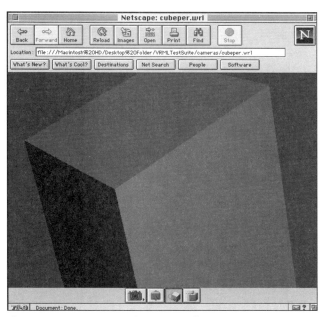

Figure 4-31: VRML Equinox at work.

By attaching itself to both your browser and the Apple QuickDraw 3D system extensions, VRML Equinox takes advantage of the object-oriented nature of the Macintosh architecture to create an excellent plug-in VRML browser (see Figure 4-31.

Early versions of the plug-in — the ones available at this writing — did not support hyperlinks and textures.

 You should be aware that VRML Equinox doesn't support .GZIP compression — a form of compression used on many VRML files. Make sure that any file you try to open with VRML Equinox has the filename extension .WRL, not .GZIP.

Plug-in Power Rating: ★★

Installing VRML Equinox

To install VRML Equinox on a Macintosh:

1. Before you download VRML Equinox, make sure you have installed Apple's QuickDraw 3D. It's on the Web at `http://QuickDraw3D.apple.com/`.
2. Point your browser at `http://www.northplains.com/downloads.html`.
3. Click on the link labeled as the plug-in download link.
4. Fill in the registration form.
5. Click on the Download button.
6. Click on one of the download links.
7. Use StuffIt Expander to decompress the downloaded file. Your browser may be configured to do this automatically.
8. Shut down your browser.
9. Drag the VRML Equinox PlugIn file to your browser's Plugins folder.
10. Re-start your browser. VRML Equinox will be ready to go.

Using VRML Equinox

You'll use four basic controls to manipulate objects with VRML Equinox. They're labeled in Figure 4-32. The controls are

✦ **View selector.** Click on this button to reveal a list box that enumerates preprogrammed views of the scene, as well as an option to return to your original vantage point.

✦ **Zoom.** Click on this to use your mouse to zoom in and out.

✦ **Rotation.** Click on this to spin the scene around an axis that runs vertically, out of your desk and through your monitor.

✦ **Left-Right.** Click on this so you can drag the scene left and right in front of you.

To move the scene in a particular way, click on the button that corresponds to the type of motion you want, then click on and drag the scene to move it the way you want.

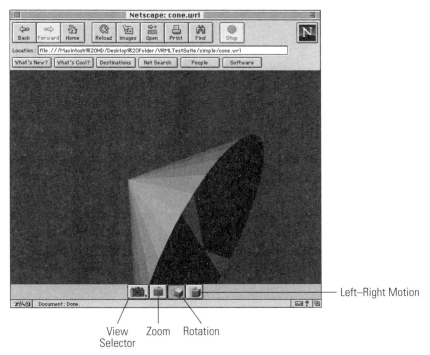

Figure 4-32: VRML Equinox's controls, labeled.

Plugged-in sites

North Plains posts links to some objects that work well with its plug-in at `http://www.northplains.com/EquiInfo.html`. Two of the best appear in Figures 4-33 and 4-34.

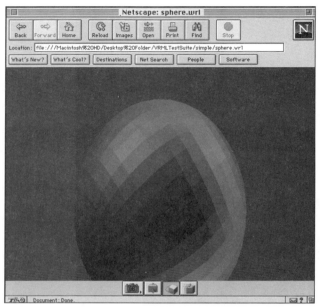

Figure 4-33: A sphere, seen through VRML Equinox.

Figure 4-34: A VRML Equinox cylinder.

Authoring for VRML Equinox

You can create worlds for exploration with VRML Equinox with any VRML-authoring program, such as QuickDraw 3D for the Macintosh. You can get QuickDraw 3D at `http://product.info.apple.com/qd3d/`.

Attach your VRML files to Web pages with the `<EMBED>` tag and its mandatory attributes: `SRC`, `WIDTH` and `HEIGHT`.

Web-Active

Creator: Plastic Thought

Function: Displays Web VR files

Home Site: `http://www.PlasticThought.com/`

Supported Platforms: All Macintosh systems

Authoring Tool: Web VR Maker or any VRML authoring tool

Good Examples: Watch `http://www.PlasticThought.com/pages/links.html` for Web-Active links

Though it escaped my attention until it was too late to include a complete write-up, Web-Active is a virtual reality plug-in for the Macintosh. Be sure to explore what it can do if you're a Macintosh jockey looking to see what your computer can do with three-dimensional space.

Installing Web-Active

To install Web-Active

1. Point your browser at `http://www.PlasticThought.com/`.
2. In the navigation menu in the uppermost frame, click on the WebWorks button.
3. Under the Web-Active heading, click on the Download Self Extracting Archive button.
4. Shut down your browser.
5. Use StuffIt to decompress the file you downloaded.
6. Move the plug-in file to your Plug-ins folder.
7. Re-start your browser. Web-Active will be ready to go.

Using Web-Active

Manipulating models with Web-Active is a matter of mouse magic. Move your mouse pointer to the center of a still object and click, and it will start to tumble. Move your pointer to the edge of an image, and it will rotate around an axis — which one depends upon where you click on.

You can also long-click on an image to bring up a pop-up menu containing artist-defined commands.

Plugged-in sites

Plastic Thought maintains a list of links relevant to Web-Active at `http://www.PlasticThought.com/pages/links.html`.

Authoring for Web-Active

To create files for Web-Active to read, you'll need Web VR Maker. You can download a demonstration version of that program from `http://www.PlasticThought.com/`.

With Web VR Maker, you can convert a .3DMF file — a standard QuickDraw 3D file — to a .WVR file. Web VR files can be made to rotate, tilt, or tumble, unlike plain .3DMF files.

To attach a Web VR file to a Web page, use the `<EMBED>` tag. In addition to the standard `SRC`, `WIDTH` and `HEIGHT` commands, Web-Active understands a number of optional attributes. They are

- ✦ SPIN. Set to TRUE or FALSE, SPIN determines whether the image rotates.
- ✦ SPIRAL. Set to TRUE or FALSE, SPIRAL determines whether the image spins on an axis perpendicular to your screen.
- ✦ VERTWRAP. Set to TRUE or FALSE, VERTWRAP determines how much navigational freedom viewers have. If VERTWRAP is set to FALSE, viewers of the image cannot make the image flip over.
- ✦ HORZWRAP. Setting HORZWRAP to FALSE prevents the viewer from spinning all the way around.
- ✦ MENU. Allows you to add functions to the Web-Active menu. Use the syntax MENU=TITLE;COMMAND PARAMETERS.
- ✦ NAVIGATE. Determines the viewer's ability to rotate the Web-Active image.
- ✦ CLICK. CLICK=FALSE causes Web-Active to ignore all mouse actions.

✦ PICTURE. Setting PICTURE=FILL causes the Web-Active image to fill the space allocated to it by the WIDTH and HEIGHT attributes. Setting it to CENTER centers it in the box.

✦ DELAY. Set to an integer between 0 and 120, DELAY determines how fast an image spins. 10 is the default value.

✦ DOUBLE. Set equal to a command, DOUBLE defines what the image does when it is double-clicked on.

✦F SINGLE. Set equal to a command, SINGLE defines what the image does when it is clicked on.

In Web-Active's <EMBED> statements, TRUE is the same as ON and 1, and FALSE is the same as OFF and 0. You can use those values interchangeably.

If you're going to serve content for Web-Active, make sure your server is configured for MIME type and x-world and x-wvr with the .WVR filename extension.

Whurlplug

Creator: John Louch

Function: Displays VRML 1.0 worlds

Home Site: http://product.info.apple.com/qd3d/viewer.html

Supported Platforms: Power Macintosh

Authoring Tool: QuickDraw 3D

Touted by Apple itself, one would expect Whurlplug to be the king of the Macintosh VRML browsers. Maybe so — but for the life of me, I couldn't get it to work on my Power Macintosh. The BinHex compression Apple used on it seems to have been faulty, and despite several hours' attempts to unscramble the problem on two different sessions a week apart, I could not get Whurlplug to go.

For this reason, I've omitted a Plug-in Power Rating here. Check it out for yourself and make your own decision.

Installing Whurlplug

To install Whurlplug:

1. Make sure you have QuickDraw 3D installed on your machine. If not, get it from http://quickdraw3d.apple.com/.

2. Point your browser at `http://product.info.apple.com/qd3d/viewer.html`.

3. Scroll to the bottom of the page.

3. Click on the WHURLPLUG link at the top of the description of the plug-in.

4. Use StuffIt to unpack the file you download. Your Macintosh may be configured to do this automatically.

5. Shut down your browser.

6. Move the plug-in file to your Plugins folder.

7. Re-start your browser. Whurlplug will be ready to go.

Using Whurlplug

Odds are, you use Whurlplug in a manner similar to the way you use ExpressVR and VRML Equinox (both covered earlier in this chapter).

Plugged-in sites

Try the archive at `http://vrml.arc.org/worlds` as a test-bed for Whurlplug.

Authoring for Whurlplug

You can create worlds for exploration with ExpressVR with any VRML-authoring program, such as QuickDraw 3D for the Macintosh. You can get QuickDraw 3D at `http://product.info.apple.com/qd3d/`.

Attach your VRML files to Web pages with the `<EMBED>` tag and its mandatory attributes: `SRC`, `WIDTH` and `HEIGHT`.

WIRL

Creator: VREAM

Function: Displays VRML worlds

Home Site: `http://www.vream.com/`

Supported Platforms: Windows 95

Authoring Tool: Any VRML 2.0 authoring package

Good Examples: The Space Shuttle at `http://www.vream.com/worlds/shuttle/shuttle.html`; a drag strip at `http://www.vream.com/worlds/races.html`

To get an idea of what WIRL can do, check out the Camaro in Figure 4-35. Not only does the WIRL plug-in display the car in an attractive way, it races from one end of the quarter-mile to the other, while your point of view moves from one prime location to the next. What's more, you can pick up the racer with your mouse pointer, let it go, and watch virtual gravity do its stuff — complete with a little bounce after the car hits the ground the first time. Try for yourself at `http://www.vream.com/worlds/races.html`.

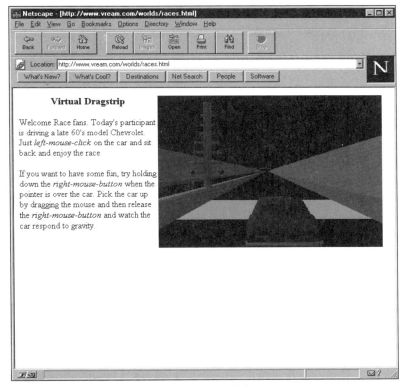

Figure 4-35: WIRL's virtual hemi-powered drone.

WIRL's an excellent VRML 2.0 browser that would benefit from sound support but otherwise stacks up well against the best virtual reality Web tools. Both *Wired Magazine* and *PC Magazine* named it to their lists of top Web tools.

Plug-in Power Rating: ★★★★

Installing WIRL

To install WIRL on a Windows machine:

1. Point your browser at `http://www.vream.com/3dll.html`.
2. Scroll almost all the way down the page. Click on one of the download sites.
3. Save the file by itself in a temporary directory.
4. When the file has downloaded completely, shut down your browser.
5. Run the file you downloaded. It's an automated installation routine, so respond to the prompts as needed and let it do the work.
6. Save all your work and reboot your computer.
7. Re-start your browser. WIRL will be ready to go.

Using WIRL

Navigating with WIRL is a lot like navigating with other VRML browsers — you have a set of arrows for each plane of movement, and you can drag your mouse around the screen to cause a change in your perspective.

The neat thing about navigation in WIRL, though, is the support the plug-in has for interaction. For example, in the world shown in Figure 4-36, you can press the 7 key to move away from the bird and into a kayak on a virtual river — and then use the 1, 2, 3, and 4 keys to paddle around.

Like Topper, WIRL features Start and Stop buttons for its animated movie-like sequences. Labeled in Figure 4-36, these buttons let you pause animations at critical points to examine details.

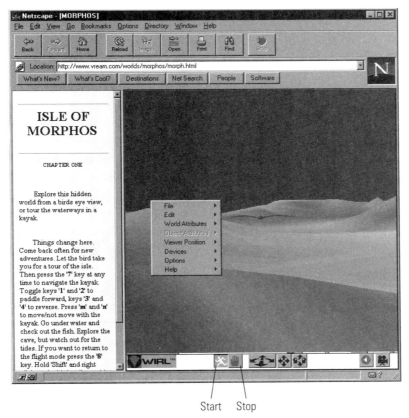

Start   Stop

Figure 4-36: WIRL's controls.

Plugged-in sites

WIRL will should display practically any VRML 2.0 world. One of the best such worlds, though, resides on the VREAM site. Don't pass up...

✦ **The Space Shuttle (**`http://www.vream.com/worlds/shuttle/shuttle.html`**).** This depiction of the space shuttle (see Figure 4-37) can play like a movie — or like a video game. Use your mouse and keyboard to manipulate the shuttle's robot arm and try to retrieve a satellite; then re-enter the Earth's atmosphere.

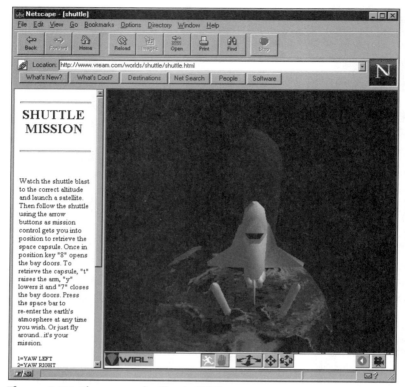

Figure 4-37: The space shuttle via WIRL.

Authoring for WIRL

Like all the VRML plug-ins, WIRL lets you use any of several authoring tools — from a text editor (with which you can write straight VRML code) to an elaborate three-dimensional-modeling package — to create and edit your worlds and models.

Here's a typical `<EMBED>` tag for WIRL:

```
<EMBED SRC="MAZE.VRML WIDTH=150 HEIGHT=70>
```

That statement fits the file MAZE.VRML into a box 150 pixels wide by 70 pixels high.

At this writing, VREAM is developing an authoring tool called VRCreator that probably will be extremely well-integrated with WIRL.

CHAPTER 5

Document and Image Viewers

The electronic office always has concerned itself with documents — page layout documents, spreadsheet documents, presentation documents, drawings — the list could go on all day. Ever since engineers figured out the idea of saving electronic information in "files," the metaphor of the document has been part of the computing lexicon.

The Web, likewise, has everything to do with documents. We talk about home pages and welcome pages. We sometimes use "document" as a synonym for "Web page." The most common way to explain the Web is to compare it to a pile of pages torn from books that you can navigate in any order you want.

It makes sense, then, that there would be a way to integrate the documents that populate our offices with the documents that comprise the global (or not-so-global, as in the case of intranets) network. That way involves plug-ins. By equipping your browser with the plug-ins described in this chapter — many of which appear on the included CD-ROM, by the way — you can view AutoCad drawings that reside on a computer in California, or Microsoft Word documents on a hard drive in Baltimore, all from your Web-savvy computer in Duluth. These plug-ins make your browser aware of dozens of common and specialized file formats and teach the browser how to display information encoded in those formats in its window.

These plug-ins may foretell a day when entire computing environments center on a browser-like tool that you can use to view everything from word-processing documents to proprietary engineering data simply by calling up the appropriate data and letting your browser figure out how to display it. Imagine: not just a common interface for everything (as Windows and the Macintosh already provide) but a single tool you can use for all your computing tasks. Once you play with these plug-ins, it's hard to convince yourself that this isn't the future of the operating system!

Acrobat

Creator: Adobe

Function: Displays and prints documents encoded in the Acrobat (.PDF) format

Home Site: `http://www.adobe.com/Acrobat/`

Supported Platforms: All Windows and Macintosh systems and UNIX for Netscape Navigator; Windows 95 and Windows NT for Microsoft Internet Explorer

Authoring Tool: Acrobat Distiller or Acrobat Exchange in conjunction with practically any page-layout or word-processing application

Good Examples: A sample of *The New York Times Internet Edition* at `http://www.adobe.com/cgi-bin/byteserver3/acrobat/3beta/PDFS/Times.pdf`; a sample of *PCWeek* at `http://www.adobe.com/cgi-bin/byteserver3/acrobat/3beta/PDFS/Pcweek.pdf`

Formerly called Amber, the Acrobat plug-in works with the other Acrobat programs to help you distribute Acrobat-formatted documents worldwide to users with any of several computing platforms (see Figure 5-1).

Acrobat was originally designed before the popularization of the Internet to allow people in a single building to share elaborately formatted documents across a variety of machines, and has flourished on the global network. The original Acrobat Reader program was a common helper application before plug-ins came into being. Now that it's possible to integrate Acrobat compatibility with your browser, you can enjoy the world's collection of Portable Document Format (.PDF) documents. Since Acrobat Exchange also can be downloaded from the Web, you can become an Acrobat publisher almost as easily as you can equip yourself to read the publications of others.

Plug-in Power Rating: ★★★★

Installing Acrobat

To install Acrobat:

1. Point your browser at `http://www.adobe.com/acrobat/3beta/`.
2. Scroll down to the link that corresponds to your computer and the package you want. You may want to download Acrobat Exchange, which includes the Acrobat Reader software, rather than just the Reader. Click on the link.
3. Click on the DOWNLOAD link.
4. Save the file to a temporary directory by itself.
5. Shut down your browser.

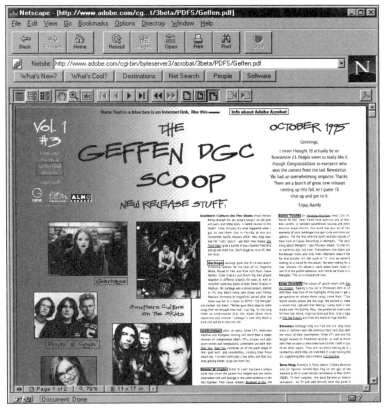

Figure 5-1: Adobe Acrobat displaying a Geffen Records newsletter.

6. Run the file you downloaded. It's an installation program that handles the details of installing Acrobat. Respond to its prompts as needed.

7. Restart your browser. Acrobat will be ready to go.

Using Acrobat

Using Acrobat is intuitive. If you've used Exchange before, you're all set, since the toolbar you're used to working with has migrated to the Acrobat plug-in. If you're new to the Acrobat world, it won't be long before you're navigating documents like a pro. Figure 5-2 shows the most important Acrobat controls, labeled.

When viewing Acrobat documents, remember that you're exploring a web of documents within the Web itself. Documents can contain links — both to other points in the same document and to Web URLs. Links are boxed in blue. When you pass your mouse pointer over a link, the pointer turns into a hand with its index finger extended. In the case of Web links, the hand has a *W* tattooed on its back.

Figure 5-2: Acrobat's controls, labeled.

The basic tools for navigating through a multipage Acrobat document mimic the controls on a CD player's control panel. The right-pointing triangle calls up the next page; the left-pointing triangle goes back a page; the two left- and right-pointing triangles next to bars go to the first and last pages of a document, respectively. If you want a thumbnail view of all the pages in a document, click on the thumbnail button; you can then click on a page's thumbnail view to call it into the full-size window.

Clicking anywhere on a displayed page zooms in on the point you clicked.

Plugged-in sites

What do you do with your Acrobat plug-in now that you've installed it? Fortunately, Acrobat is a fairly popular system for publishing things on the Web. You should be able to find lots to look at. Check out Adobe's directory at `http://www.adobe.com/acrobat/3beta/amexamp.html` for the latest and sharpest Acrobat publications. Some of the best:

✦ **The New York Times Internet Edition** (`http://www.adobe.com/cgi-bin/ byteserver3/acrobat/3beta/PDFS/Times.pdf`). Though this is an old version of the *Times*, it gives you an idea of what the paper is doing on the Web (see Figure 5-3). Head to `http://www.nytimes.com` to register for access to current editions.

Figure 5-3: *The New York Times Internet Edition*, in Acrobat format.

✦ **PCWeek Magazine** (`http://www.adobe.com/cgi-bin/byteserver3/ acrobat/3beta/PDFS/Pcweek.pdf`). Again, an old version of a periodical — but one that illustrates the color capability of Acrobat. Check out the captioned graphics and the embedded logos — things that aren't easy to create with HTML, if they're feasible at all (see Figure 5-4).

Figure 5-4: *PCWeek* Magazine, in Acrobat format.

Authoring for Acrobat

You can create Acrobat documents in several ways. The easiest and least-expensive is to use the PDF Writer feature of Acrobat Exchange. This feature works in the same way as a printer driver — you create a document in any word-processing or page-layout program, then select the PDF Writer from your list of available printers. Instead of printing to paper, PDF Writer will "print" your work to a .PDF file, which can then be read by Acrobat Exchange or by the Acrobat plug-in — perhaps on a machine many thousands of miles distant.

You can expand the functionality of Acrobat Exchange with special add-on programs called — yep, you guessed it — plug-ins! These plug-ins have nothing to do with your Web browser, but they can aid your publishing efforts. Plug-ins exist to help you do such things as add video to your Acrobat documents and index multi-page documents. Read all about them at http://www.adobe.com/acrobat/plugins.html.

If PDF Writer doesn't translate your documents properly — and it sometimes has problems with graphics — try Acrobat Distiller. This program, which you buy from Adobe, translates PostScript files into .PDF format. Most page layout programs, such as PageMaker and Quark Xpress, can generate Postscript files. Usually, you choose the program's Print to File option to create a PostScript file.

Unlike most other plug-ins, Acrobat does not use the <EMBED> tag to designate part of a Web page for use by the plug-in. Instead, the Acrobat plug-in uses the entire browser window to display an Acrobat document.

Page-at-a-time viewing, one of the special features of the latest versions of Acrobat, allows you to start looking at the first page of a .PDF document while subsequent pages continue to download. Basically, it's streaming for Acrobat documents. To take advantage of page-at-a-time viewing, you need a Web server program that supports it or a special Common Gateway Interface (CGI) script attached to your current server. No server supports page-at-a-time viewing at this writing, though Adobe says that future versions of Netscape's servers will. A copy of the CGI script needed to convert a generic server can be found on Adobe's Web site.

Don't forget to add the MIME type document/x-pdf, with the filename extension .PDF, to your server.

ASAP WebShow

Creator: SPC

Function: Lets you display graphically rich ASAP WebShow presentations

Home Site: http://www.spco.com/asap/asapwebs.htm

Supported Platforms: All Windows systems

Authoring Tool: ASAP WordPower

Good Examples: Graphicsland at http://www.graphicsland.com/asapshow. htm; U.S.-Russian Information Bureau at http://homepage.interaccess.com/ ~cognito/czar/asap.html (see Figure 5-5); Visone Corvette at http://www. visone.com/visone.asp.

Designed to enhance Web pages with frame presentations that site visitors can examine at their own speed, ASAP WebShow is one option for site developers who want to use elaborate formatting and fancy graphics without having to use awkward graphics or stretch HTML to the limit.

Plug-in Power Rating: ★★★

Figure 5-5: ASAP WebShow at the U.S.-Russian Information Bureau.

Installing ASAP WebShow

To install ASAP WebShow on a Windows machine:

1. Point your browser at `http://www.spco.com/asap/websdnld.htm`.
2. Click on the link that corresponds to your operating environment.
3. Fill in the form that appears, specifying your browser type.
4. Click on the Download button.
5. Click on the Download Now link.
6. Save the file to a temporary directory by itself.
7. When the file has downloaded completely, shut down your browser.
8. Run the file you downloaded. It's an installation program that handles the details of installing ASAP WebShow. Respond to its prompts as needed.
9. Restart your browser. ASAP WebShow will be ready to go.

Using ASAP WebShow

Watching a slide show with ASAP WebShow is a pleasure; most of the process is automated, and the controls are easy to master. Figure 5-6 shows the controls labeled. The controls are

- ✦ **Previous Slide.** Goes back one slide.

- ✦ **Slide List.** Shows a list of the slides in the presentation from which you can choose the one you want to view.

- ✦ **Next.** Goes forward one slide.

- ✦ **Pause.** Halts the progress of an automatic presentation.

- ✦ **Full Page.** When pressed, causes ASAP WebShow to disregard the height and width specifications in the <EMBED> tag (see the Authoring section) and fill the entire browser window with the ASAP WebShow display.

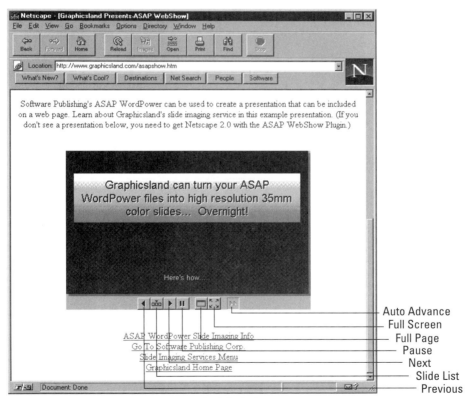

Figure 5-6: ASAP WebShow's controls, labeled.

✦ **Full Screen.** When pressed, fills your entire screen with the slide show —
displacing your browser's controls and everything else. You can return to the
window-sized display mode by right-clicking on the presentation and selecting the Show Embedded option from the pop-up menu.

✦ **Auto Advance Status.** When this is green, the slides will display in sequence
automatically. Turn off Auto Advance by right-clicking on the presentation
and choosing Disable Auto Advance from the pop-up menu.

Plugged-in sites

You'll find a collection of links to exemplary uses for ASAP WebShow at `http://
www.spco.com/asap/asapgalcust.htm`. These are real-life examples, not demon-
strations put together by SPC. Some of the best:

✦ **Visone Corvette** (`http://www.visone.com/visone.asp`). Visone Corvette
sells Chevrolet Corvettes of all vintages — and the dealer uses ASAP
WebShow to display prime examples. A photograph and explanatory text for
each of half a dozen cars show visitors what Visone has to offer (see Figure 5-7).

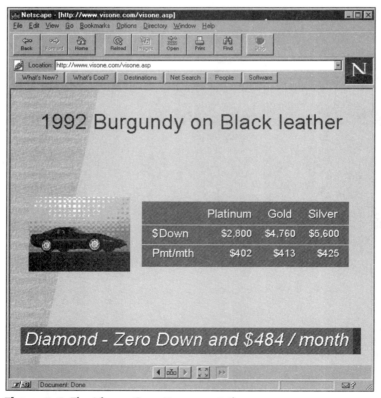

Figure 5-7: The Visone Corvette presentation.

✦ **PC World Online** (http://www.pcworld.com/resources/promos/asap-presentation.html). Here's a straightforward marketing presentation that lists the merits of the PC World information service (see Figure 5-8).

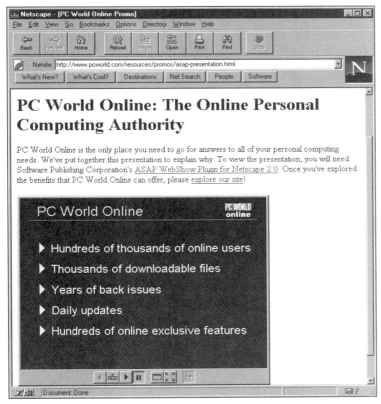

Figure 5-8: PC World Online.

Authoring for ASAP WebShow

To create content for ASAP WebShow, you use ASAP WordPower — which you have to purchase from SPC for $129. Read all about it on the SPC site at http://www.spco.com/asap/presentkit/index.htm.

Once you've built a presentation, you must use the <EMBED> tag to attach it to your Web page. A minimal statement looks like this:

```
<EMBED SRC="SALES.ASP" HEIGHT=100 WIDTH=250>
```

That makes the presentation SALES.ASP play in a box 100 pixels high by 250 pixels wide. In addition to the mandatory attributes, <EMBED> tags for ASAP WebShow can take on some additional attributes.

Don't forget to configure your server to handle MIME type application/x-asap, with extension .ASP.

CMX Viewer

Creator: Corel

Function: Allows you to view embedded .CMX files

Home Site: `http://www.corel.com/corelcmx/index.htm`

Supported Platforms: Windows 95 and Windows NT

Authoring Tool: CorelDRAW!

Good Examples: A Corel demo at `http://www.corel.com/corelcmx/realcmx.htm`; a fancy car at `http://www.corel.com/corelcmx/cmx/luxury59.cmx`; a unicorn at `http://www.corel.com/corelcmx/cmx/unicorn.cmx`

Vector-based images — that is, images based on mathematically defined shapes rather than on pixel-by-pixel renderings — came to the desktops of the business world with CorelDRAW!, Corel's flagship drawing program. The program allowed graphic artists to create exquisite drawings, and it saved its output in .CMX format. Until now, Web publishers had to translate their .CMX drawings into GIF or JPEG format. Now, CMX Viewer lets Web publishers place .CMX files directly in Web pages (see Figure 5-9).

Installing CMX Viewer

To install CMX Viewer on your Windows machine:

1. Point your browser at `http://www.corel.com/corelcmx/index.htm`.
2. Click on the download the viewer now link near the bottom of the page.
3. Save the file to a temporary file by itself.
4. When the file has downloaded completely, shut down your browser.
5. Run the file you downloaded. It's a self-extracting .ZIP archive.
6. Run SETUP.EXE. It's an installation program that handles the details of installing CMX Viewer. Respond to its prompts as needed.
7. Restart your browser. CMX Viewer will be ready to go.

Plug-in Power Rating: ★★★★

Figure 5-9: CMX Viewer announces itself to the world.

Using CMX Viewer

Nothing to it — just call up a page with a .CMX picture embedded in it and let the plug-in do the rest.

If you want to do something exotic, such as save the image to your hard disk or rotate the image, use your right mouse button to call up a pop-up menu. You can select any of a dozen file- and image-manipulation commands from the pop-up menu. One of the niftiest options is the Pop-Up command, which causes the image to be displayed in a separate window in which you can perform image rotations without messing up the rest of the Web page.

Plugged-in sites

Looking for something to do with CMX Viewer? You'll find a directory of other CMX-enhanced sites at `http://www.corel.com/corelcmx/samples.htm`. Here are a couple of good examples

✦ **Unicorn** (`http://www.corel.com/corelcmx/cmx/unicorn.cmx`). The unicorn, mythical beast of the forest, appears in Figure 5-10. This full-page graphic can be downloaded in just a few seconds over a 28.8 Kbps dialup connection.

Figure 5-10: A unicorn, spotted by CMX Viewer.

♦ **The CMX Logo** (`http://www.corel.com/corelcmx/cmx/cmx.cmx`). Here's an example of how your company's logo can look fantastic with the help of CMX Viewer. Though this drawing appears on a page by itself, it could just as easily have been embedded in a larger Web page (see Figure 5-11).

Authoring for CMX Viewer

Create .CMX files with CorelDRAW! or any other vector-drawing program that can handle the .CMX extension. CorelDRAW!, a popular art program, is available from almost any software store or mail-order outlet. To insert your .CMX drawings into a Web page, use the `<EMBED>` tag with only its mandatory attributes:

```
<EMBED SRC="RODENT.CMX" WIDTH=40 HEIGHT=20>
```

This statement embeds the file RODENT.CMX in a box 40 pixels wide by 20 pixels high. Don't forget that you can make your embedded images larger and smaller — without introducing graininess or blockiness — by adjusting the `WIDTH` and

HEIGHT attributes. That's the big advantage of vector-based file formats such as .CMX as opposed to pixel-based formats such as .TIF or .BMP.

Figure 5-11: The CMX Logo.

Yep, it's that pesky MIME type issue again. Configure your server to handle type image/x-cmx, and assign extension .CMX to that type.

If you want to include .CMX art on your site but don't have CorelDRAW!, point your browser at http://www.corel.com/corelcmx/cmxfiles.exe. That's a self-extracting .ZIP archive that includes about 50 handy pieces of .CMX clip art.

DWG/DXF Viewer

Creator: SoftSource

Function: Displays AutoCad .DWG and .DXF files

Home Site: http://www.softsource.com/softsource/

Supported Platforms: Windows 95 and Windows NT

Authoring Tool: AutoCad

Good Examples: Bio-engineering drawings at the U.S. Department of Agriculture's Natural Resource Conservation Service at `http://www.wsdot.wa.gov/EESC/cae/bioengr/default.htm`; various details (frequently used images) at the Tri-Service CADD GIS Technology Center at `http://mr2.wes.army.mil/`

AutoCad is the *lingua franca* of engineering. Whether one expert needs to communicate ideas for a turbofan engine or plans for a city park, the chances are excellent that the information will come in the form of an AutoCad drawing.

With the appearance of DWG/DXF Viewer (and a couple of other AutoCad file viewers covered later in this chapter), it's no longer necessary for AutoCad information to be printed or stored on disk before it can be communicated (see Figure 5-12). This plug-in lets you view AutoCad .DWG and .DXF files right in your browser window — a real benefit to people who make their living out of making things work.

Plug-in Power Rating: ★★★★

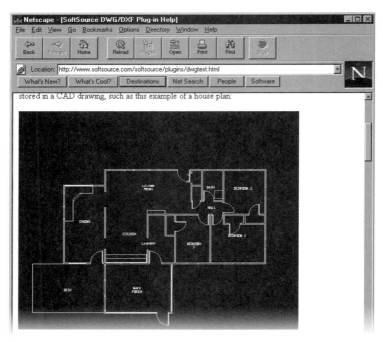

Figure 5-12: DWG/DXF Viewer at work.

Installing DWG/DXF Viewer

To install DWG/DXF Viewer on your Windows machine:

1. First, understand that you can use the plug-in only for noncommercial purposes. If you want to use DWG/DXF Viewer to try to make money, you have to pay $50 per copy to SoftSource.

2. Point your browser at `http://www.softsource.com/softsource/plugins/dwg-plugin.html`.

3. Click on the download the Windows 95/NT DWG/DXF Plug-in link about halfway down the page.

4. Save the file by itself in a temporary directory.

5. When the file has downloaded completely, shut down your browser.

6. Double-click on the file you downloaded. The file is a self-extracting .ZIP archive that runs the setup routine automatically. Respond to its prompts as needed.

7. When the installation program finishes its work, restart your browser. DWG/DXF Viewer will be ready to go to work.

Using DWG/DXF Viewer

The first time you call up a .DWG or .DXF file with DWG/DXF Viewer, you'll be transferred to SoftSource's registration form. Fill in the form, click on the Register button at the bottom, and then use your browser's Back button to return to the drawing you wanted to examine.

Plugged-in sites

At the bottom of the page from which you downloaded the plug-in (`http://www.softsource.com/softsource/plugins/dwg-plugin.html`), you'll find a list of the sites that use DWG/DXF Viewer to put AutoCad drawings on the Web. Here are a couple of excellent examples:

✦ Architectural, mechanical, and electrical details at the Tri-Service CADD GIS Technology Center (`http://mr2.wes.army.mil/`). Loads and loads of utilitarian parts for those who spend their days designing guided missiles, tank treads, and barracks toilets. A water pump appears in Figure 5-13.

✦ Bio-engineering drawings at the U.S. Department of Agriculture's Natural Resource Conservation Service (`http://www.wsdot.wa.gov/EESC/cae/bioengr/default.htm`). Take a look at these drawings (one is shown in Figure 5-14) of methods that government engineers use to provide protection against erosion and other environmental problems.

Authoring for DWG/DXF Viewer

DWG/DXF Viewer works with the `<EMBED>` tag. You must specify the name of the file you want to embed and the dimensions of the box in which the embedded drawing is to appear. Here's an example:

```
<EMBED SRC="DRAWING.DWG" WIDTH=200 HEIGHT=200>
```

The contents of the file DRAWING.DWG appear in a box 200 pixels square.

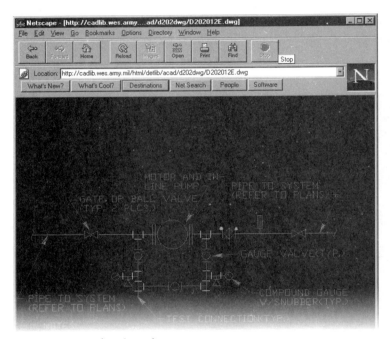

Figure 5-13: A drawing of a water pump.

You can specify the WIDTH and HEIGHT attributes with percentage figures, such as HEIGHT=50% and WIDTH=80%. Percentages enlarge or shrink an AutoCad drawing to the stated percentage of their original size.

In addition to the mandatory attributes, DWG/DXF Viewer supports a number of optional attributes. Web publishers find these handy for exercising control over how their embedded drawings appear to site visitors. The optional tags are

- ✦ **LAYERON.** Specifies which layers are to be presented — the layers not listed after LAYERON won't be displayed. LAYERON=RIVERS,LAKES,PONDS would display those three layers of your drawing. Note that there are no spaces between the listed layers.

- ✦ **LAYEROFF.** The opposite of LAYERON. Layers not listed after LAYEROFF *will* be displayed. LAYEROFF=PLUMBING,HVAC,AC would hide those three layers of your drawing. Note that again there are no spaces between the listed layers.

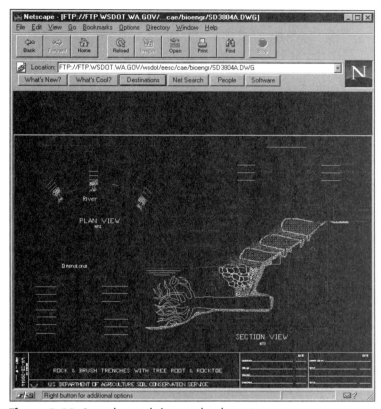

Figure 5-14: An enhanced river embankment.

✦ **NAMEDVIEW.** If you defined and named a special view in your drawing, you can tell DWG/DXF Viewer to use it by using the NAMEDVIEW attribute. NAMEDVIEW=EAST is a typical usage.

✦ **STATUS.** Defines a short text message that appears in the status bar. If the message is more than one word in length, put quotes around it. STATUS="Proposed plan" is a legal usage.

✦ **ZOOM.** Normally TRUE, setting ZOOM=FALSE disables the Zoom feature in the pop-up menu.

✦ **PAN.** Normally TRUE, setting PAN=FALSE disables the Pan feature in the pop-up menu.

✦ **LAYERS.** Normally TRUE, setting LAYERS=FALSE disables the Layers feature in the pop-up menu.

AutoCad drawings require your Web server to know about special MIME types. Have your server administrator configure the server to handle MIME type image/x-dwg, with the .DWG filename extension, and MIME type image/x-dxf, with the .DXF filename extension.

Envoy

Creator: Tumbleweed Software

Function: Displays documents in the Envoy cross-platform format

Home Site: `http://www.twcorp.com/plugin.htm`

Supported Platforms: All Windows and Macintosh systems

Authoring Tool: Any word processing, page layout or graphics-creation program

Good Examples: An embedded cardinal at `http://www.twcorp.com/tech/ tnpiembl.htm`; a newsletter at `http://www.twcorp.com/evy/wp.evy`; a document with many fonts at `http://www.twcorp.com/evy/truedoc.evy`

In the portable-document wars, most experts will tell you that Acrobat (covered earlier in this chapter) has the upper hand. Envoy, though, has some significant tricks up its virtual sleeves, and it's definitely worth a try if you're looking for a multiplatform, application-independent way to convey elaborately formatted documents to a widely distributed audience (see Figure 5-15).

Netscape Plug-in Power Rating: ★★★★

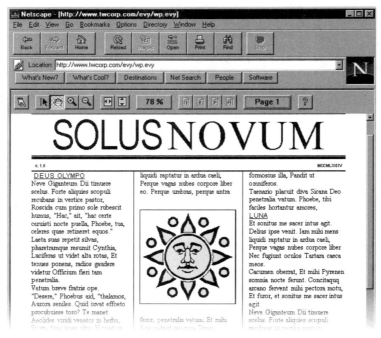

Figure 5-15: An Envoy newsletter.

Installing Envoy

To install Envoy:

1. Point your browser at `http://www.twcorp.com/download.htm`.

2. Click on the radio button next to the product you want — the plug-in for the operating environment you use.

3. Fill in the registration form at the bottom of the page and click on the Download button.

4. Click on the Download button about halfway down the page that appears next.

5. Save the file by itself in a temporary directory.

6. When the file has downloaded completely, shut down your browser.

7. Run the file you downloaded; it's an automated installation routine. Respond to its prompts as needed.

8. Restart your browser. Envoy will be ready to go.

Using Envoy

Envoy displays documents without much intervention from you. If you want to manipulate those documents, though, all the controls appear on the control bar at the top of the Envoy document, unless the page designer has turned them off (you'll learn how to do that in the Authoring section).

The important controls aren't hard to figure out. The arrow buttons move you forward and backward in a document, and the arrows that point to rectangular bars move you to the beginning and end of the document. Alternately, you can click on the large button labeled Page X and specify the page you want to see. You can zoom in and out of a document by clicking on one of the two magnifying-glass buttons and then clicking on the document or by clicking on the button labeled X % and specifying the magnification you want.

Instead of using the scroll bars to view hidden parts of the document, click on the button with the hand on it. Then, click on the document and drag until you see the portion you need.

Plugged-in sites

What can Envoy do in real life? Take a look at these two examples — one of an Envoy-encoded graphic, the other of a full-blown, full-page Envoy document:

✦ **A cardinal** (`http://www.twcorp.com/tech/tnpiembl.htm`)**.** This page demonstrates both Envoy's capacity for handling vector images and its ability to display documents embedded in a Web page. The cardinal appears in Figure 5-16.

Figure 5-16: An Envoy cardinal.

✦ **A book chapter (**`http://www.twcorp.com/evy/frame4.evy`**).** This document demonstrates the power of stand-alone Envoy documents. By incorporating graphics with carefully laid-out text, the book chapter surpasses the capabilities of HTML and makes Envoy an excellent choice for online publication projects. A page from the chapter appears in Figure 5-17.

Authoring for Envoy

Envoy documents come from any application that can print to the Envoy printer driver. The result of printing to the Envoy driver is an .EVY file ready for viewing as a stand-alone document or embedded in an HTML document.

You have three basic options for embedding Envoy documents. First, you can embed the document with no scrollbars and no toolbars. Here's the code for that:

```
<EMBED SRC="CAT.EVY" WIDTH=300 HEIGHT=250>
```

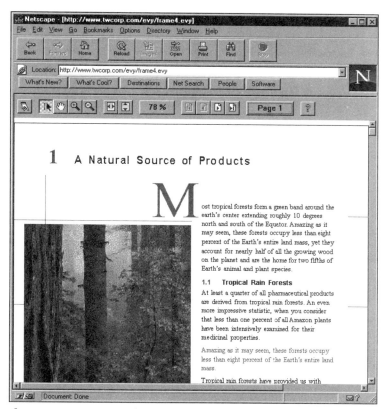

Figure 5-17: An Envoy-based book chapter.

The second way to display an Envoy document is with a scrollbar only:

```
<EMBED SRC="WORD6.EVY" WIDTH=600 HEIGHT=300 INTERFACE=SCROLL
    BORDER=1>
```

Alternately, you can surround the document with a toolbar and scrollbar. Here's the <EMBED> statement for that purpose:

```
<EMBED SRC="ROBIN.EVY" WIDTH=500 HEIGHT=300 ZOOM=FITWIDTH
    INTERFACE=FULL>
```

Don't forget to add the MIME type document/x-envoy, with the filename extension .EVY, to your server.

FIGleaf Inline

Creator: Carberry Technology

Function: Displays graphics in several formats

Home Site: http://www.ct.ebt.com/figinline/

Supported Platforms: All Windows and Macintosh systems

Authoring Tool: Practically any graphics program

Good Examples: A sextant at http://www.ct.ebt.com/figinline/gallery/ sextant.cgm; a robot arm at http://www.ct.ebt.com/figinline/gallery/ robot.cgm

An all-purpose still-graphics viewer, FIGleaf lets you view more than a dozen popular and not-so-popular graphics files (see Figure 5-18). It also gives you some ability to rotate, zoom, and scroll around the images. Supported formats include

+ Computer Graphics Metafile (.CGM)
+ Tagged Image File Format (.TIFF and .TIF)
+ Encapsulated PostScript (.EPSI and .EPSF)
+ CCITT Group 4 Type I (.G4)
+ CCITT Group 4 Type II (.TG4)
+ Microsoft Windows Bitmap (.BMP)
+ Microsoft Windows Metafile (.WMF)
+ Portable Network Graphics (.PNG)
+ Portable Pixmap (.PPM)
+ Portable Greymap (.PGM)
+ Portable Bitmap (.PBM)
+ Sun Raster files (.SUN)
+ Graphics Interchange Format (.GIF)
+ Joint Photographic Experts Group (.JPEG and .JPG)
+ Silicon Graphics RGB (.RGB)

If you need to display one of the obscure file formats in this list, FIGleaf Inline is for you (though you should check into KEYview, covered later in this chapter). Even if you don't have any pressing need to display .PPM files, though, consider equipping your browser with FIGleaf Inline for its handy image-manipulation tools.

Plug-in Power Rating: ★★★

Figure 5-18: A sextant displayed by FIGleaf.

Installing FIGleaf Inline

To install FIGleaf Inline:

1. Point your browser at `http://www.ct.ebt.com/figinline/download.html`.

2. Click on one of the Download links.

3. Save the file by itself in a temporary directory.

4. When the file has downloaded completely, shut down your browser.

5. Run the file you downloaded. It's an automated installation routine, so respond to its prompts as needed.

6. Restart your browser. FIGleaf Inline will be ready to go.

Using FIGleaf Inline

There really are only two conventions you need to understand: the zoom-in convention and the zoom-out convention. To zoom in on a portion of a drawing, hold down the Ctrl key and drag a rectangle over (or around) what you want to view close-up. To zoom back out, press Ctrl-Shift and click on the image. You can also access those features by right-clicking on (or long-clicking on, for Macintosh users) the image.

Plugged-in sites

The best place to try out FIGleaf Inline is at the Carberry Technology site's CGM Gallery at `http://www.ct.ebt.com/figinline/custcgm.html`. Here are a couple of highlights from the several images you can make appear on that page:

✦ **A robot arm** (`http://www.ct.ebt.com/figinline/gallery/robot.cgm`). Shown in Figure 5-19, the robot arm is handy for demonstrating FIGleaf Inline's Zoom features.

Figure 5-19: A FIGleaf robot arm.

✦ **The space shuttle** (http://www.ct.ebt.com/figinline/ gallery/ shuttle.cgm). A cool rendering of everyone's favorite reusable spacecraft, shown in Figure 5-20.

Figure 5-20: A FIGleaf space shuttle.

Authoring for FIGleaf Inline

You can use practically any graphics tool to create files that FIGleaf Inline can interpret, thanks to the plug-in's broad knowledge of image formats (a list of valid formats appears at the beginning of this write-up, you'll recall).

The catch comes when you try to embed your graphics in your Web pages. You need to use the <EMBED> tag, even if your graphics are in a format (such as .JPEG or .GIF) that most browsers understand without plug-ins. That's because browsers only consult their arsenal of plug-ins when confronted with a file type they don't recognize either by itself (not embedded) or attached to an HTML document with the <EMBED> tag. Therefore, if you want to give visitors to your site the ability to use FIGleaf Inline's advanced features, you need to start embedding images with statements such as `<EMBED SRC="CAT.GIF" WIDTH=100 HEIGHT=50>` rather than `<IMG SRC="CAT.GIF" WIDTH=100 HEIGHT=50>`.

In addition to the mandatory attributes, FIGleaf inline supports optional attributes:

✦ `ACTUALSIZE`. Set to `TRUE`, `ACTUALSIZE` tells the plug-in to represent the embedded image with no scaling, even if part of the image gets hidden behind the borders you define. Set to `FALSE` — the default setting — `ACTUALSIZE` scales the image to fit the box you define with the `WIDTH` and `HEIGHT` attributes.

✦ `BORDER`. Set to an integer value, `BORDER` adds a border to your image. A setting of `BORDER=4` would create a border four pixels thick around your image.

✦ `COLORMAP`. Set to `PRIVATE`, the `COLORMAP` attribute lets FIGleaf Inline use whatever colors it needs to represent the colors in an image. Set to `DITHERED`, the attribute limits the plug-in to a 16-color palette. `PRIVATE` is the default setting.

✦ `PICTNUM`. Set to an integer value, `PICTNUM` specifies which image in a multi-image file is displayed. Unless you specify otherwise, the first image in the file is displayed.

✦ `ROTATION`. Set to `0`, `90`, `180` or `270`, `ROTATION` spins your image around its center. The default value is `0`.

✦ `VFLIP`. Set to `TRUE`, `VFLIP` inverts your image. `FALSE` is the default setting.

✦ `ZOOMAREA`. Defines a rectangle to zoom into. The first number to follow the `=` is the number of pixels from the left that the top-left corner of the zoom rectangle is located. The second number is the number of pixels from the top that the top-left corner occurs. The next two numbers define the lower-right corner: the number of pixels from the right and from the bottom, respectively. `ZOOMAREA=10,15,30,10` is a valid syntax — note that there are no spaces after the commas.

FIGleaf Inline rotates your image (if you specified to rotate it) before it zooms. Be sure to figure out your `ZOOMAREA` coordinates after the image rotates.

Formula One/Net

Creator: Visual Components

Function: Displays spreadsheets and charts

Home Site: `http://www.visualcomp.com/f1net/download.htm`

Supported Platforms: All Windows systems

Authoring Tool: Any visual software development environment, plus the Formula One OLE control

Good Examples: Several examples at `http://www.visualcomp.com/f1net/live.htm/`

So much of what you've learned about in this book seems like puffery — a video player here, a sound player there, a chat plug-in over there. Formula One/Net, which lets you share spreadsheet data via browser windows, is a plug-in that should get every workaholic's blood flowing (see Figure 5-21). And it's not a rinky-dink VisiCalc-revisited spreadsheet, either. Formula One/Net can do almost everything full-blown spreadsheet packages can do (to import and modify Microsoft Excel files, you'll need to pay $79 for Formula One/Net Pro).

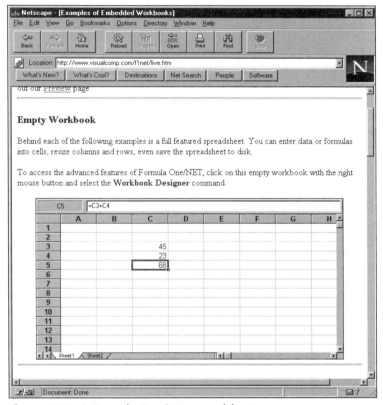

Figure 5-21: A Formula One/Net spreadsheet.

If your business works by the numbers — and whose doesn't? — this plug-in needs a test drive on your desktop.

Plug-in Power Rating: ★★★★

Installing Formula One/Net

To install Formula One/Net on a Windows machine:

1. Point your browser at `http://www.visualcomp.com/f1net/download.htm`.

2. Click on the link near the bottom of the page that corresponds to your operating environment.

3. Read the license agreement.

4. If you agree to abide by its terms, click on the link — under the InstallShield header, unless you're in a big hurry — that corresponds to your operating environment.

5. Save the file by itself in a temporary directory.

6. When the file has downloaded completely, shut down your browser.

7. Run the file you downloaded. It's an automated installation routine that will set up Formula One/Net automatically. Respond to its prompts as needed.

8. Restart your browser. Formula One/Net will be ready to use.

Using Formula One/Net

Formula One/Net is a spreadsheet application, not a viewer or player. It's a fully functional spreadsheet program that you can use to build mathematical models of complex phenomena or design interactive forms.

Formula One/Net doesn't include any sort of multiple-copy reconciliation. If you download a copy of a spreadsheet from a server and modify that spreadsheet, the modified spreadsheet resides only on your machine. You can save your modified copy back to the server; but if someone else was working on a copy of the spreadsheet at the same time, you have a real problem.

Plugged-in sites

A gimmick? Not. Look at these examples:

✦ **Loan Calculator** (`http://www.visualcomp.com/f1net/live.htm`). The fastest way to realize that you're working with a real, live spreadsheet application and not some kind of viewer plug-in is to play with this calculator.

Enter the amount you're borrowing and the loan term and immediately see your monthly payment. This looks like Java — but it's better. The Loan Calculator appears in Figure 5-22.

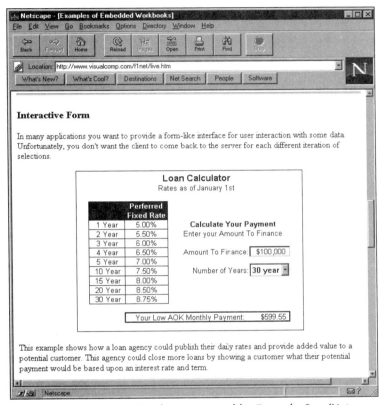

Figure 5-22: An interactive form powered by Formula One/Net.

✦ **Formatted spreadsheet** (`http://www.visualcomp.com/f1net/live.htm`). On the same page as the Loan Calculator, you'll find a spreadsheet that will convince you Formula One/Net isn't a toy. This spreadsheet, which compares the performance of various mutual funds over time, employs fancy formatting and buttons that are hyperlinked to the fund companies' Web pages. The spreadsheet appears in Figure 5-23.

Authoring for Formula One/Net

Unless you purchase Formula One/Net Pro, you develop spreadsheets for Formula One/Net with the Formula One OLE control. You can use this control in several visual development environments, including Visual Basic, Delphi, or PowerBuilder.

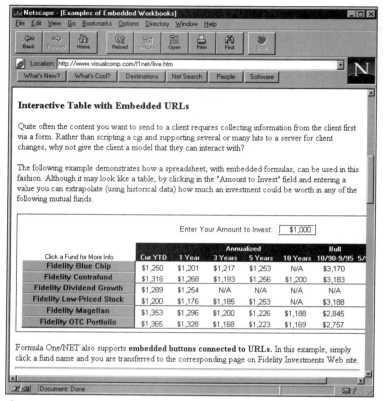

Figure 5-23: A Formula One/Net workbook with fancy formatting.

To embed Formula One/Net spreadsheets in Web pages, use the `<EMBED>` tag with the `SRC`, `HEIGHT`, and `WIDTH` attributes.

Fractal Viewer

Creator: Iterated Systems

Function: Displays Fractal Image Format (.FIF) files (see Figure 5-24)

Home Site: `http://www.iterated.com/fracview/fv_home.htm`

Supported Platforms: All Windows and Macintosh systems

Authoring Tool:

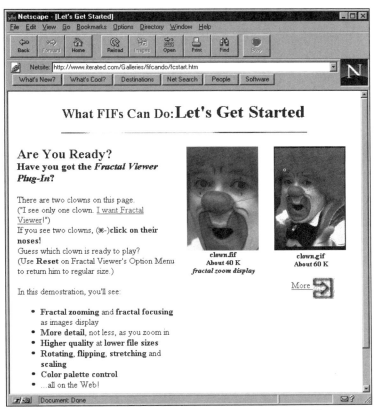

Figure 5-24: A Fractal Image Format clown, compared with a .GIF clown.

Good Examples: A hot-air balloon at http://www.iterated.com/Galleries/ images/colorbal.fif; a butterfly at http://www.iterated.com/Galleries/ images/butterfl.fif; a virtual tour of the U.S. at http://www.iterated.com/ Galleries/usamap/usamap.html

Plug-in Power Rating: ★★★★

Installing Fractal Viewer

To install Fractal Viewer on a Windows machine:

1. Point your browser at http://www.iterated.com/fracview/fv_home.htm.

2. Click on the link that corresponds to your computer and browser.

3. Fill in the registration form and click on the Continue button.

4. Click on the Get the File Right Now button.

5. Save the file by itself in a temporary directory.

6. When the file has downloaded completely, shut down your browser.

7. Run the file you downloaded. It's a self-extracting .ZIP archive that will place a handful of files in your temporary directory.

8. Run the file SETUP.EXE. It's an automated installation routine that will install Fractal Viewer on you computer and integrate it with your browser. Respond to its prompts as needed.

9. Restart your browser. Fractal Viewer will be ready to go.

Using Fractal Viewer

Want to view a .FIF file without starting your browser? The Fractal Viewer plug-in download package comes with a helper application, too. Look in the FIFVIEW folder for the Fractal Viewer executable — called FIFVIEW.EXE in Windows systems.

Plugged-in sites

Want to see what Fractal Image Format is all about? Don't pass up the directory of fractal sites at http://www.iterated.com/Galleries/. There's another directory of images at http://www.iterated.com/Galleries/images/gallery.htm. Here are a couple of good examples:

✦ **U.S. Tour** (http://www.iterated.com/Galleries/usamap/usamap.htm). Here's a .FIF file with embedded hyperlinks — click on the cities and see Web pages with information about those places. The map appears in Figure 5-25.

✦ **Hot Air Balloons** (http://www.iterated.com/Galleries/images/colorbal.fif). A plain photograph, encoded in .FIF (see Figure 5-26). Check out that download speed in comparison to .GIFs and .JPEGs.

Authoring for Fractal Viewer

You can create fractal images and convert images in other formats to .FIF with the aid of Fractal Imager, another Iterated Systems product you can examine at http://www.iterated.com/FractalImager/.

The power of the Fractal Image system comes in embedding .FIF files in Web pages. In addition to mandatory attributes SRC, WIDTH, and HEIGHT, Fractal Viewer supports a optional attributes that let you tailor the appearances of your images.

✦ CROPX. Set to an integer, CROPX defines the number of pixels (from the left) at which an image is cut off.

Figure 5-25: A mouse-driven fractal tour of the U.S.

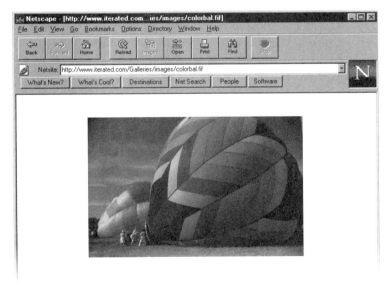

Figure 5-26: Hot-air balloons in fractal image format.

- ✦ CROPY. Set to an integer, CROPY defines the number of pixels (from the top) at which an image is cut off.

- ✦ CROPWIDTH. The equivalent of CROPX.

- ✦ CROPHEIGHT. The equivalent of CROPY.

- ✦ STANDARDPALETTE. Since it optimizes color palettes among several images on the same page, STANDARDPALETTE should be used when you have more than one embedded .FIF file.

- ✦ OPTIMIZEDPALETTE. Optimizes the color palette for a single .FIF on a page.

- ✦ INTERNALPALETTE. Tells the Fractal Image plug-in to use the color palette that is embedded with all .FIF files.

- ✦ TOPLEFT. Aligns the image in the top-left corner of the frame defined by the WIDTH and HEIGHT attributes.

- ✦ TOPRIGHT. Aligns the image in the top-right corner of the frame defined by the WIDTH and HEIGHT attributes.

- ✦ TOPCENTER. Aligns the image in the upper center of the frame defined by the WIDTH and HEIGHT attributes.

- ✦ CENTERLEFT. Aligns the image in the center of the left edge of the frame defined by the WIDTH and HEIGHT attributes.

- ✦ CENTERCENTER. Aligns the image in the center of the frame defined by the WIDTH and HEIGHT attributes. This is the default positioning attribute.

- ✦ CENTERRIGHT. Aligns the image in the center of the right edge of the frame defined by the WIDTH and HEIGHT attributes.

- ✦ BOTTOMLEFT. Aligns the image in the bottom-left corner of the frame defined by the WIDTH and HEIGHT attributes.

- ✦ BOTTOMCENTER. Aligns the image in the lower center of the frame defined by the WIDTH and HEIGHT attributes.

- ✦ BOTTOMRIGHT. Aligns the image in the bottom-right corner of the frame defined by the WIDTH and HEIGHT attributes.

- ✦ TOP. Same as TOPCENTER.

- ✦ CENTER. Same as CENTERCENTER.

- ✦ BOTTOM. Same as BOTTOMCENTER.

- ✦ LEFT. Same as LEFTCENTER.

- ✦ RIGHT. Same as RIGHTCENTER.

- ✦ FLIPHORIZONTAL. Set to TRUE, FLIPHORIZONTAL inverts an image across its horizontal axis.

- ✦ FLIPVERTICAL. Set to TRUE, FLIPVERTICAL inverts an image across its vertical axis.

✦ ROTATE90CW. Rotates the image 90 degrees clockwise.

✦ ROTATE180. Rotates the image 180 degrees.

✦ ROTATE90CCW. Rotates the image 90 degrees counterclockwise.

✦ NOPROGRESSIVE. Causes the image to be downloaded fully and then displayed, rather than displayed in increasingly larger or sharper steps.

✦ FOCUSPROGRESSIVE. Causes the image to be displayed with increasing sharpness as more information downloads.

✦ EXPANDPROGRESSIVE. Causes the image to be displayed larger as more information downloads.

✦ STEP1. Displays only the first of the five progressive steps during download.

✦ STEP2. Displays only the first two of the five progressive steps during download.

✦ STEP3. Displays only the first three of the five progressive steps during download.

✦ STEP4. Displays only the first four of the five progressive steps during download.

✦ STEP5. Displays all five progressive steps during download.

✦ DITHER. Tells the plug-in to use dithered color, rather than true color, to make the best use of the available color palette.

✦ GRAYSCALE. Converts a color image to shades of gray.

✦ INVERTCOLORS. Creates a color negative of the image.

✦ MAP. Lets you create a clickable map. MAP must be set equal to the full URL of a CERN or NCSA imagemap file. A valid example is http://foo.com/ncsa/clickon.mpp.

✦ FTT. Set equal to a full URL, FTT specifies the .FTT file associated with the .FIF file.

Don't forget to configure your server to handle fractal image files. Set it up to handle MIME type image/fif with filename extension .FIF.

KEYview

Creator: FTP Software

Function: Displays and prints files in more than 200 formats

Home Site: http://www.ftp.com/mkt_info/evals/kv_dl.html

Supported Platforms: Windows 95

Authoring Tool: You name it, KEYview can read it.

Good Examples: Look around on your own hard disk for obscure files and ask KEYview to open them.

An all-purpose blowtorch for opening practically every kind of file, KEYview can handle everything from Wang word-processing files to advanced MPEG video (see Figure 5-27). It's a Swiss Army knife of a plug-in that doesn't handle everything gracefully, but handles it well enough to get the information you need.

Plug-in Power Rating: ★★★★

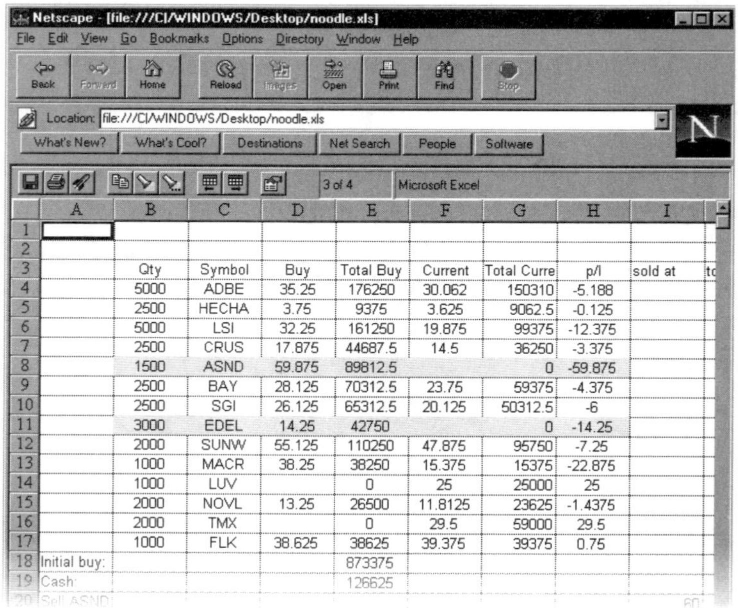

Figure 5-27: KEYView displaying a Microsoft Excel file.

Installing KEYview

To install KEYview on a Windows machine:

1. Point your browser at http://www.ftp.com/mkt_info/evals/.
2. Click on the KEYview 5.0 link.

3. Read the license agreement. If you agree to its terms, click on the Agree link at the bottom of the page.

4. Fill in the registration form and click on the Register button.

5. Click on the Click on here link.

6. Click on the link that corresponds to your operating environment.

7. Save the file by itself in a temporary directory.

8. Run the file you downloaded. It's a self-extracting .ZIP archive that will unpack several files into your temporary directory.

9. Run SETUP.EXE. It is an automated installation routine that will install the main KEYview program for you. Respond to its prompts as needed.

10. Point your browser at `http://www.ftp.com/mkt_info/evals/kv_dl.html`.

11. Click on the link in the Download section.

12. Save the file by itself in a temporary directory, separate from the temporary directory you used for the main KEYview program files.

13. When the file has downloaded completely, shut down your browser.

14. Run the file you downloaded. It's a self-extracting .ZIP archive.

15. Run SETUP.EXE. It's an automated setup routine. Respond to its prompts as needed.

16. Restart your browser. KEYview will be ready to go.

Using KEYview

A viewer with a few controls added in, KEYview is more of a skeleton key for opening files than a tool for doing anything with them. The most useful features that KEYview adds when it displays a file are its Save button and its Print button — the first two buttons on the KEYview button bar.

Plugged-in sites

Writing about sites that feature KEYview-compatible files is similar to writing about people who breathe air — they're not hard to come by at all. Rather than show you what KEYview will do on the Web, I looked around my own hard disk for some files and asked my browser, with the KEYview plug-in installed, to display them. Here are the results:

✦ **A text file.** Your browser will display these without help, but KEYview adds a Save button and some display options. A text file displayed by KEYview appears in Figure 5-28.

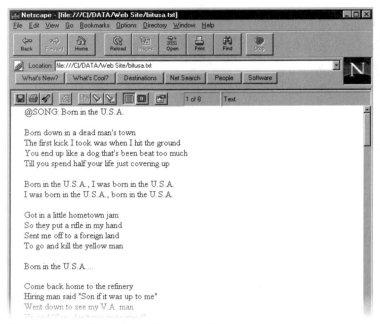

Figure 5-28: KEYview handling a text file.

✦ **A Microsoft Word file.** Here's where browsers run into trouble — with
application-specific file formats. Though other plug-ins can read Word files
(look at Inso's Word Viewer, covered later in this chapter), KEYview can read
Word files and dozens of others. A Word file appears in Figure 5-29.

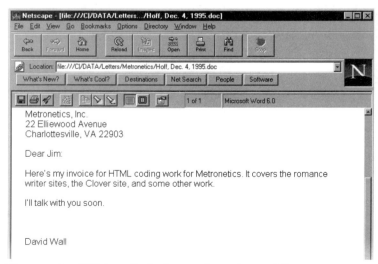

Figure 5-29: KEYview displaying a Microsoft Word file.

Authoring for KEYview

You can author material for KEYview with any of about 150 applications, at least one of which surely resides on your desktop.

Most of the time, you'll use KEYview to display entire documents; so you don't have to worry about <EMBED> statements. If you do want to embed a document for KEYview, use EMBED with only its three mandatory attributes: SRC, WIDTH, and HEIGHT.

Lightning Strike

Creator: Infinet

Function: Displays Lightning Strike graphics

Home Site: http://www.infinop.com/html/infinop.html

Supported Platforms: All Windows and Macintosh systems and UNIX

Authoring Tool: Lightning Strike

Good Examples: A cowboy at http://www.infinop.com/html/comphoto_htmls/cowboy.html; a portrait at http://www.infinop.com/html/comphoto_htmls/laura.html; a flower at http://www.infinop.com/html/comphoto_htmls/flower.html

Like Fractal Image graphics, Lightning Strike graphics are suitors to the throne of Internet Graphics Standard — the image format everybody uses to encode the images on their Web pages. Lightning Strike is an excellent option in applications in which download speed is all-important — its compression is phenomenal, even though image quality isn't the best available. Even the largest pictures download in seconds (see Figure 5-30).

Key to Lightning Strike's speed is technology based on wavelets, mathematical approximations of image characteristics around certain points in a graphic image.

Plug-in Power Rating: ★★

Installing Lightning Strike

To install Lightning Strike:

1. Point your browser at http://www.infinop.com/html/extvwr_pick.html.

2. Fill in the registration form and click on the Display Download Sites buttons when you're done.

Figure 5-30: A large, highly compressed Lightning Strike portrait.

3. Click on one of the Download links about halfway down the page.

4. Save the file by itself in a temporary directory.

5. When the file has downloaded completely, shut down your browser.

6. Run the file you downloaded. It's a self-extracting .ZIP file.

7. Move NPCOD32.DLL (for Windows 95 and Windows NT) or NPCOD16.DLL (for Windows 3.*x*) to your browser's plug-in directory.

8. Restart your browser. Lightning Strike will be ready to go.

Using Lightning Strike

Nothing to it — just call up a page with an embedded Lightning Strike image, and the plug-in will display it for you.

Lightning Strike requires your browser to have a disk cache of at least one megabyte. Use your browser's Options menu to adjust the cache, then restart your browser.

Plugged-in sites

Graphics viewers don't usually lend themselves to dramatic demonstrations, but this one may be the exception. Point your browser at the portrait of the woman in Figure 5-33 (`http://www.infinop.com/html/comphoto_htmls/laura.html`) or at the cowboy in Figure 5-31 (`http://www.infinop.com/html/comphoto_htmls/cowboy.html`). Notice how fast the images download, and how large they are. Equivalent JPEG images would take much longer to download, equivalent GIFs longer still. But note the weird "computerish" color gradations, too — Lightning Strike doesn't have the image quality of GIF or JPEG yet.

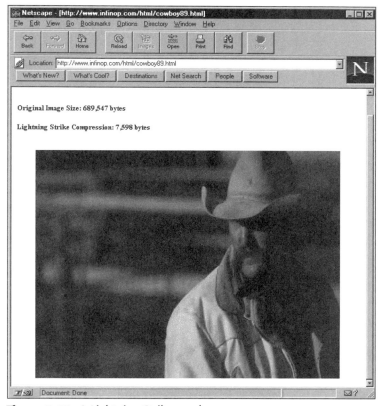

Figure 5-31: A Lightning Strike cowboy.

Authoring for Lightning Strike

You can create Lightning Strike graphics with the Lightning Strike encoder — for sale at the Infinet Web site (`http://www.infinop.com/html/infinop.html`).

Embedding Lighting Strike Graphics is simple — just use the `<EMBED>` tag with the `SRC`, `WIDTH`, and `HEIGHT` attributes.

Don't forget to configure your server to handle MIME type image/cis-cod with file-name extension .COD.

MapGuide

Creator: AutoDesk

Function: Displays MapGuide (.MWF) files

Home Site: `http://www.mapguide.com/`

Supported Platforms: All Windows systems

Authoring Tool: MapGuide Author (with MapGuide Server)

Good Examples: A map of the U.S. at `http://www.mapguide.com/maps/usa.mwf`; a map of Canada at `http://www.mapguide.com/maps/canada.mwf`

Lots of map-related schemes for the Web have been put forth in recent months. MapGuide plug-in lets you view maps in Autodesk's .MWF format over the network (see Figure 5-32). The potential is huge — imagine being in a foreign city and calling up a local map on your laptop via the Web. The potential intranet market also looms large. If your company works with maps, give MapGuide a trial run.

Installing MapGuide

To install MapGuide on a Windows system:

1. Point your browser at `http://www.mapguide.com/mbr_dnld.htm`.
2. Click on the MapGuide Viewer Plug-in link that corresponds to your operating environment.
3. Save the file by itself in a temporary directory.
4. When the file has downloaded completely, shut down your browser.
5. Run the file you downloaded. It's an automated installation routine, so respond to its prompts as needed.
6. Restart your browser. MapGuide will be ready to go.

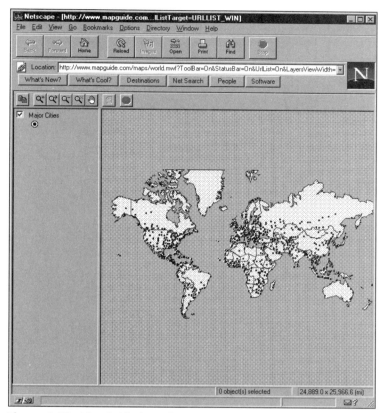

Figure 5-32: MapGuide in action.

Using MapGuide

Basically, you just enter the map's URL into your browser's URL box and let the plug-in take care of the rest. MapGuide has a button bar that's used mainly for defining the function of the mouse cursor. Click on one of the magnifying-glass buttons to zoom in or out. Most of the time, you'll probably want to have the hand pointer selected so you can click on the map and drag it around.

In many maps, you can turn on and off certain features, such as cities, rivers, and place names, by clicking on check boxes to the left of the map itself.

Plugged-in sites

Don't miss the Virtual World. It's an elaborate collection of framed demonstrations of the MapGuide plug-in. You can reach the Virtual World from the Argus home page — http://www.mapguide.com/

✦ **United States** at http://www.mapguide.com/maps/usa.mwf. A map of 48 of the 50 nifty United States (see Figure 5-33). You can turn off the state capitals, too — a handy feature for places like Bismarck and Dover.

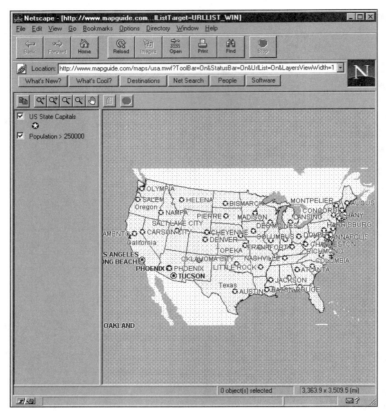

Figure 5-33: MapGuide's United States.

✦ **Canada** at http://www.mapguide.com/maps/canada.mwf. A map of the Great White North, just in case you need to get from Calgary to Prince Edward Island by airplane. You can see the map of Canada in Figure 5-34.

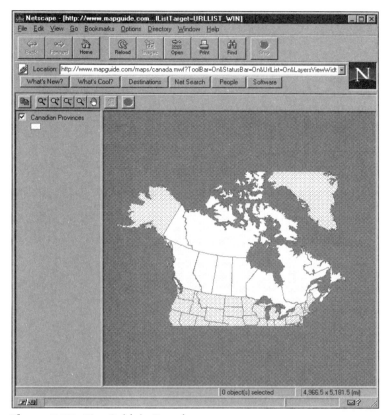

Figure 5-34: MapGuide's Canada.

Authoring for MapGuide

MapGuide Author — available in a 30-day trial version on the Argus Technologies Web site at http://www.mapguide.com/ — is the key application for creating maps for the MapGuide plug-in. You usually don't embed maps in Web pages; you view them independently, as files.

Don't forget to configure your server to handle MIME type image/mwf with file-name extension .MWF.

PointPlus

Creator: Net-Scene

Function: Displays Microsoft PowerPoint presentations

Home Site: http://www.net-scene.com/

Supported Platforms: All Windows systems

Authoring Tool: Microsoft PowerPoint and Net-Scene's PointPlus Maker

Good Examples: A Net-Scene corporate presentation at http://www.net-scene.com/demo2.htm (see Figure 5-35); some animated advertisements at http://www.net-scene.com/demo3.htm; a promotion for the El Fajiita Food Company at http://www.net-scene.com/demo6.htm

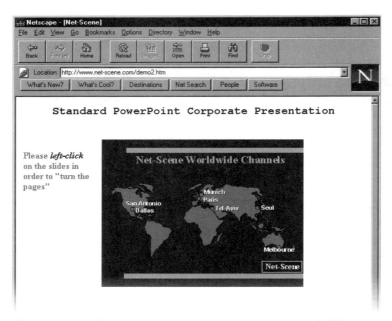

Figure 5-35: PointPlus showing a Net-Scene promotional slide show.

If you're like a lot of business people, you bought Microsoft Office for Excel or Word and got PowerPoint as a side benefit. Since this full-featured business presentation package was sitting there on your desktop, you decided to use it to build a couple of presentations. Now instead of just showing those presentations to all the people who can fit in a conference room, you need to display your handiwork to people all across the global network. No problem. PointPlus lets you embed PowerPoint presentations in Web pages, then view them from within your browser window. This plug-in really lends some credence to the idea that the next generation of computer operating systems will be modeled after browsers, allowing you to hop from one piece of information on your hard disk to another, just as you navigate from one Web page to the next on the Internet.

Plug-in Power Rating: ★★★★

Installing PointPlus

To install PointPlus on a Windows machine:

1. Point your browser at `http://www.net-scene.com/down2.htm`.
2. Click on the link for the operating environment you use — either Windows 95 or Windows 3.
3. Click on the link in the paragraph that begins "Download. . ." near the top of the page.
4. Save the file by itself in a temporary directory.
5. When the file has downloaded completely, shut down your browser.
6. Run the file you downloaded. It's an automated installation program. You should respond to its prompts as needed.
7. Restart your browser. PointPlus will be ready to go.

Using PointPlus

Are you familiar with the operation of your mouse's left button? Yes? Then you're ready to use PointPlus. To advance from one page of a PowerPoint presentation to the next, simply click on the slide.

Plugged-in sites

There's a directory of PointPlus-enabled sites at `http://www.net-scene.com/demos2.htm`. Here are a couple of prime examples:

✦ **Animated slide show** (`http://www.net-scene.com/demo5.htm`). Here's a PowerPoint slide show that features animated graphics. This demonstration appears in Figure 5-36.

Figure 5-36: Another PointPlus presentation — this one animated.

✦ **El Fajiita** (`http://www.net-scene.com/demo5.htm`). This demonstration, pictured in Figure 5-37, features music and animation in the form of an advertisement for a fictional restaurant supply company.

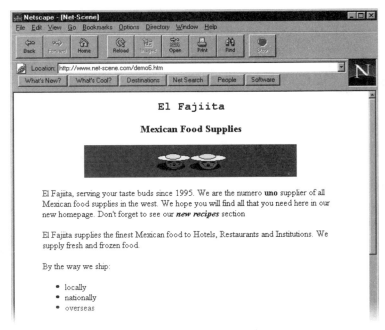

Figure 5-37: A PointPlus-enhanced Web site advertising El Fajiita.

Authoring for PointPlus

Microsoft PowerPoint is much too complex to cover here. If you're interested in PointPlus, you probably know all about authoring with PowerPoint anyway.

In addition to PowerPoint, you'll need PointPlus Maker, which converts plain PowerPoint files to a format more compatible with the network. You can get PointPlus Maker (in demonstration form) from the Net-Scene Web site at `http://www.net-scene.com/try_it.htm`. The company claims that PointPlus Maker can shrink a 2.1 MB, 57-slide PowerPoint file to 123 KB.

Embedding PowerPoint content relies on the `<EMBED>` tag with its `SRC`, `WIDTH` and `HEIGHT` attributes only.

Don't forget to configure your server to handle MIME type application/x-pointplus with filename extension .CSS.

QuickSilver

Creator: Micrografx

Function: Displays ABC QuickSilver and ABC Graphics Suite files

Home Site: `http://www.micrografx.com/quicksilver.html`

Supported Platforms: All Windows systems

Authoring Tool: ABC Graphics Suite

Good Examples: A chess game at `http://www.micrografx.com/gallery/abcqsgallery/chess.htm`; a paintable motorcycle at `http://www.micrografx.com/gallery/abcqsgallery/bike.dsf`; clickable tabs at `http://www.micrografx.com/gallery/abcqsgallery/tabs.htm`

Based on layers of objects that comprise graphics, QuickSilver lets you create and use interactive graphics for the Web — graphics that change in response to mouse movements and other user actions (see Figure 5-38). QuickSilver displays are easy to create, fun to use, and much smoother than the sort of crude Java applications that exist at this writing.

Plug-in Power Rating: ★★★

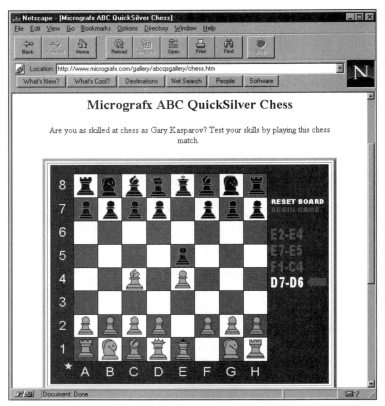

Figure 5-38: QuickSilver plays chess.

Installing QuickSilver

To install QuickSilver on a Windows machine:

1. Point your browser at http://www.micrografx.com/
   download/qsd1.html.

2. Fill out the registration form at the bottom of the page and click on the
   button below the form to submit the information by electronic mail.

3. Click on the Download ABC Components Now link at the bottom of the page.

4. Click on the link that corresponds to the browser you use — there's a version of the plug-in optimized for Netscape Navigator and another optimized
   for Microsoft Internet Explorer.

5. Save the file by itself in a temporary directory.

6. When the file has downloaded completely, shut down your browser.

7. Run the file you downloaded. It's an automated setup routine that will install the plug-in for you. Reply to its queries as needed.

8. Restart your browser. QuickSilver will be ready to go.

Using QuickSilver

How you use a particular QuickSilver object depends upon how the author configured his or her product. Some interfaces feature buttons, others have sliders, and still others have movable objects for you to drag around. Every QuickSilver product is different, and you have to rely on intuition and the creator's documentation.

Plugged-in sites

There are a couple of really cool demonstrations of QuickSilver's capabilities that branch from the Micrografx welcome page. Look at the chess game shown in Figure 5-38. You can click on the board to watch the progress of the match. You'll find the chess game on the Web at `http://www.micrografx.com/gallery/abcqsgallery/chess.htm`.

Also look at the paintable motorcycle shown in Figure 5-42. You can click on buttons to define the color of both the flames and the body, and there's a button at the bottom of the page that resets both flames and body to white. It's on the Web at `http://www.micrografx.com/gallery/abcqsgallery/bike.htm`.

Authoring for QuickSilver

ABC QuickSilver breaks the creation process into two important parts: defining the objects that will make up your display and defining how those objects will behave under certain conditions. You can download a demonstration version from `http://www.micrografx.com/download/qsdl.html`.

You attach QuickSilver content to Web pages with the `<EMBED>` tag. The `SRC`, `HEIGHT` and `WIDTH` tags are all mandatory, as they are with all plug-ins. QuickSilver also supports some additional tags:

✦ `ALIGN`. Set to `LEFT`, `RIGHT` or `CENTER`, `ALIGN` defines where on a page the embedded object appears.

✦ `ANTIALIAS`. Normally a good attribute to include in your `<EMBED>` statement since it smoothes diagonal lines and curves, `ANTIALIAS` doesn't work when used on displays with 256 or fewer available colors and can cause problems with objects that move.

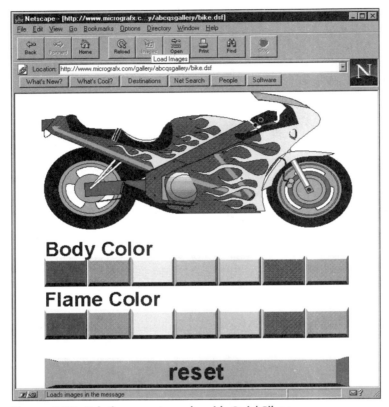

Figure 5-39: Painting a motorcycle with QuickSilver.

QuickSilver also lets you define custom attributes. If you tell your embedded objects to look for a parameter with a certain name, you can use an attribute with that name in your <EMBED> statement.

Don't forget to configure your server to handle MIME type application/x-quicksilver with filename extension .DSF.

RapidVue

Creator: Pegasus

Function: Displays compressed images

Home Site: http://www.jpg.com/

Supported Platforms: All Windows systems

Authoring Tool: IMPACJ and IMPAC4

Good Examples: An F-15 Eagle at `http://www.jpg.com/pictures/pic/010.pic`; a Shelby AC Cobra at `http://www.jpg.com/pictures/pic/001.pic`; a frog at `http://www.jpg.com/pictures/pic/006.pic`

A new version of the old JPEG graphics standard, RapidVue combines minuscule download times with excellent image quality (see Figure 5-40). RapidVue is the best of the general-purpose, still-image plug-ins covered in this chapter.

Figure 5-40: A RapidVue-compressed F-15.

RapidVue is a new kind of JPEG that takes advantage of a characteristic of your brain's vision system (you can more readily see variations in brightness than variations in color) and can compress big images into very small packages.

Plug-in Power Rating: ★★★★

Installing RapidVue

To install RapidVue on a Windows machine:

1. Point your browser at `http://www.jpg.com/snapshots.html`.

2. Click on the link that corresponds to your operating environment. If you're running Windows 3.*x*, get the 16-bit plug-in. For Windows 95 or Windows NT, get the 32-bit version.

3. Save the file by itself in a temporary directory.

4. When the file has downloaded completely, shut down your browser.

5. Run the file you downloaded. It's an automated installation routine that will handle the gory details of installing the plug-in. Respond to its prompts as needed.

6. Restart your browser. RapidVue will be installed.

Using RapidVue

There's nothing to use — once you've installed the RapidVue plug-in, you're all set to view images. Move on to the examples in the next section.

Plugged-in sites

Okay, so what can this new image-compression scheme do for you and your Web site? Navigate over to `http://www.jpg.com/snapshots.html`, where you'll find a directory of example graphics. The F-15 in Figure 5-40 is a good start; you should also check out these highly detailed images:

✦ **A Shelby AC Cobra** (`http://www.jpg.com/pictures/pic/001.pic`). One of the greatest American sports cars ever made, this Cobra downloads almost as fast as the real thing runs the quarter mile (see Figure 5-41).

Figure 5-41: A RapidVue Cobra.

✦ **A frog** (`http://www.jpg.com/pictures/pic/006.pic`). Though it has nothing to fear from the Cobra above, this frog shows that even complex patterns — such as the rock he's resting on — can be rendered in a hurry. The frog appears in Figure 5-42.

Figure 5-42: A RapidVue frog.

Authoring for RapidVue

You can create images for RapidVue in any graphics package. To compress those images so they're compatible with the RapidVue plug-in, though, you must use IMPACJ (for 24-bit and 8-bit grayscale images) or IMPAC4 (for images with 16 or fewer colors). You can find out more about the authoring tools at http://www.jpg.com/developers.html.

To embed for RapidVue, use the <EMBED> tag with its mandatory attributes SRC, WIDTH, and HEIGHT.

Don't forget to configure your server to handle MIME type image/pic with filename extension .PIC.

Shockwave for Freehand

Creator: Macromedia

Function: Displays Macromedia Freehand graphics

Home Site: http://www.macromedia.com/shockwave/

Supported Platforms: All Windows and Macintosh systems

Authoring Tool: Macromedia Freehand

Good Examples: Magellan Geographix at `http://www.magellangeo.com/telescope/shockwave.html`; Latter Day Garage Band at `http://rampages.onramp.net/~bware/neoldgb.html`

Part of the Shockwave family of plug-ins that includes Shockwave for Director and Shockwave for Authorware, Shockwave for Freehand serves as a viewer plug-in for files created with Macromedia Freehand (see Figure 5-43). It does a fine job of displaying these vector-based files.

Plug-in Power Rating: ★★★

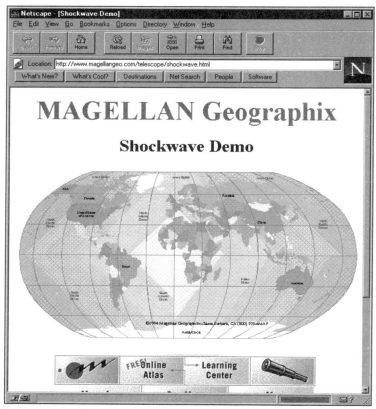

Figure 5-43: Shockwave for Freehand at Magellan Geographix.

Installing Shockwave for Freehand

Macromedia makes you install all of its Shockwave plug-ins at one time. You have to install Shockwave for Director (covered in Chapter 3) and Shockwave for Authorware (covered in Chapter 8) along with Shockwave for Freehand. They're all pretty handy. To install Shockwave for Freehand:

1. Point your browser at `http://www.macromedia.com/shockwave/plugin/plugin.cgi`.
2. Fill in the registration form at the bottom of the page and click on the Get Shockwave button at the bottom of the form.
3. Click on one of the links to Macromedia's FTP site. If one link doesn't work, try another.
4. Save the file by itself in a temporary directory.
5. When the file has downloaded completely, shut down your browser.
6. Run the file you downloaded. It's a self-extracting .ZIP archive.
7. Run the file SETUPEX.EXE, which sprang forth from the file you downloaded. It's an automated setup routine; so reply to its prompts, and it will take care of the dirty work.
8. Restart your browser. All the Shockwave plug-ins, including Shockwave for Freehand, will be ready for use.

Using Shockwave for Freehand

Since Shockwave for Freehand is basically a viewer for a certain kind of image file, there's not much for you to diddle with. You can, however, use your mouse and keyboard in combination to adjust your view of the file.

Macintosh users should press Command and click on the image to zoom in, Command-Option and click on to zoom out, and Control and click on to pan. Windows users should press Ctrl and click on to zoom in, Ctrl and Alt and click on to zoom out, and spacebar and click on to pan.

Plugged-in sites

You'll find an excellent directory — of Freehand files as well as other Shocked sites — at `http://www.macromedia.com/shockwave/epicenter/vanguard/`. Each of the Freehand files is marked with a special icon.

Figure 5-44 shows a Web page for Latter Day Garage Band that features an embedded Freehand file.

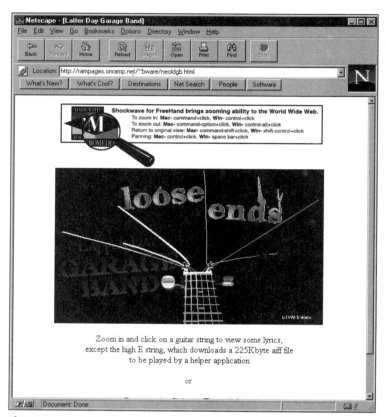

Figure 5-44: Latter Day Garage Band viewed with Shockwave for Freehand.

Authoring for Shockwave for Freehand

Embed Freehand images in Web pages with the <EMBED> tag and its three manda-tory attributes: SRC, WIDTH, and HEIGHT.

 Don't forget to configure your server to handle MIME type image/x-freehand with filename extension .FH5.

SVF Viewer

Creator: SoftSource

Function: Displays .SVF-format graphics

Home Site: http://www.softsource.com/softsource/

Supported Platforms: Windows 95

Authoring Tool: AutoCad, or any other program that can generate .SVF files

Good Examples: A stock chart, a house plan, a locomotive and some other example drawings at http://www.softsource.com/softsource/svf/svftest.html

The Simple Vector Format (SVF) is a vector-based image format that, like other AutoCad files, supports layers and, unlike .DWG and .DXF files, supports hyperlinks, too. SVF is an excellent format for those who want to enable people to navigate through drafted data. This plug-in enables that information to be published on the Web and shared with millions of people.

Plug-in Power Rating: ★★★

Installing SVF Viewer

To install SVF Viewer on a Windows machine:

1. Point your browser at http://www.softsource.com/softsource/ plugins/svf-plugin.html.
2. Click on the link that says "Download the SVF Plug-in."
3. Save the file by itself in a temporary directory.
4. When the file has downloaded completely, shut down your browser.
5. Run the file you downloaded. It's an automated installation routine, so reply to its prompts as needed.
6. Restart your browser. SVF Viewer will be ready to go.

Using SVF Viewer

To use SVF Viewer, you simply call up a page with an embedded .SVF graphic and let the plug-in do the work (see Figure 5-45). You can, however, right-click on the graphic to display a pop-up menu that lets you zoom in to and out from the point you right-clicked on and pan around the graphic if it is larger than the window it fills.

If you want to view the entire graphic, right-click on the graphic to summon the pop-up menu, then choose Zoom Extents from the list of options. Zoom Extents is a command from drafting programs that shows the entire area of a drawing.

Since .SVF files also can contain hyperlinks, you'll find that clicking on certain areas of particular drawings can have surprising consequences. If you end up at a Web page unexpectedly, click on your browser's Back button and start over.

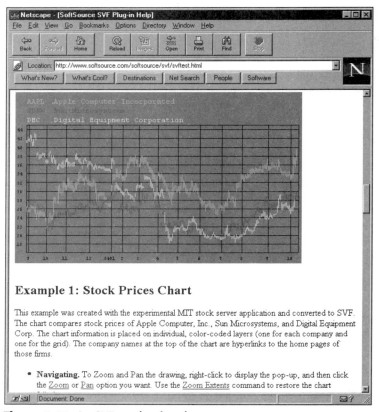

Figure 5-45: An SVF stock price chart.

Plugged-in sites

Grand Central Station for SVF files is a page on the SoftSource Web site: http://www.softsource.com/softsource/svf/svftest.html. Go there to test SVF Viewer. If the plug-in is working properly, you'll see a locomotive (shown in Figure 5-46) and a floor plan for a house (shown in Figure 5-47).

Authoring for SVF Viewer

Most late-model computer drafting tools can generate output in .SVF format. You'll need such a program to create content for SVF Viewer.

Embed .SVF files in your Web pages with the <EMBED> tag and its mandatory attributes, SRC, WIDTH, and HEIGHT. There are a couple of optional attributes, too. With SVF, the left mouse button usually activates a hyperlink or zooms to the cursor. To disable link activation, use the following tags:

✦ LINKS. Set to FALSE, LINKS disables all hyperlinks and instead causes the display to zoom in on a clicked on point. Normally, LINKS=TRUE.

✦ SHOWURL. Unless SHOWURL is set to TRUE, SVF Viewer can display the text associated with hyperlinks in .SVF files instead of the URL itself when the mouse pointer is passed over a link. SHOWURL=TRUE guarantees that the URL, not the text, is shown.

Don't forget to configure your server to handle MIME type image/x-svf with file-name extension .SVF.

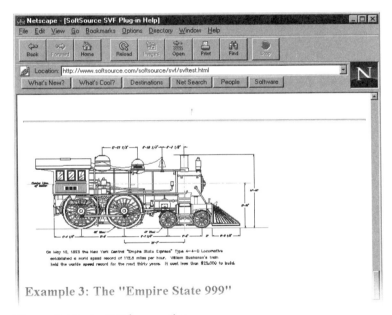

Figure 5-46: An SVF locomotive.

techexplorer

Creator: IBM

Function: Displays TeX and LaTeX information

Home Site: http://www.ics.raleigh.ibm.com/ics/techexp.htm

Supported Platforms: Windows 95 and Windows NT

Authoring Tool: TeX and LaTeX

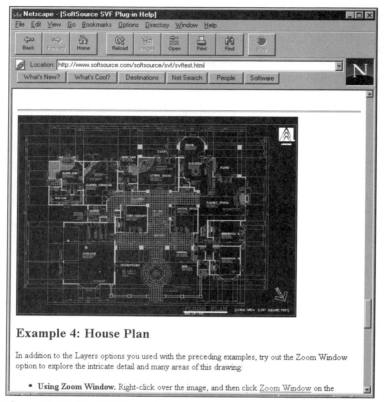

Figure 5-47: An SVF floor plan.

Good Examples: The Calculation of Some Geometric Monodromy Groups at `http://www.ics.raleigh.ibm.com/pub/diss.tex`; user-defined pop-up menus at `http://www.ics.raleigh.ibm.com/pub/techpop.tex`

TeX and LaTeX (pronounced, by the way, "tech" and "lay-tech," hence the name of this plug-in), are long-popular standards for encoding mathematical and scientific expressions and have a loyal following in research enclaves the world over. Techexplorer makes it possible for the people who work with TeX and LaTeX to post their information on the Internet or on an intranet that uses Internet communications protocols and have it available to others without hassle (see Figure 5-48). techexplorer is an example of how an older technology can be brought into the modern age with plug-ins.

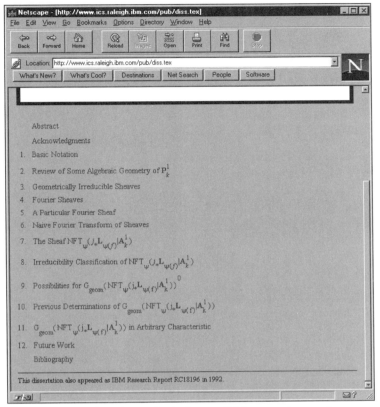

Figure 5-48: techexplorer displaying an IBM research report.

Installing techexplorer

To install techexplorer on a Windows machine,

1. Point your browser at `http://www.ics.raleigh.ibm.com/ics/techexp.htm`.
2. Click on the Download techexplorer now link.
3. Fill out the registration form and click on the Register me now! button at the bottom of the form.
4. Click on the radio button next to techexplorer.
5. Click on the Download this product button.
6. Read the license agreement. If you agree with its terms, enter your electronic mail address in the box and click on the YES button.
7. Save the file by itself in a temporary directory.

8. When the file has downloaded completely, shut down your browser.

9. Run the file you downloaded. It's a self-extracting archive file that will place a group of files in your temporary directory.

10. Double-click on SETUP.EXE. It's an automated installation routine that installs the techexplorer plug-in on your machine. Respond to its prompts as needed.

11. Restart your browser. techexplorer will be ready to go.

Plug-in Power Rating: ★★★★

Using techexplorer

There's only one semi-tricky feature of techexplorer that keeps the plug-in from being a simple viewer. Try right-clicking at various important points in a TeX document viewed with techexplorer. The plug-in supports custom pop-up menus that act as hyperlinks that can take you to explanatory material.

Plugged-in sites

You probably know of some networked TeX files you'd like to view, but IBM has posted some of its research papers for you to use as test subjects.

You'll find The Calculation of Some Geometric Monodromy Groups at `http://www.ics.raleigh.ibm.com/pub/diss.tex`. The paper also appears in Figure 5-48, interpreted by techexplorer. Note the elaborate Greek letters and mathematical notation that makes TeX so useful to scientists and engineers.

The page shown in Figure 5-49 demonstrates a cool feature of techexplorer — the ability to embed hyperlinks in TeX documents. Take a look for yourself at `http://www.ics.raleigh.ibm.com/pub/techpop.tex`.

If you're interested in authoring for techexplorer, the file at `http://www.ics.raleigh.ibm.com/pub/techpop.tex` explains how to add pop-up menus to your documents.

Authoring for techexplorer

You won't embed TeX or LaTeX documents in Web pages — you'll use techexplorer and your browser as tools for viewing entire documents. TeX and LaTeX generate documents that work with techexplorer.

Don't forget to configure your server to handle MIME type document/tex with file-name extension .TEX.

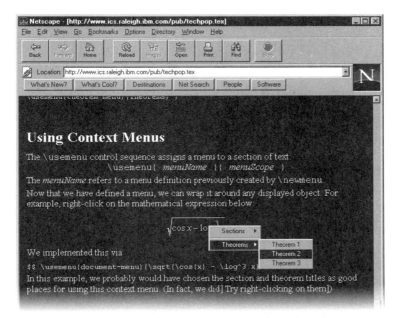

Figure 5-49: Context-sensitive pop-up menus in techexplorer.

TMSSequoia ViewDirector

Creator: TMSSequoia

Function: Displays images in TIFF and other file formats

Home Site: http://www.tmsinc.com/plugin/

Supported Platforms: All Windows systems

Authoring Tool: Any graphics package capable of generating output in TIFF form

Good Examples: Several samples at http://www.tmsinc.com/plugin/ sample/sample.htm

One of the most popular formats for scanned images and other continuous-tone graphics, the Tagged Image File Format has long been taboo on the Web, largely because files encoded in it are so enormous and therefore take a long time to download. Browser makers shunned the format, leaving those who used it to choose between converting images to JPEG format or using helper applications.

TMSSequoia ViewDirector now makes it possible to view TIFF files — and a handful of other file formats — from within your browser window (see Figure 5-50). They're still big, but there's no longer a need for a helper application.

Plug-in Power Rating: ★★★

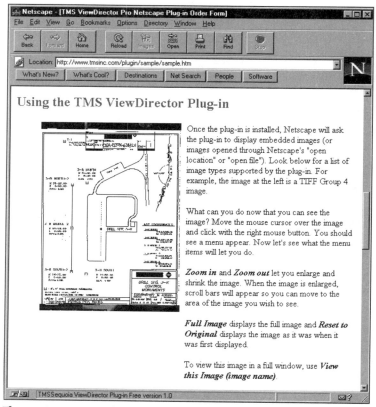

Figure 5-50: A TIFF image displayed with TMSSequoia ViewDirector.

Installing TMSSequoia ViewDirector

To install TMSSequoia ViewDirector on a Windows machine:

1. Point your browser at http://www.tmsinc.com/plugin/download.htm.

2. Fill in the registration form, specifying your operating environment via the radio buttons at the top of the page. Click on the Download button when you've complete the form.

3. Click on the link that corresponds to your operating environment and the download site that's geographically closest to you.

4. Save the file by itself in a temporary directory.

5. When the file has downloaded completely, shut down your browser.

6. Run the file you downloaded. It's an automated installation program. Respond to its prompts as needed.

7. Restart your browser. TMSSequoia ViewDirector will be ready to go.

Using TMSSequoia ViewDirector

As an image viewer, TMSSequoia ViewDirector does most of the work for you when you access a page with an embedded image in a format the plug-in understands. You can, however, pan around an image that's partly obscured by the borders of its frame by using the scroll bars or zoom in on a point in an image by clicking on.

You can also rotate the image and print it by right-clicking on the image and selecting from the pop-up menu.

Plugged-in sites

To see what TMSSequoia ViewDirector can do on TIFFs and JPEGs, call up `http://www.tmsinc.com/plugin/sample/sample.htm`. There, you'll see an embedded TIFF file and a JPEG image (see Figure 5-51).

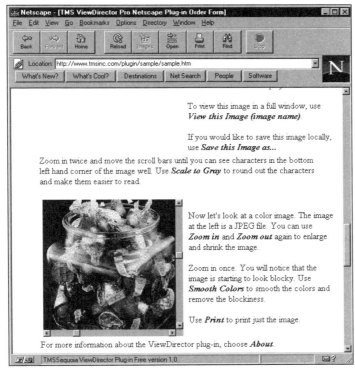

Figure 5-51: A JPEG image displayed with TMSSequoia ViewDirector.

Authoring for TMSSequoia ViewDirector

You can create graphics for TMSSequoia ViewDirector with any graphics package that generates graphics in a format that the plug-in understands.

To embed those images in your Web pages, use the `<EMBED>` tag with the basic attributes: `SRC`, `HEIGHT`, and `WIDTH`.

Vertigo

Creator: Lari Software

Function: Displays Macintosh Lightning Draw illustrations

Home Site: `http://www.larisoftware.com/Products/WebPlugin.html`

Supported Platforms: All Macintosh systems

Authoring Tool: Vertigo

Good Examples: Kanjii characters at `http://www.larisoftware.com/Products/PlugIn/japanese.html`; an animated drawing at `http://www.larisoftware.com/Products/PlugIn/texttrails.html`

Lari Software's Vertigo plug-in takes advantage of the framework established by Apple's QuickDraw GX system addition (see Figure 5-52). By enabling Web publishers to animate their QuickDraw GX drawings, this plug-in adds an extra level of usefulness to an already-handy Macintosh tool.

Plug-in Power Rating: ★★★

Installing Vertigo

To install Lightning Draw GX on a Windows machine:

1. Make sure you have QuickDraw GX installed (it comes with System 7.5 and later). If you don't, get it from Apple's site at `ftp://ftp.info.apple.com/Apple.Support.Area/Apple.Software.Updates/US/Macintosh/System/QuickDraw_GX/`.
2. Point your browser at `http://www.larisoftware.com/Products/WebPlugin.html`.
3. Save the file by itself in a temporary directory.
4. When the file has downloaded completely, shut down your browser.
5. Use StuffIt to decompress the downloaded file.

6. Drag the plug-in file into your Plugins folder.

7. Restart your browser. Vertigo will be ready to go.

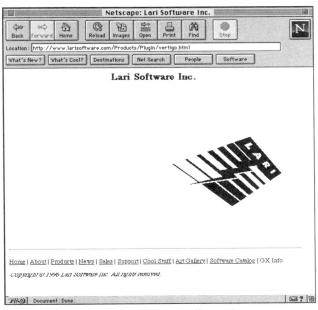

Figure 5-52: Vertigo displaying an illustration.

Using Vertigo

A no-brainer. Just load up a page that contains a QuickDraw GX illustration, and let Vertigo display it for you.

Plugged-in sites

Check out http://www.larisoftware.com/Products/PlugIn/ japanese.html for some Japanese Kanjii characters in a QuickDraw GX file. Look at http://www. larisoftware.com/Products/PlugIn/texttrails.html to see those same characters spinning back and forth in an animated sequence. These two examples appear in Figures 5-53 and 5-54.

Authoring for Vertigo

To create illustrations for Vertigo, use Vertigo. You can get a copy of Lightning Draw from http://www.larisoftware.com/Products/LightningDraw.html. Alternately, use LightningDraw Electric, available at http://www.larisoftware. com/Products/LDElectric/.

Figure 5-53: Vertigo demonstrating its capabilities.

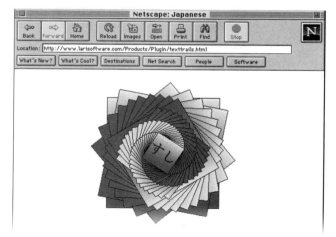

Figure 5-54: Vertigo animating a picture.

To attach Lightning Draw illustrations to your Web pages, use the `<EMBED>` tag with its standard `SRC`, `WIDTH` and `HEIGHT` attributes to identify the attached file and define the page real estate it occupies.

Vertigo also supports some optional attributes. They are

✦ BGCOLOR. Defines the background color of an embedded picture. If you do not specify a background color, Vertigo uses the same background color as your browser. Use BGCOLOR like this: BGCOLOR=#RRGGBB, where RR, GG and BB are hexadecimal values for the red, green, and blue components of the background color, respectively.

✦ SCALE. Set equal to an integer, SCALE determines how large Vertigo should draw the embedded picture. The integer represents a scaling percentage. By default, SCALE=100.

✦ ROTATE. Set equal to an integer, ROTATE determines how many degrees clockwise to turn an image.

✦ STRETCH. Set equal to an integer scaling percentage, STRETCH defines how large an image grows during an animation sequence.

✦ SPIN. Determines the angle, in clockwise degrees from vertical, at which an animation stops.

✦ MOVE. Determines how a spinning image spins into its final position. OFF, the default, eliminates all movement. H moves the image from left to right. V moves it from top to bottom. HV moves it from the top-right corner to the bottom-left corner. HVPERSPECTIVE moves it from left to right in perspective, while VPERSPECTIVE moves it from top to bottom in perspective.

✦ TRAILS. When TRAILS is set to ON, the spinning image leaves a trail of old images in its wake. When TRAILS=OFF, no old images are left.

✦ LOOP. Determines what happens when an animation sequence ends. When LOOP=ON, the animation plays forward, then backward, repeatedly (like the PALINDROME attribute in many other plug-ins). When LOOP=FORWARD, the animation plays over and over, but from beginning to end each time. LOOP=OFF, the default, eliminates all looping.

✦ TIME. Set equal to an integer, TIME determines how long it takes to complete an animation sequence. The integer is the number of 1/60-second ticks needed to complete the animation. 300 is the default.

Don't forget to configure your server to handle MIME type image/x-qdgx with file-name extension .QDGX.

Whip

Creator: AutoDesk

Function: Displays AutoCad .DWF files

Home Site: http://www.autodesk.com/products/autocad/whip/whip.htm

Supported Platforms: Windows 95

Authoring Tool: AutoCad

Good Examples: Neutrino Property Management at `http://www.autodesk.com/products/autocad/whip/site07/neut01.htm`; Napa Valley wine tour at `http://www.autodesk.com/products/autocad/whip/site02/napa01.htm`; Zephyr Tech at `http://www.autodesk.comproducts/autocad/whip/site06/index.htm`.

Whip was made by the people who developed the granddaddy of all computer-aided drafting programs, AutoCad. It uses .DWF, a new, compressed form of the venerable .DWG file format, to speed images across the Web (see Figure 5-55).

Plug-in Power Rating: ★★★

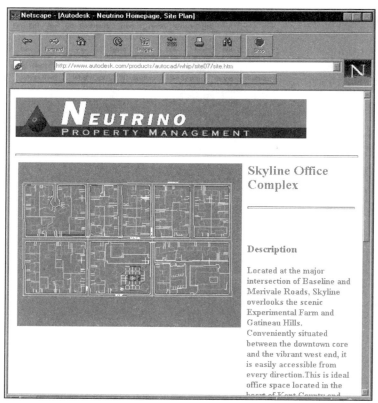

Figure 5-55: Whip displays part of the sample Neutrino Property Management site.

Installing Whip

To install Whip on a Windows machine:

1. Point your browser at `http://www.autodesk.com/products/autocad/whip/whpndwn.htm`.

2. Click on the Download Now! button at the top of the page.

3. Click on the Read License Agreement link to review the terms of AutoDesk's plug-in license agreement.

4. Click on the I Accept link to accept the terms of the agreement and download the plug-in.

5. Save the file by itself in a temporary directory.

6. When the file has downloaded completely, shut down your browser.

7. Run the file you downloaded. It's an automated installation routine. Respond to its prompts as needed.

8. Restart your browser. Whip will be ready to go.

Using Whip

A simple tool for displaying files, Whip has few controls. You can rotate and save .DWF files via the pop-up menu that appears when you right-click on the image.

Plugged-in sites

Take Whip for a spin through the Napa Valley wine country at `http://www.autodesk.com/products/autocad/whip/site02/napa01.htm`, or call up the Zephyr Tech machine tools demonstration page at `http://www.autodesk.com/products/autocad/whip/site06/index.htm`. The Zephyr Tech page appears in Figure 5-56.

Authoring for Whip

Users of AutoCad release 13c4 can save files in .DWF format. Users of other programs can use utilities available at `http://www.autodesk.com/products/autocad/whip/whippubl.htm` to convert .DWG and .DXF files to .DWF format.

To embed .DWF files in Web pages, use the `<EMBED>` tag with nothing more than the `SRC`, `WIDTH`, and `HEIGHT` attributes.

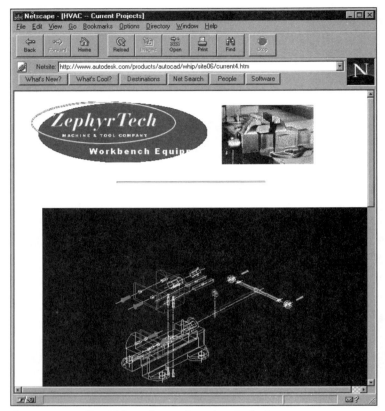

Figure 5-56: The Whip-enhanced Zephyr Tech site.

Make sure your Web server is configured to understand MIME type drawing/x-dwf with the filename extension .DWF.

Communications

From its earliest days, the Internet has been a communications medium, facilitating two-way conversations between people. The first Internet application was electronic mail, soon followed by mailing lists and Usenet newsgroups. People loved the Net because it brought them closer in spirit to others who were physically distant.

Lately, though, the Web has gotten away from its communications roots. The Web, multimedia wonder though it may be, has become more like television. You can sit and absorb data from the Web, but it's really hard to contribute anything. The early Web was — sadly — a one-way communications medium.

These plug-ins are changing that. By making it possible to communicate via Web sites, the plug-ins in this chapter are returning the Internet to its fun, community-based origins.

CyberSpell

Creator: Inso

Function: Checks spelling in Netscape Mail messages

Home Site: http://www.inso.com/consumer/cyberspell/democybr.htm

Supported Platforms: All Windows systems

Authoring Tool: The mail editor in Netscape Navigator

Good Examples: Any mail message you can create (especially if you're a poor speller)

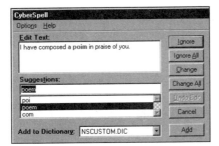

Figure 6-1: CyberSpell critiques a lover's missive.

Though technically not a plug-in under the strict definition set forth by the plug-in API, CyberSpell expands the capabilities of Netscape Navigator and for that reason is included in these pages (see Figure 6-1). CyberSpell does not work with Microsoft Internet Explorer.

At your command, CyberSpell checks the words you've written in Netscape Navigator's mail editor and highlights the words it can't find in its dictionary. By protecting you from spelling, punctuation, and grammar errors, CyberSpell saves you the embarrassment of dashing off e-mail filled with dumb mistakes — at least, dumb mistakes of the lexical variety.

Plug-in Power Rating: ★★★★

Installing CyberSpell

To install CyberSpell on a Windows machine equipped with Netscape Navigator:

1. Point your browser at `http://www.inso.com/consumer/cyberspell/democybr.htm`.

2. Read the license agreement.

3. Click on the link that indicates you accept the terms of the agreement and want to download the version of CyberSpell for your operating environment.

4. Fill in the registration form and click on the Send button.

5. Click on one of the Continue DOWNLOADING CyberSpell links.

6. Save the downloaded file by itself to a temporary directory.

7. When the file has downloaded completely, shut down your browser.

8. Double-click on the file you downloaded. It's a fully automated installation routine; respond to its prompts as needed.

9. Restart your browser. The next time you run Netscape's mail client, CyberSpell will be in effect.

 CyberSpell won't work with the version of Netscape Navigator that AT&T distributes to its Internet users. If you have an AT&T edition of Netscape Navigator, head over to Netscape's site at http://www.netscape.com and get a standard version of Netscape Navigator.

Using CyberSpell

You'll notice CyberSpell's presence on a machine only when you're in a Netscape Mail message, composing or editing text. Figure 6-2 shows the new Spelling addition to the menu bar.

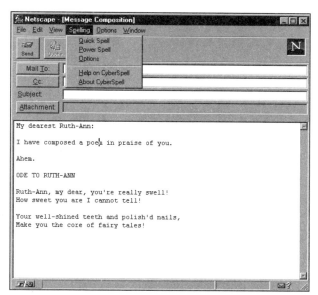

Figure 6-2: CyberSpell's Spelling menu.

There are two key items in the spelling menu: the Quick Spell command and the Power Spell command. When you want to check your message, select the option you want from the Spelling menu.

Quick Spell gives your mail message the once-over for common writing mistakes. Quick Spell checks for

- ✦ **Spelling errors** — Quick Spell won't let you mess up "embarrass" again.

- ✦ **"A" versus "An" errors** — Quick Spell protects you from writing about "a apple" or "an browser."

- ✦ **Capitalization errors** — Quick Spell makes sure you spell common proper nouns with capitals.

- ✦ **Compounding errors** — Quick Spell won't let you write "antifreeze" as "anti-freeze," or "cannot" as "can not."

- ✦ **Doubled-word errors** — Quick Spell won't let, "I went to the the courthouse" slip by again. It makes exceptions for the sometimes-legitimate "had had" and "that that."

Power Spell takes checking to the next level by doing everything Quick Spell does, plus the following:

- ✦ **Some formatting errors** — Power Spell makes sure you put dollar signs before, not after, money figures, verifies that you use commas to separate digits in large numbers, and catches some other common errors.

- ✦ **Some punctuation errors** — Power Spell won't let you have an opening parenthesis without a closing one — unless it's part of a smiley :-)!

- ✦ **Some grammar errors** — Power Spell catches double negatives, inappropriate prepositions (no more "borrow off" instead of "borrow from"), and some other mistakes.

Plugged-in sites

There are no sites plugged-in for CyberSpell. It works with Netscape Navigator's mail client, not the Web.

Authoring for CyberSpell

CyberSpell works with Netscape Navigator's mail client.

Worldgroup Manager

Creator: Galacticomm

Function: Lets you use a browser as a global conferencing tool

Home Site: http://www.gcomm.com/show/plugin.html

Supported Platforms: All Windows systems

Authoring Tool: Various

Good Examples: The Galacticomm Demo System at `http://www.gcomm.com/walk/client/launch/galtlc.html`

Calling Worldgroup Manager a plug-in is like calling Windows 95 a program — yes, that's what it is, but only in the most technical sense.

Worldgroup Manager uses the `<EMBED>` tag in a Web page to call up a whole set of groupware programs, including an electronic mail system and a chat program. Once the groupware programs have started, the Web is secondary to what goes on among the various people running those programs. A company might use Galacticomm to, say, run a technical support operation or to facilitate a conference among distant consultants.

Plug-in Power Rating: ★★★★

Installing Worldgroup Manager

To install Worldgroup Manager on a Windows machine:

1. Point your browser at `http://www.gcomm.com/show/plugin.html`.
2. Click on the link that says, Download the Worldgroup Manager.
3. Save the file by itself in a temporary directory.
4. When the file has downloaded completely, shut down your browser.
5. Run the downloaded file. It's an automated installation routine that takes care of the details of installing Worldgroup Manager. Respond to its prompts as needed.
6. Save all your work and re-boot your system.
7. Restart your browser. Worldgroup Manager will be ready for use.

Using Worldgroup Manager

Worldgroup Manager consists of several complicated programs. Explaining how to use all of the Galacticomm tools falls outside the scope of this book.

Your navigation through the Worldgroup Manager environment begins with the Main System Menu shown in Figure 6-3. By clicking on the buttons in that window, you can call up the various programs you will use to do business with the Worldgroup Manager conferencing system.

Some features to note:

- ✦ The E-Mail & Forums button takes you to Worldgroup's messaging systems, including its electronic mail program and chat clients.
- ✦ The File Libraries button calls up a file-downloading tool.
- ✦ You can jump directly to any program or information page by clicking on the Go To button at the top of the Main System Menu.

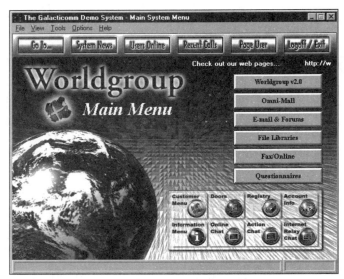

Figure 6-3: The Worldgroup Manager window.

Plugged-in sites

Organizations ranging from the U.S. Veterans Administration to Symantec Corporation have put Worldgroup Manager to work for them. The best way to see what the plug-in can do, though, is to head for Galacticomm's own demonstration site at `http://www.gcomm.com/walk/client/launch/galtlc.html`. When you load that page, the Worldgroup Manager programs will start automatically. Figure 6-4 shows an Internet Relay Chat-like conference going on in the Worldgroup Manager Teleconference tool. A useful business discussion could occur in this program just as easily as the test chatter you see in the illustration.

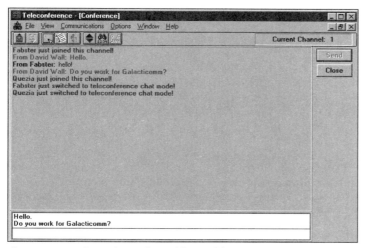

Figure 6-4: Teleconferencing with Worldgroup Manager.

Authoring for Worldgroup Manager

Like all plug-ins, Worldgroup Manager relies upon the <EMBED> tag. In this case, though, <EMBED> is only a command to launch the Galacticomm Worldgroup suite of programs.

Here's a typical usage:

```
<EMBED SRC="launch.wg" HEIGHT=0 WIDTH=2 HOST="gcomm.com"
       APP="GALTLC">
```

In this example, your browser looks on server gcomm.com for an executable file called GALTLC.

Groupscape

Creator: Brainstorm

Function: Lets you embed Lotus Notes information in Web documents

Home Site: http://www.braintech.com/

Supported Platforms: All Windows systems

Authoring Tool: Lotus Notes

Good Examples: Your own machine, if you have Notes data residing there

Not long ago, computer industry pundits were predicting the downfall of Lotus' flagship conferencing and information-sharing system, Lotus Notes. Web browsers, the columnists and thinkers said, did the same thing Notes did — without all the hassle of setting up a custom server and using information clients that cost lots of money.

Brainstorm's Groupscape proves that it's possible for Notes and the Web to coexist by complimenting one another. The marriage is a good one because Notes has lots of capabilities the Web lacks, and the global reach of the Web turns Notes into the backbone of global corporations for minimal cost. Groupscape is a key component in intranets for organizations running Notes.

Plug-in Power Rating: ★★★★

Installing Groupscape

To install Groupscape on a Windows machine:

1. Install OneWave's OneWave plug-in according to the instructions in Chapter 8.
2. Point your browser at `http://www.braintech.com/Brainstorm/register.htm`.
3. Check the box next to Free Groupscape Demo and fill in all the data fields.
4. Click on the Submit button.
5. Click on the link that says Free Groupscape Demo.
6. Click on the icon next to the words Groupscape ActiveX & HTML Demo files.
7. Save the file by itself in a temporary directory.
8. When the file has downloaded completely, shut down your browser.
9. Unpack the file with WinZip. Your browser may be configured to do this automatically.
10. Windows 95 and NT users should run the file REGDLL.BAT to register the plug-in.
11. Windows 3.*x* users should add the directory into which they unpacked the downloaded file to the PATH statement in AUTOEXEC.BAT.
12. Make sure your Notes data directory appears in the PATH statement also.
13. Open the file BROWSER.HTM, which came in the .ZIP file you downloaded.

Using Groupscape

At the core of Groupscape is Windows' Object Linking and Embedding technology, which means that a full copy of the Notes client actually embeds itself in your browser via the Groupscape plug-in. Therefore, all the Notes commands and controls you're used to working with will appear in your browser window.

Plugged-in sites

There aren't any Groupscape sites — this plug-in is designed for use on your computer or across the network on which your organization runs Notes. Ask your Notes administrator for help using the network if you run into trouble.

Authoring for Groupscape

Use Groupscape to examine information Lotus Notes creates. Lotus Notes is a huge program — and you probably know something about creating information files with it if you're interested in Groupscape.

To embed a Notes application in an HTML document, use this syntax:

```
<EMBED SRC="FILE.OPP" WIDTH=300 HEIGHT=240 FORM="Component1">
```

In this example, the Notes application FILE.OPP is embedded in a box 300 pixels wide by 240 pixels high.

IChat

Creator: IChat

Function: Acts as an embedded Chat client

Home Site: http://www.ichat.com/

Supported Platforms: All Macintosh systems, Windows 95 and Windows NT

Authoring Tool: Keep an eye on the Ichat site.

Good Examples: A directory at http://www.ichat.com/chatsites.htm; Itropolis, at http://itropolis.net:4080; Treasure Quest at http://www.treasurequest.com

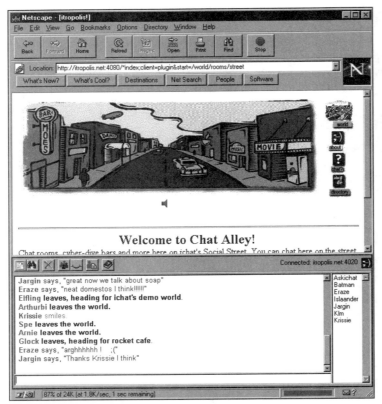

Figure 6-5: IChat in action at Itropolis.

Once upon a time, playing with the only real-time group conferencing system on the Internet meant using a clunky Internet Relay Chat client program — a dinosaur of a program that operated with arcane keyboard commands and featured an interface that was far from intuitive.

IChat changes the paradigm. By allowing Web publishers to embed Chat links in their pages and giving it a friendly interface, IChat makes real-time conferencing — for fun or for serious purposes — a real possibility (see Figure 6-5).

Plug-in Power Rating: ★★★★

Installing IChat

To install IChat on a Windows or Macintosh machine:

   1. Point your browser at http://www.ichat.com/download.htm.

2. Click on the link for your operating environment.

3. Click on the Activate IChat icon.

4. Save the file by itself in a temporary directory.

5. When the file has downloaded completely, shut down your browser.

6. Run the file you downloaded. It's an automated installation routine. Respond to its prompts as needed.

7. Restart your browser. IChat will be ready to go.

Using IChat

The key to using IChat is simple — you simply type the words you want to broadcast to the people in your chat room. IChat does, however, have a series of advanced features that make it more fun.

The best of these is the Emotions button — the one with the smile on it, above the dialog window. When the Emotions button is pressed, you get a menu of emotions on the right side of the chat window, and you can express one of those emotions by double-clicking on it. For example, you can show you're happy by double-clicking on the Smile entry in the emotions list. It adds color to an otherwise potentially dry communications medium.

Also check out IChat's Name List button (just to the left of the Emotions button). When that button is down, a list of everyone in your chat room appears on the right side of the dialog window. Double-click on a name in the list, and you can send a private message to that person — what other chat programs call whispering.

You'll find that when you're asked to register your character at the various chat sites, there's a space on the registration form for your telephone number. Don't fill in that space! Lots of the Web's seamier characters hang out at chat sites, and you're inviting trouble if you give your number to one of these clowns.

Plugged-in sites

IChat maintains a directory of IChat plug-in-aware sites at `http://www.ichat.com/chatsites.htm`. Make that your first stop in your late-night searches for playful banter.

Here are a couple of great servers:

✦ **Itropolis** (`http://itropolis.net:4080`). IChat's own chat city, Itropolis features lots of clickable maps, ever-present talkative crowds, and a really cool integration of chat, graphics, and sound. It's IRC taken to the extreme. Figure 6-5 shows part of Itropolis.

✦ **Treasure Quest** (http://www.treasurequest.com). Also on the IChat site, Treasure Quest Chat is supposed to center on discussions of the Myst-like game Treasure Quest (see Figure 6-6). In truth, it's a verbal free-for-all. That's fun, though, and it's something the Web wouldn't have without the IChat plug-in.

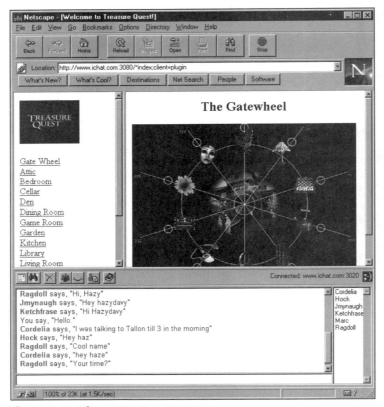

Figure 6-6: IChat at Treasure Quest.

Authoring for IChat

You don't really create content for the IChat plug-in — the people using IRC do that for you. To date, only IChat has built sites that feature the IChat plug-in; so the details of building them remain sketchy.

CHAPTER 7

Navigation

The plug-ins in this chapter aren't viewers for certain kinds of computer files or even applications you can embed in Web pages to perform specific tasks. Instead, the plug-ins covered here extend the capabilities of your browser, making navigation on the Web easier and more intuitive.

All of these plug-ins use some variation on the record-all-the-sites-visited-and-display-them theme. The displays take the form of trees and simple lists. One plug-in, Table of Contents, examines a site before you explore it and gives you a map of the pages to be found there.

All of the plug-ins in this chapter are designed to enable you to use the Web more effectively by helping you find the information you want immediately.

HindSite

Creator: ISYS/Odyssey Development

Function: Makes a record of all the sites you visit

Home Site: http://www.rmii.com/isys_dev/hindsite. html

Supported Platforms: Windows 3.*x* only

Authoring Tool: None

Good Examples: Any collection of pages you've visited

It sounds like a good thing, but HindSite suffers a lot from its lack of a 32-bit version. Limited to the waning Windows 3.*x* operating environments, HindSite is bound to suffer from a declining market. One bright note for Windows 95 and Windows NT users: The HindSite plug-in comes with a stand-alone helper application that, though it uses 16-bit code, works just fine on 32-bit machines.

Plug-in Power Rating: ★★

Installing HindSite

To install HindSite:

1. Point your browser at `http://www.rmii.com/isys_dev/hindsite.html`.
2. Click the link that says, "Download FREE for a limited time!"
3. Fill in the registration form and click the Submit button.
4. Click one of the links for a self-extracting .ZIP file.
5. Save the file by itself in a temporary directory.
6. When the file has downloaded completely, shut down your browser.
7. Run the file you downloaded. It's a self-extracting .ZIP file that will place several more files in your temporary directory.
8. Run the file SETUP.EXE. It's an automated installation routine that will install HindSite for you. Respond to its prompts as needed.
9. Restart your browser. HindSite will be ready to use.

When the installation routine asks you which directory it should install to, make sure you specify the directory that contains your browser's executable file, not your plug-ins directory.

Using HindSite

HindSite looks in your Netscape Navigator cache (it works only with Netscape Navigator) and records the sites you've visited as they are recorded in the cache files. It records not only the URLs, but the contents of the pages, too — though the developers of the plug-in claim that the HindSite index file (called HINDSITE.ISY, and kept in your plug-ins directory) doesn't duplicate the contents of the cache files.

When you want to use HindSite to find information you found on the Web at some point in the past, open HINDSITE.ISY — to which you should assign a bookmark — and use it to locate the material you want. You can search for information in the HindSite database via plain-English queries (Where was that information about Symantec Café?) or Boolean searches (Springsteen AND Bittan AND Clemons AND NOT Alford).

HindSite has some intelligence — it can identify tenses and forms of regular verbs. By using a search string followed by a tilde (~), you can specify that you want HindSite to return all variations on that word. The search string "read~," for example, will return "readers," "reading," and "read," but not "readjusted."

Plugged-in sites

Because it's a navigation plug-in, there's really no site better suited to HindSite than any other.

Authoring for HindSite

There is no authoring tool for HindSite.

HistoryTree

Creator: SmartBrowser

Function: Records sites you visit and displays them as a tree

Home Site: http://www.smartbrowser.com/

Supported Platforms: All Windows systems

Authoring Tool: None

Good Examples: Any collection of pages you visit.

Chances are, you spend a fair amount of time playing with little enhancements for your computer, trying to get it to serve your needs better. You try shareware and often discard it, and you try all the little hints that the computer magazines publish each month. Usually, you end up disappointed with the performance of the latest gimmick.

HistoryTree will not disappoint you (see Figure 7-1). It is a valuable tool that really does enhance the usefulness of your browser. You'll be able locate information faster and with greater ease when you have HistoryTree installed on your machine.

Strictly speaking, HistoryTree is not a plug-in, since it doesn't place a .DLL file in the plug-ins directory. But it does work with your browser — you can rig it to start every time you start your browser — and therefore it's included in this book.

Plug-in Power Rating: ★★★★

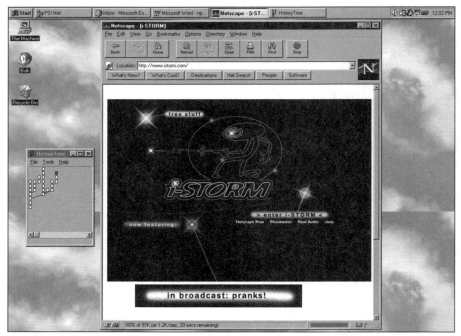

Figure 7-1: HistoryTree in use.

Installing HistoryTree

To install HistoryTree:

1. Point your browser at http://www.smartbrowser.com/histb5.zip.

2. Click the link that says, "HistoryTree."

3. Save the file by itself in a temporary directory.

4. When the file has downloaded completely, shut down your browser.

5. Decompress the .ZIP file you downloaded with WinZip.

6. Run the file SETUP.EXE. It's an automated installation routine that will install HistoryTree for you. Respond to its prompts as needed.

7. Restart your browser. HistoryTree will be ready to use.

Using HistoryTree

HistoryTree takes the form of a window that sits on your desktop, recording every page you visit as a little rectangle on a gray background. The site presently displayed by your browser is represented by a red rectangle; the other rectangles are white. Lines connect the rectangles, showing the paths you followed to reach each.

The rectangles act as a superior sort of bookmark. When you pass your mouse pointer over a rectangle, a box containing the page's title, URL, and the date and time of your last visit appears, as shown in Figure 7-2. Click a rectangle, and your browser goes back to the page it represents.

Why is HistoryTree superior to your browser's Bookmarks or Favorite Places feature? In a word, comprehensiveness. When you backtrack through a Web site, then branch out in a different direction, the Bookmarks list drops all the sites you visited before returning to the central page. You're out of luck if you want to go back to one of those pages.

You can save a tree by choosing File, Save as Snapshot from the menu bar. Bear in mind, however, that the same tree will be in the HistoryTree window the next time you start your browser, regardless of whether you save it.

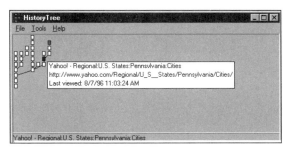

Figure 7-2: A description of a site recorded by HistoryTree.

Plugged-in sites

Because it's a navigation plug-in, there's really no site better suited to HistoryTree than any other.

Authoring for HistoryTree

There is no authoring tool for HistoryTree.

Table of Contents

Creator: InternetConsult

Function: Provides a graphical navigation aid for the Web

Home Site: http://www.InternetConsult.com/toc.html

Supported Platforms: All Windows systems

Authoring Tool: Table of Contents Creator

Good Examples: A map of the InternetConsult site at http://www.InternetConsult.com/intcnslt.toc; a map of the Netscape Communications site at http://www.InternetConsult.com/netscp.toc.

By placing the burden of mapping on site administrators rather than on surfers, Table of Contents offers a key advantage over plug-ins such as HistoryTree: You get to see the structure and organization of a site before you surf through it. Table of Contents is a true plug-in that gives you a map of a site.

With Table of Contents' advantage, though, comes a curse. It's only effective on sites where someone has taken the time to use Table of Contents Creator to map the pages in the site and create a .TOC guide file. Outside of the InternetConsult demo pages, there aren't any such public sites; and so for now, Table of Contents is best suited for intranets.

Plug-in Power Rating: ★★★

Installing Table of Contents

To install Table of Contents:

1. Point your browser at http://www.InternetConsult.com/tocplug.html.
2. Click the download link that corresponds to your operating environment.
3. Save the file by itself in a temporary directory.
4. When the file has downloaded completely, shut down your browser.
5. Run the file you downloaded. It's a self-extracting .ZIP file that will place several more files in your temporary directory.
6. Run the file SETUP.EXE. It's an automated installation routine that will install Table of Contents for you. Respond to its prompts as needed.
7. Restart your browser. Table of Contents will be ready to use.

Using Table of Contents

When you call up a .TOC file in your browser, the browser doesn't display the file itself. Instead, the plug-in opens a separate window for the Table of Contents application.

In that window, you'll see a line for each of the pages on the site (see Figures 7-3 and 7-4 for examples). Pages that contain links to subordinate pages are depicted as books; pages that have no pages below them on the hierarchy have sheet-of-paper icons.

To access a page depicted in the Table of Contents window, double-click on its line, and your browser will display the page. You can also use the buttons on the button bar to save or print the .TOC file.

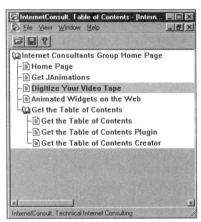

Figure 7-3: A Table of Contents site map for the InternetConsult site.

Plugged-in sites

There are, at this writing, only two publicly accessible .TOC files out there for the Table of Contents plug-in, and both are on the InternetConsult site. The first, shown in Figure 7-3, contains a map of the pages on the InternetConsult site itself. The other, shown in Figure 7-4, provides a graphical depiction of the oft-confusing Netscape Communications site.

Figure 7-4: The Table of Contents map of the Netscape site.

Authoring for Table of Contents

To enable people to navigate around your site with Table of Contents, you'll have to map your site with Table of Contents Creator, available at http://www.InternetConsult.com/toccreat.html.

Table of Contents Creator examines all the pages that make up your site and lists them in a special .TOC file that can be read across the network by the Table of Contents plug-in.

The best way to publish your .TOC file is to have a link to it on your site's regular welcome page. Label it with a sentence such as, "For users of the Table of Contents plug-in," and have a link to the download page for those who want to try it out.

Try experimenting with FirstFloor's SmartMarks — read all about it at http://www.firstfloor.com — or Freeloader, at http://freeloader.com, as tools to help create .TOC navigation files

Utilities

What? You thought your browser was only for fun? A mere toy for you to use to travel from one fun site to the next, playing video clips, listening to audio files and exploring three-dimensional renderings of the Taj Mahal? Hah!

Sorry, cyber-sports, but your browser is a real working tool. It can do everything from facilitate business meetings to enable you to control applications that are running on someone else's machine. This chapter shows you some of the utilitarian stuff plug-ins can enable your browser to do.

Of course, the nice thing about browsers is that when you're through filling in online forms and building interactive applications, you *can* scurry off to the entertainment site of your choice.

EarthTime

Creator: Starfish Software

Function: Tells the time in different locations worldwide

Home Site: http://www.starfishsoftware.com/getearth.html

Supported Platforms: Windows 95 and Windows NT

Authoring Tool: None

Good Examples: None — but you need to open the file EARTHTIM.ETC to start the plug-in

They used to say that the sun never set on the British Empire. As of next year, with the return of Hong Kong to China, that will no longer be the case. But the sun always remains aloft over the Internet — a fact that can cause some problems if you're trying to coordinate people in Melbourne, San Francisco, Washington, and Zurich.

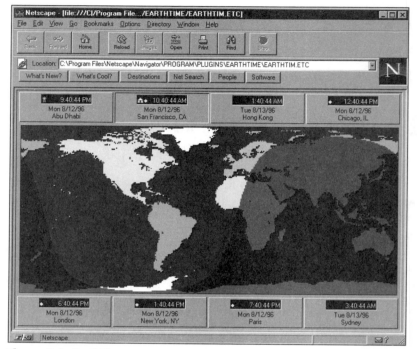

Figure 8-1: EarthTime.

EarthTime to the rescue! This plug-in shows you a map of the world and tells you with a click of your mouse what time it is at specific locations (see Figure 8-1). A version that sells for $19.95 gives you more cities to click on and information about such things as local languages and holidays.

Plug-in Power Rating: ★★★

Installing EarthTime

To install EarthTime:

1. Point your browser at http://www.starfishsoftware.com/products/et/get_earth.html.

2. Fill out the registration form and click on the Sign Me Up! button.

3. Click on one of the download links.

4. Save the file by itself in a temporary directory.

5. When the file has downloaded completely, shut down your browser.

6. Run the file you downloaded. It's an automated installation routine that handles the details of installation for you. Respond to its prompts as needed.

7. Restart your browser. EarthTime will be ready to use.

Using EarthTime

To see EarthTime information, you need to point your browser at a file called EARTHTIM.ETC in your EarthTime directory. The first time you use EarthTime, the plug-in will ask you to specify your home city, the city in which you currently are, and six other cities that interest you (the demonstration version of the plug-in — the one that you can get from the Web — can track the time in only eight cities).

One of the handiest features of the plug-in is its ability to instantly compare the time of day in two cities (see Figure 8-2). By clicking on one city's time display and dragging to another city, you get a dialog box that explains the time differential between the two cities.

You can center the map on a specific location by right-clicking on the map and clicking on the Center Map Here command in the pop-up menu that appears.

To get information about a particular city, right-click on the name of the city and select the information you want from the pop-up menu. You can get general information (such as currency and language) as well as conversion information from the pop-up menu.

Plugged-in sites

The only file that matters for running EarthTime is EARTHTIM.ETC, which lives on your hard disk.

Authoring for EarthTime

You can't create content for EarthTime — unless you know something about time that I don't.

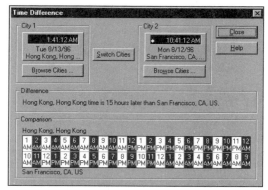

Figure 8-2: EarthTime comparing times in different cities.

JetForm Filler

Creator: JetForm

Function: Makes creation and use of Web forms easier

Home Site: `http://www.jetform.com/product/web/jfwebov.html`

Supported Platforms: All Windows systems

Authoring Tool: JetForm Design (with JetForm Server)

Good Examples: A purchase order at `http://www.jetform.com/product/web/jetfrmpo.html`; a survey at `http://www.jetform.com/product/web/survey.html`; an expense report at `http://www.jetform.com/product/web/survey.html`

Tired of clunky, plain-vanilla Web forms with the same old white backgrounds, gray buttons, and nondescript controls? JetForm Filler can help you get around your form-design doldrums. By enabling you to create smartly formatted forms with clever controls, JetForm lets you take your Web site — or intranet operation — out of the realm of the boring and into the world of the cool.

Plug-in Power Rating: ★★★

Installing JetForm Filler

To install JetForm Filler:

   1. Point your browser at `http://www.jetform.com/product/web/webdload.html`.

2. Follow the link to the JetForm license agreement and make sure you agree to its terms.

3. Click on the link at the bottom of the page that corresponds to your operating environment.

4. Save the file by itself in a temporary directory.

5. When the file has downloaded completely, shut down your browser.

6. Run the file you downloaded. It's a self-extracting .ZIP archive that will place a number of additional files in your temporary directory.

7. Run the file SETUP.EXE. It's an automated installation routine that handles the details of installation for you. Respond to its prompts as needed.

8. Restart your browser. JetForm will be ready to use.

Using JetForm Filler

Much of how you use JetForm Filler depends upon how the form designer has done his or her work — every form is different. Still, there are some features of the JetForm display that remain constant — namely, the seven buttons in the button bar. They are

✦ **Print.** Prints the form and any information in it.

✦ **Submit-Web.** The same as the Submit button that appears on many Web forms. This button sends in your information.

✦ **Cut.** Performs the Windows Cut function.

✦ **Copy.** Performs the Windows Copy function.

✦ **Paste.** Performs the Windows Paste Function.

✦ **Zoom.** Increases or decreases the level of magnification.

✦ **About.** Displays information about the plug-in.

Plugged-in sites

The odds are excellent that you've used a plain old Web form before; so you're familiar with JetForm Filler's competition. To see what it can do, point your browser at `http://www.jetform.com/product/web/webdemo.html`, where there's a directory of demonstration forms. Some of the best:

✦ **Purchase Order**
(`http://www.jetform.com/product/web/jetfrmpo.html`).. This page shows the power of JetForm in designing multi-column charts that incorporate elaborate graphics. The purchase order appears in Figure 8-3.

✦ **Survey** (http://www.jetform.com/product/web/survey.html) This page
shows that JetForm can handle much better-looking check boxes than regular HTML forms can. Rather than being big and clunky, these boxes are tight
and attractive. The survey form appears in Figure 8-4.

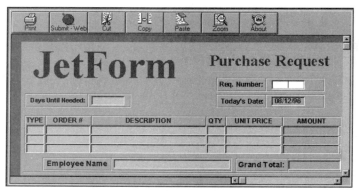

Figure 8-3: JetForm Filler displaying a purchase order.

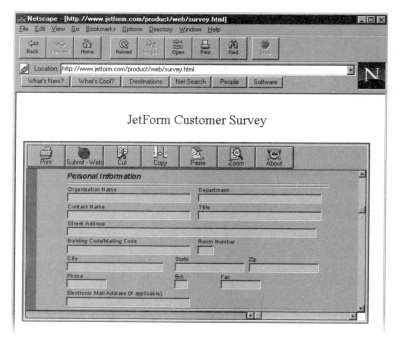

Figure 8-4: A JetForm-powered survey.

Authoring for JetForm Filler

To create forms for JetForm Filler, you need JetForm Design — which you can read about on the JetForm site.

You can also use pre-made forms from the Virtual Forms Warehouse at `http://www.jetform.com/wareh/waremain.html`.

Embedding forms in Web pages relies on the `<EMBED>` tag with the basic `SRC`, `HEIGHT`, and `WIDTH` tags.

In order to server JetForm document, you need to configure your server to handle MIME type application/x-jetform-plugin, with filename extension .MDX.

OneWave

Creator: OneWave

Function: Aids in developing applications based on your browser

Home Site: `http://www.onewave.com/`

Supported Platforms: All Windows and Macintosh systems

Authoring Tool: OneWave Development Environment

Good Examples: Groupscape, covered in Chapter 6

Programmers, particularly those who work with object-oriented languages, are big believers in *hooks*. Hooks are features of computer code that allow other programmers to attach new pieces of code to existing programs. Microsoft Windows, with its Windows Application Program Interface, is, in some sense, one big hook that allows all Windows programs to have similarly styled dialog boxes and toolbars.

Plug-in Power Rating: ★★★

Installing OneWave

To install OneWave:

1. Point your browser at `http://www.onewave.com/download/f_down.htm`.

2. Click on the link that corresponds to your operating environment. Users of Windows 3.*x* should use the 16-bit version of the plug-in; users of Windows 95 and Windows NT should use the 32-bit version. Download the run-time

version of the plug-in unless you plan to develop applications with OneWave — the download file that contains the development environment is much larger than the run-time-only download file.

3. Fill in the registration form and click on the Signup button.

4. Read the license agreement. If you agree to abide by its terms, click on the I Agree button.

5. Save the downloaded file by itself in a temporary directory.

6. When the file has downloaded completely, shut down your browser.

7. Run the file you downloaded. It is an automated installation routine that installs OneWave. Respond to its prompts as needed.

8. Restart your browser. OneWave will be ready to go.

Using OneWave

Groupscape, which you learned about in Chapter 6, makes good use of the OneWave environment. Take a look at it at `http://www.braintech.com/grpdemo.htm` for some idea of what OneWave can facilitate. The people at Braintech used OneWave as a basis for integrating Lotus Notes into Web browser software.

Plugged-in sites

Because OneWave was designed mainly for proprietary applications, there aren't any sites that show it off well — except for the GroupScape site (`http://www.braintech.com/grpdemo.htm`) covered in Chapter 6.

Authoring for OneWave

To create tools based on the OneWave framework, use the OneWave Development Environment, which you must purchase. There's lots of information on the OneWave Development Environment on the OneWave Web site. In order for your server to work with OneWave, you need to configure your server to handle MIME type x-form/x-onewave, with filename extension .OPP.

PenOp

Creator: PenOp

Function: Provides signature-like verification of electronic transactions

Home Site: `http://www.penop.com/download.htm`

Supported Platforms: Windows 95

Authoring Tool: PenOp

Good Examples: There's a demo at `http://www.penop.com/files/penopdem.exe`.

As an increasing amount of commerce takes place on the Internet, the need for authentication of the identity of the people grows more important. Traditionally, authentication has been done with signatures — distinctive marks made on paper with a pen. PenOp brings the signature into the network age by encoding it in a machine-readable form, transmitting it across the Web, and verifying its authenticity.

If you already use pen computers, PenOp is an excellent way to bring your operation onto the Web.

 PenOp authentication is based on real, handwritten signatures; so its acceptability as legal documentation is likely, the company says. Still, there's never been a test of the validity of a PenOp signature in an actual court of law.

Plug-in Power Rating: ★★★

Installing PenOp

To install PenOp:

1. Point your browser at `http://www.penop.com/download.htm`.
2. You must install PenOp/Base, the core PenOp program, on your computer before you install the PenOp plug-in. Click on the link that corresponds to PenOp/Base for your machine.
3. Save the file by itself in a temporary directory.
4. When the file has downloaded completely, shut down your browser.
5. Run the file you downloaded. It's a self-extracting .ZIP archive that will place a handful of files in your temporary directory.
6. Run SETUP.EXE. It's an automated installation routine that will install the PenOp/Base files on your machine.
7. Go back to `http://www.penop.com/download.htm`.
8. Click on the link for the plug-in download file that corresponds to your operating environment (it's located near the bottom of the page).
9. Save the file by itself in a temporary directory.
10. When the file has downloaded completely, shut down your browser.

11. Run the file you downloaded. It's a self-extracting .ZIP archive that will place several files in your temporary directory.

12. Run SETUP.EXE. It is an automated installation routine that will install the PenOp plug-in on your machine.

13. Restart your browser. PenOp will be ready for use.

Using PenOp

The PenOp signature verification window usually appears as a result of a script. When it prompts you for a signature, make sure you read the text above the signature window, then sign your name with a stylus attached to your computer. After you sign your name, the plug-in submits information about your signature — in a package called a *biometric token* — to a server, where it rates the signature's similarity to a copy of your signature on file. If the signatures match, the server executes a script file that can do whatever you want.

Figures 8-5 and 8-6 show PenOp verifying an identity by signature.

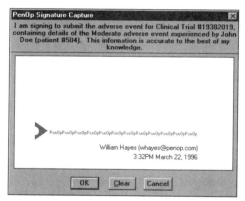

Figure 8-5: PenOp requesting a signature.

Plugged-in sites

There aren't a lot of sites that use PenOp, and it's tough to check it out without a pen-equipped computer. Check out the demo, though — its available at `http://www.penop.com/files/penopdem.exe`. Figures 8-5 and 8-6 came from the demonstration.

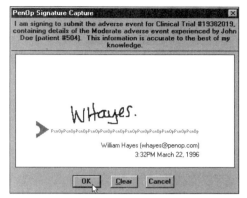

Figure 8-6: A PenOp signature.

Authoring for PenOp

PenOp uses the <EMBED> tag to attach signature files to Web pages. In addition to the WIDTH and HEIGHT attributes, PenOp uses the SRC in an unusual way and has several optional attributes:

✦ SRC. If a signature is to be displayed, SRC specifies the file that contains the signature. If a signature is to be captured, set SRC equal to the file that *will* contain the signature.

✦ ACTION_URL. The URL of the script that will be executed after PenOp verifies the signature. ACTION_URL is a mandatory attribute.

✦ METHOD. Set to GET or POST, METHOD specifies how the signature information will be sent to the script. The default value is GET.

✦ PROMPT. Set PROMPT equal to the text, in quotes, that is to be displayed when the cursor is in the area defined by the WIDTH and HEIGHT values.

✦ GRAVITY. GRAVITY defines the words that are displayed while the signature is being captured. GRAVITY often is set equal to something similar to, "I agree to pay $500 to the bearer."

✦ CLAIMED_ID. CLAIMED_ID is set equal to the name of the person who is supposed to sign the document.

PointCast

Creator: PointCast

Function: Brings a customized news summary to your browser

Home Site: `http://www.pointcast.com/`

Supported Platforms: Windows 3.*x* and Windows 95 systems

Authoring Tool: PointCast I-Server

Good Examples: None

Numerous Web pundits have said that the future of news delivery is in personalization — no more generic newscasts sent out to millions of people over the airwaves. Instead of broadcasting, information will be delivered to particular interest groups (such as elderly people or Cubs fans) by narrowcasting, or to individuals (such as someone who owns stock in AT&T, follows the Rangers, and wants to track the weather in Philadelphia) by *pointcasting*.

PointCast brings pointcasting to your browser. By letting you select which stocks you want to follow, what sort of news you care about, and other details about the information that matters to you, PointCast enables you to create a custom information package. Though the information often downloads slowly from PointCast's overloaded servers, this plug-in belongs on your desktop.

Plug-in Power Rating: ★★★★

Installing PointCast

To install PointCast:

1. Point your browser at `http://www.pointcast.com/cgi-bin/download.pl`.
2. Click on the download site that corresponds to your geographic region.
3. When the file has downloaded completely, shut down your browser.
4. Run the file you downloaded. It's an automated installation routine that will do the dirty work of installing the PointCast stand-alone application and plug-in. Respond to its prompts as needed.
5. Restart your browser. PointCast will be ready to go.

Using PointCast

Unlike many plug-ins that read content embedded in pages all over the Web, PointCast relies on a single URL to activate it. When you want to use PointCast, direct your browser to `http://www.pointcast.com/viewpoint/run.pcn`.

You'll probably want to set a bookmark for `http://www.pointcast.com/viewpoint/run.pcn` so you can get to it quickly.

When the PointCast display appears, note its general layout: There's a strip of buttons down the left side, a set of tabs in the top-left corner, an information window on the bottom, and an advertising window in the top-right corner.

Use the buttons on the left side to select the general type of information you want to view — there's a button for general news, a button for news and stock quotes for companies you select, a button for industry news, a button for sports scores and information, along with a couple of others. You'll also find a button labeled Update, which you click on to get current information, and buttons labeled Personalize and Options, which you use to get details about the information you need and the way PointCast behaves.

Figure 8-7 shows PointCast in action.

The PointCast package comes with a stand-alone application and a screen saver. Both of these tools can be handy information-display media.

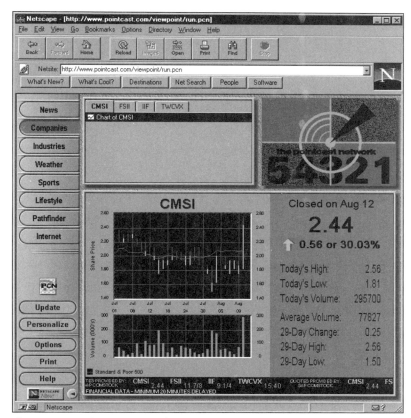

Figure 8-7: PointCast at work.

Plugged-in sites

Just one: http://www.pointcast.com/viewpoint/run.pcn. That's the URL you use to activate the PointCast plug-in and update your information. Another view of the plug-in in action appears in Figure 8-7.

Authoring for PointCast

PointCast recently came out with PointCast I-Server, a news server for corporate intranets that allows network administrators to broadcast news to PointCast users. The network administrator authors for a special channel that appears alongside the regular News, Sports, Companies, and Weather channels.

Few details are available at this writing, but look for news at http://www.pointcast.com/products/iserver.html.

QuickServer

Creator: Wayfarer

Function: Helps develop applications

Home Site: http://www.wayfarer.com/

Supported Platforms: Windows 95

Authoring Tool: None

Good Examples: StockWatcher, available for download at http://www.wayfarer.com/demonstration/19.htm

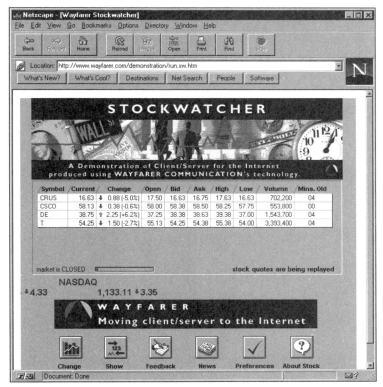

Figure 8-8: StockWatcher, a QuickServer application.

A set of hooks similar in concept to OpenScape, QuickServer is a server/plug-in combination that lets you create applications that update very speedily. StockWatcher, a plug-in based on the QuickServer system that you can download from the Wayfarer site, demonstrates how fast QuickServer applications can track continuously updating information (see Figure 8-8). Wayfarer ran a QuickServer application called Medalwatcher that kept Web surfers informed about the outcomes of events at the Atlanta Olympics almost as soon as they were over.

Plug-in Power Rating: ★★★

Installing QuickServer

You can download a 60-day trial version of QuickServer for use with Visual Basic. To install QuickServer:

1. Point your browser at `http://www.wayfarer.com/products/18.htm`.

2. Fill in the registration form and click on the ACCEPT button.

3. Click on the button that says, Download the Wayfarer SDK.

4. Run the file you downloaded. It's an automated installation routine that installs the SDK for you.

5. Use Visual Basic to develop applications based on the QuickServer system.

Using QuickServer

The best way to get a taste of what QuickServer can do is to point your browser at `http://www.wayfarer.com/demonstration/19.htm` and download StockWatcher, a QuickServer-based plug-in. StockWatcher allows you to specify companies whose shares you want to follow and keeps in contact with a server that provides continuously updated stock prices.

Plugged-in sites

If you've installed StockWatcher on your machine, point your browser at `http://www.wayfarer.com/demonstration/run.sw.htm`, select some stocks to follow, and see what QuickServer can do.

Authoring for QuickServer

QuickServer is an authoring tool itself — you can't create content for QuickServer.

Using the CD-ROM

The key to using the CD-ROM that accompanies this book is a Web page called PLUGINS.HTM. You find that file in the root directory of the CD-ROM, and you should open it with your browser. With PLUGINS.HTM, you can easily access three things:

♦ The plug-ins encoded on the CD-ROM

♦ The home sites of all plug-ins covered in this book and the home sites of some plug-ins that came out too late for inclusion in *Netscape Plug-in Power*

♦ Plug-ins clearinghouses, such as BrowserWatch Plug-in Plaza

To use the plug-ins on the CD-ROM, open PLUGINS.HTM and click on the link that corresponds to the plug-in you want. When your browser prompts you to save the file, specify an empty temporary directory on your hard disk. After the file has transferred to the new location, run the file or use a decompression utility to unpack the file's contents (you may have configured your browser to decompress files automatically). You find detailed instructions for installing most plug-ins in the pages of this book.

What's on the Disc

What plug-ins are on the disc? Here's a list.

Adobe's tool for reading Acrobat .PDF files.

✦ Acrobat Reader Weblink for Macintosh

✦ Acrobat Reader Weblink for Windows

Iterated Systems' Video for Windows player.

✦ ClearFusion for Windows 95

SoftSource's viewer for AutoCad files.

✦ DWG/DXF Viewer for Windows 95

EchoSpeech's player for compressed speech files.

✦ EchoSpeech for Windows 3.x

✦ EchoSpeech for Windows 95

Narrative Communications' interactive animation plug-in.

✦ Enliven for Windows 95

Tumbleweed Software's viewer for Envoy portable documents.

✦ Envoy for Windows 3.x

✦ Envoy for Windows 95

✦ Envoy for Power Mac

* Envoy for 68K Mac

Visual Components' plug-in for viewing networked spreadsheets.

✦ Formula One/NET for Windows 3.x

✦ Formula One/NET for Windows 95

ISYS/Odyssey Development's handy tool for keeping track of sites you visit.

✦ HindSite for Windows 3.x

Ichat's plug-in for real-time Web chat.

✦ Ichat for Windows 3.x

✦ Ichat for Windows 95

✦ Ichat for Power Mac

Intergraph's viewer for .CGM files.

✦ InterCAP Inline for Windows 95

FTP Software's all-purpose file opener.

✦ KeyView for Windows 95

Sseyo's generative music plug-in.

✦ Koan Net Player Plugin for Windows 3.x

✦ Koan Web Player

Infinet's compressed-image viewer.
- ✦ Lightning Strike for Windows 3.*x*
- ✦ Lightning Strike for Windows 95

mBED's animation viewer.
- ✦ mBED for Windows 3.*x*
- ✦ mBED for Windows 95
- ✦ mBED for 68K Mac
- ✦ mBED for Power Mac

A QuickTime viewer from Intelligence at Large.
- ✦ Movie Star for Windows 3.*x*
- ✦ MovieStar for Windows 95
- ✦ MovieStar for all Macintoshes

OpenScape's utility for making applications browser-aware.
- ✦ OneWave for Windows 3.*x*
- ✦ OneWave for Windows 95

A viewer for Microsoft PowerPoint files from Net-Scene.
- ✦ PointPlus for Windows 3.*x*
- ✦ PointPlus for Windows 95

InterVu's MPEG video viewer.
- ✦ PreVu for Windows 95

Allegiant's viewer for SuperCard-authored multimedia.
- ✦ Roadster for 68K Mac
- ✦ Roadster for Power Mac

A demonstration of Wayfarer's QuickServer technology.
- ✦ Stockwatcher (Quickserver Demo) for Windows 95

FastMan's player for highly compressed audio.
- ✦ \Rapid Transit for Windows 95

Digital Dreams' plug-in for adding spoken commands to Shockwave for Director.
- ✦ ShockTalk for all Macintoshes

The plug-ins that started it all — Shockwave for Director, FreeHand, and Authorware. Animation, vector graphics and multimedia from Macromedia.
- ✦ Shockwave for Windows 3.*x*
- ✦ Shockwave for Windows 95
- ✦ Shockwave for 68K Mac
- ✦ Shockwave for Power Mac

SoftSource's viewer for .SVF drawing files.
- ✦ SVF Viewer for Windows 95

MVP Solutions' plug-in for making Web sites talk.
+ Talker for all Macintoshes

Lari Software's viewer for QuickDraw GX graphics.
+ Vertigo for all Macintoshes

Vivo Software's QuickTime video viewer.
+ Vivo for Windows 3.x

+ Vivo for Windows 95

+ Vivo for all Macintoshes

Integrated Data Systems' VRML explorer.
+ VRealm for Windows 95

Great Plains Software's Macintosh VRML browser.
+ VRML Equinox for all Macintoshes

A VRML browser from Chaco Communications.
+ VR Scout for Windows 95

Summus' compressed-image viewer.
+ Wavelet Image for Windows 3.x

+ Wavelet Image for Windows 95

+ Wavelet Image for Power Mac

+ Wavelet Image for 68K Mac

Galacticomm's browser-based conferencing tool.
+ Worldgroup Manager for Windows 95

And a Bonus...

You'll also find Eudora Light, an excellent e-mail program!

Directory of Plug-in Developers

Here's a quick guide to available plug-ins. Check here for information about where to look for the latest information on plug-in modules.

This appendix was put together after most of the rest of *Netscape Plug-in Power*. Therefore, some plug-ins mentioned here don't have full coverage elsewhere in this book.

AboutTime

Creator: Now Software

Home site: http://www.nowsoft.com

Acrobat

Creator: Adobe

Home site: http://www.adobe.com/Acrobat/

Action

Creator: Open2U

Home site: http://www.open2u.com/action/action.html

Allegiant Roadster

Creator: Allegiant

Home site: http://www.allegiant.com/

ASAP WebShow

Creator: SPC

Home site: http://www.spco.com/asap/asapwebs.htm

Astound Web Player

Creator: Gold Disk

Home site: http://www.golddisk.com/awp.html

Beacon

Creator: Oarsman
Home site: http://www.oarsman.com/choices.html

BusinessWeb

Creator: MSA
Home site: http://www.msa.com/

Carbon Copy/Net

Creator: Microcom
Home site: http://www.microcom.com/cc/ccdnload.htm

Chemscape Chime

Creator: MDL Information Systems
Home site: http://www.mdli.com/chemscape/chime/chime.html

CMX Viewer

Creator: Corel
Home site: http://www.corel.com/corelcmx/index.htm

Concerto

Creator: Alpha Software
Home site: http://www.alphasoftware.com/concerto/plugin.htm

ClearFusion

Creator: Iterated Systems
Home site: http://webber.iterated.com/

Cosmo Player

Creator: Silicon Graphics
Home site: http://webspace.sgi.com/cosmoplayer/

CPC View

Creator: Cartesian
Home site: http://www.cartesianinc.com/

Crescendo

Creator: LiveUpdate
Home site: http://www.liveupdate.com/crescendo.html

CyberSpell

Creator: Inso
Home site: http://www.inso.com/consumer/cyberspell/democybr.htm

DWG/DXF Viewer

Creator: SoftSource
Home site: http://www.softsource.com/softsource/

EarthTime

Creator: Starfish Software
Home site: http://www.starfishsoftware.com/getearth.html

EchoSpeech

Creator: Echo Speech
Home site: http://www.echospeech.com/plugin.htm

Emblaze

Creator: Interactive Media Group

Home site: `http://Geo.inter.net/Geo/technology/emblaze/downloads.html`

Enliven

Creator: Narrative Communications

Home site: `http://www.narrative.com/`

Envoy

Creator: Tumbleweed Software

Home site: `http://www.twcorp.com/plugin.htm`

Express VR

Creator: Brad Anderson

Home site: `http://www.cis.upenn.edu/~brada/VRML/ExpressVR.html`

FIGleaf Inline

Creator: Carberry Technology

Home site: `http://www.ct.ebt.com/figinline/`

Formula One/Net

Creator: Visual Components

Home site: `http://www.visualcomp.com/f1net/download.htm`

Fractal Viewer

Creator: Iterated Systems

Home site: `http://www.iterated.com/fracview/fv_home.htm`

GoScript GSPlugIn

Creator: LaserGo

Home site: `http://www.lasergo.com`

Groupscape

Creator: Brainstorm

Home site: `http://www.braintech.com/grpdemo.htm`

HindSite

Creator: ISYS/Odyssey Development

Home site: `http://www.rmii.com/isys_dev/hindsite.html`

HistoryTree

Creator: SmartBrowser

Home site: `http://www.smartbrowser.com/`

IChat

Creator: IChat

Home site: `http://www.ichat.com/`

JetForm Filler

Creator: JetForm

Home site: `http://www.jetform.com/product/web/jfwebov.html`

KEYview

Creator: FTP Software

Home site: `http://www.ftp.com/mkt_info/evals/kv_dl.html`

Koan

Creator: Sseyo

Home site:
http://www.sseyo.com/

Lightning Strike

Creator: Infinet

Home site: http://www.infinop.
com/html/infinop.html

ListenUp

Creator: Bill Noon

Home site: http://snow.cit.
cornell.edu/noon/ListenUp.html

Live3D

Creator: Netscape Communications

Home site: http://home.
netscape.com/comprod/
products/navigator/live3d/

Look@Me

Creator: Farallon Software

Home site: http://collaborate.
farallon.com/www/look/
ldownload.html

MacZilla

Creator: MacZilla

Home site: http://MacZilla.com/

MapGuide

Creator: Argus Technologies

Home site: http://
www.argusmap.com/

mBED

Creator: mBED Software

Home site: http://www.mbed.com/

MIDIPlug

Creator: Yamaha

Home site: http://www.yamaha.
co.jp/english/xg/html/midhm.html

MIDIPlugin

Creator: Arnaud Masson

Home site:
http://www.planete.net/
~amasson/midiplugin.html

MidiShare NetPlayer

Creator: GRAME

Home site: http://www.
grame.fr/english/MidiShare.html

MovieStar

Creator: Intelligence at Large

Home site: http://www.
beingthere.com/

Navigate with an Accent

Creator: AccentSoft

Home site: http://www.
accentsoft.com/

NET-Install

Creator: 20/20 Software

Home site: http://www.twenty.
com/Pages/NI/NIPI.shtml

OpenScape

Creator: OneWave
Home site: http://www.
onewave.com/

PenOp

Creator: PenOp
Home site:
http://www.penop.com/
download.htm

PhotoBubble

Creator: Omniview
Home site: http://www.
omniview.com/viewer.htm

PointCast

Creator: PointCast
Home site: http://www.
pointcast.com/

PointPlus

Creator: Net-Scene
Home site: http://www.
net-scene.com/

PreVU

Creator: InterVU
Home site: http://www.
intervu.com/prevu.html

Project X

Creator: Apple Computer
Home site: http://mcf.research.
apple.com/

QuickServer

Creator: Wayfarer
Home site: http://
www.wayfarer.com/

QuickSilver

Creator: Micrografx
Home site: http://www.micrografx.
com/quicksilver.html

QuickTime

Creator: Apple Computer
Home site: http://quicktime.
apple.com/

Rapid Transit

Creator: FastMan
Home site: http://monsterbit.
com/rapidtransit/RTHome.html

RapidVue

Creator: Pegasus
Home site: http://www.jpg.com/

RealAudio

Creator: Progressive Networks
Home site: http://www.
realaudio.com/products/
player2.0.html

ScriptActive

Creator: ExCITE
Home site: http://www.excite.
sfu.ca/NCompass/

ShockTalk

Creator: Digital Dreams
Home site: `http://www.`
`surftalk.com/`

Shockwave for Authorware

Creator: Macromedia
Home site: `http://www.`
`macromedia.com/shockwave/`

Shockwave for Director

Creator: Macromedia
Home site: `http://www.`
`macromedia.com/shockwave/`

Shockwave for Freehand

Creator: Macromedia
Home site: `http://www.`
`macromedia.com/shockwave/`

Sizzler

Creator: Totally Hip Software
Home site: `http://www.`
`totallyhip.com/`

Speech Plug-in

Creator: William H. Tudor
Home site: `http://www.albany.`
`net/~wtudor/speechinfo.html`

SVF Viewer

Creator: SoftSource
Home site: `http://www.`
`softsource.com/softsource/`

Table of Contents

Creator: InternetConsult
Home site: `http://www.`
`InternetConsult.com/toc.html`

Talker

Creator: MVP Solutions
Home site: `http://www.`
`mvpsolutions.com/PlugInsite/`
`Talker.html`

Tcl Plugin

Creator: Sun Microsystems
Home site:
`http://www.sunlabs.com/tcl/`
`plugin/index.html`

techexplorer

Creator: IBM
Home site:
`http://www.ics.raleigh.ibm.`
`com/ics/techexp.htm`

TMSSequoia ViewDirector

Creator: TMSSequoia
Home site:
`http://www.tmsinc.com/plugin/`

ToolVox

Creator: Voxware
Home site: `http://www.voxware.`
`com/download.htm`

Topper

Creator: Kinetix (A division of AutoDesk)

Home site: http://www.ktx.com/

TrueSpeech

Creator: DSP Group

Home site: http://www.dspg.com/plugin.htm

VDOLive

Creator: VDOnet

Home site:
http://www.vdolive.com/

Vertigo

Creator: Lari Software

Home site: http://www.larisoftware.com/Products/WebPlugin.html

ViewMovie

Creator: ICB

Home site:
http://www.well.com/user/ivanski/download.html

Viscape

Creator: Superscape

Home site: http://www.superscape.com/

Vivo

Creator: Vivo

Home site: http://www.vivo.com

VR Scout

Creator: Chaco Communications

Home site: http://www.chaco.com/vrscout/

VRealm

Creator: Integrated Data Systems

Home site: http://www.ids-net.com/

VRML Equinox

Creator: North Plains Systems

Home site: http://www.northplains.com/EquiInfo.html

WebAnimator

Creator: DeltaPoint

Home site: http://www.deltapoint.com

Whip

Creator: AutoDesk

Home site: http://www.autodesk.com/products/autocad/whip/whip.htm

Whurlplug

Creator: John Louch

Home site: http://product.info.apple.com/qd3d/viewer.html

WinFrame

Creator: Citrix Systems

Home site: http://www.citrix.com/

WIRL

Creator: VREAM

Home site: `http://www.vream.com/`

Worldgroup Manager

Creator: Galacticomm

Home site: `http://www.gcomm.com/show/plugin.html`

Index

✦ **Y** ✦

IDG BOOKS WORLDWIDE LICENSE AGREEMENT

Important — read carefully before opening the software packet. This is a legal agreement between you (either an individual or an entity) and IDG Books Worldwide, Inc. (IDG). By opening the accompanying sealed packet containing the software disc, you acknowledge that you have read and accept the following IDG License Agreement. If you do not agree and do not want to be bound by the terms of this Agreement, promptly return the book and the unopened software packet to the place you obtained them for a full refund.

1. License. This License Agreement (Agreement) permits you to use one copy of the enclosed Software program on a single computer. The Software is in "use" on a computer when it is loaded into temporary memory (i.e., RAM) or installed into permanent memory (e.g., hard disk, CD-ROM, or other storage device) of that computer.

2. Copyright. The entire contents of this disc and the compilation of the Software are copyrighted and protected by both United States copyright laws and international treaty provisions. You may only (a) make one copy of the Software for backup or archival purposes, or (b) transfer the Software to a single hard disk, provided that you keep the original for backup or archival purposes. The individual programs on the disc are copyrighted by the authors of each program respectively. Each program has its own use permissions and limitations. To use each program, you must follow the individual requirements and restrictions detailed for each in Appendix A of this Book. Do not use a program if you do not want to follow its Licensing Agreement. None of the material on this disc or listed in this Book may ever be distributed, in original or modified form, for commercial purposes.

3. Other Restrictions. You may not rent or lease the Software. You may transfer the Software and user documentation on a permanent basis provided you retain no copies and the recipient agrees to the terms of this Agreement. You may not reverse engineer, decompile, or disassemble the Software except to the extent that the foregoing restriction is expressly prohibited by applicable law. If the Software is an update or has been updated, any transfer must include the most recent update and all prior versions. Each shareware program has its own use permissions and limitations. These limitations are contained in the individual license agreements that are on the software discs. The restrictions include a requirement that after using the program for a period of time specified in its text, the user must pay a registration fee or discontinue use. By opening the package which contains the software disc, you will be agreeing to abide by the licenses and restrictions for these programs. Do not open the software package unless you agree to be bound by the license agreements.

4. Limited Warranty. IDG warrants that the Software and disc are free from defects in materials and workmanship for a period of sixty (60) days from the date of purchase of this Book. If IDG receives notification within the warranty period of defects in material or workmanship, IDG will replace the defective disc. IDG's entire liability and your exclusive remedy shall be limited to replacement of the Software, which is returned to IDG with a copy of your receipt. This Limited Warranty is void if failure of the Software has resulted from accident, abuse, or misapplication. Any replacement Software will be warranted for the remainder of the original warranty period or thirty (30) days, whichever is longer.

5. No Other Warranties. To the maximum extent permitted by applicable law, IDG and the author disclaim all other warranties, express or implied, including but not limited to implied warranties of merchantability and fitness for a particular purpose, with respect to the Software, the programs, the source code contained therein and/or the techniques described in this Book. This limited warranty gives you specific legal rights. You may have others which vary from state/jurisdiction to state/jurisdiction.

6. No Liability For Consequential Damages. To the extent permitted by applicable law, in no event shall IDG or the author be liable for any damages whatsoever (including without limitation, damages for loss of business profits, business interruption, loss of business information, or any other pecuniary loss) arising out of the use of or inability to use the Book or the Software, even if IDG has been advised of the possibility of such damages. Because some states/jurisdictions do not allow the exclusion or limitation of liability for consequential or incidental damages, the above limitation may not apply to you.

7. U.S.Government Restricted Rights. Use, duplication, or disclosure of the Software by the U.S. Government is subject to restrictions stated in paragraph (c) (1) (ii) of the Rights in Technical Data and Computer Software clause of DFARS 252.227-7013, and in subparagraphs (a) through (d) of the Commercial Computer— Restricted Rights clause at FAR 52.227-19, and in similar clauses in the NASA FAR supplement, when applicable.

SSEYO™ Koan™ Pro

The KoanMusic authoring system for the WWW

SSEYO Koan Pro Power view, where you can edit parameters and envelopes

Brian Eno

"I see Koan Pro as the most promising idea in musical technology for many years. I've been dreaming of something like this for ages. Here it is, and it works."
Brian Eno, acknowledged founder of Ambient music and producer of U2 and David Bowie

Brian Eno

SSEYO Koan Pro is a powerful and advanced 3 in 1 music software tool for musicians and non-musicians alike. Create and publish on your website music ranging from floor shaking drum 'n' bass to chillout ambient. Set free your creativity and imagination and realize brilliant new musical ideas. Or use it as a complete Zentertainment(tm) authoring environment for creating self contained, ever-changing Koan pieces. Either way, KoanMusic is the new 'generative' or 'organic' music standard for the WWW.

SSEYO Koan Pro V1.2 now comes with the SSEYO Koan Plus V1.2 player software and album editor, meaning you can create albums of your Koan pieces for playback.

Check us out at the following places below for the latest software, plugins and demos:

SSEYO Ltd, Pyramid House, Easthampstead Road, Bracknell, Berks, UK RG12 1YW   Tel: +44 (0)1344 712017 Fax: +44 (0)1344 712005
WWW: http://www.sseyo/com Email: koaninfo@sseyo.com
Email: sseyo@msn.com   MSN KoanMusic forum: GO KOAN
Compuserve: GO SSEYO

Selected highlights.....

- Create KoanMusic pieces from 1Kb that play for over 8 hours
- Over 150 real time changeable parameters
- Up to 50 separate voices (soundcard dependent)
- Rhythm templates and demo pieces provided
- 5 different voicetypes: Ambient, Rhythmic, FixedPattern, Follows or RepeatBar. Use Follow voices to 'follow' another to create fugues; use Repeatbar voices to repeat material from earlier bars; use Ambient voices to create notes with durations in milliseconds, seconds or fractions of a beat
- 4 music rule types: Scale, Harmony, Next Note and Rhythm
- Envelopes to control Volumes, Pans, Velocities, and Piece Tempo
- Controllers for Reverb/ Chorus/ Portamento/ Sostenuto/Expression/ Damper/ Softness
- Supports GM/GS/XG, AWE32/SB32 EMU8000 controllers and Gravis patches
- Import MIDI files & record your Koan piece output to a type 0 MIDI file
- Random patch changing as a voice is playing
- Mutation of patterns and phrases
- Micro-level controls for real time, subtle random changing of a voice's volume, pitch, start time and modulation
- Support for WAV files, stored externally or even used from a CD ROM
- Lists of values for every parameter
- Create encrypted .SKP demo pieces; Add pieces notes for others to see when they load your pieces
- Extensive mouse and keyboard support and comprehensive on-line help system

Never underestimate the power of a little chat.

True Interactivity

- Visitors to your web site can communicate and interact with each other.
- *ichat*™ offers real-time conversations while viewing a web site.
- *ichat* users now have the ability to share files, add sound to their chats, save their conversations and send private messages to a selected group.

More Traffic

- Builds a community around your web site.
- Increases web site traffic, attracting new visitors and encouraging more return visits to your site.
- Easily integrates with third-party solutions to add audio and video to your chat rooms.

Browser Integration

ichat offers the broadest platform support:
- *ichat* Plug-in for Netscape 2.0 & 3.0, Windows 95, NT, 3.11, and Macintosh OS
- *ichat* Active X control for Microsoft Internet Explorer 3.0
- *ichat* Java client

- People on a chat-enabled web page supported by *ichat* ROOMS™, can communicate and interact seamlessly and without concern for platform compatability.

Open Standards

- *ichat*'s open standards approach means that web administrators can add real-time communications and leverage existing web content without having to develop for a proprietary format.

Scalability

- *ichat* readily supports over 50,000 users through the distributed architecture of **ROOMS** version 2.0.
- *ichat*'s distributed architecture supports multiple chat rooms as well as large single events.
- Web sites using **ROOMS** 2.0 can create a chat network environment which allows a user to seamlessly navigate the site, chat in various areas and participate in events without having to re-enter passwords or log in and out of various servers.

8303 North Mopac Expressway • Suite A114 • Austin, Texas 78759
512-349-0339 • FAX: 512-349-0005
Come chat with us. http://**www.ichat.com**
email: **sales@ichat.com**

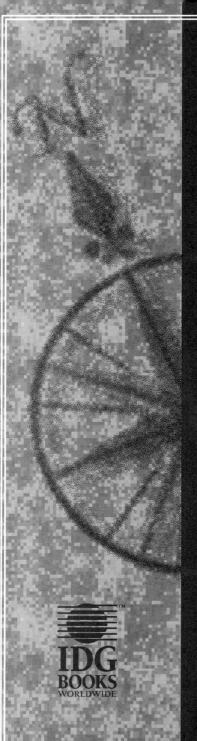

HAVE YOU BEEN TO THE EDGE?

Visit the cutting-edge at *http://www.idgbooks.com*. This value-packed site features hot, regularly updated information on books, events, and software including:

- *What's New* - Hear it here first! New books, promotions, author events, the latest information on emerging technologies, and more.

- *What's Hot* - Our hottest books, promotions, give-aways, and links.

- *Online Bookshelf* - A full catalog, searchable by title, author, or press.

- *Books Online* - Online updates to many of our printed titles, new content, book specific software, and exclusive original articles.

- *Online Events and Community* - An up-to-date listing of the latest IDG happenings and chat group, FAQs, and more.

- *Free and Downloadable* - An area full of freeware, including zip utilities and HTML editors.

- *Where to Buy* - A searchable list of retailers.

IDG BOOKS WORLDWIDE REGISTRATION CARD

RETURN THIS REGISTRATION CARD FOR FREE CATALOG

Title of this book: Netscape® Plug-in Power

My overall rating of this book: ❏ Very good [1] ❏ Good [2] ❏ Satisfactory [3] ❏ Fair [4] ❏ Poor [5]

How I first heard about this book:

❏ Found in bookstore; name: [6]

❏ Advertisement: [8]

❏ Word of mouth; heard about book from friend, co-worker, etc.: [10]

❏ Book review: [7]

❏ Catalog: [9]

❏ Other: [11]

What I liked most about this book:

What I would change, add, delete, etc., in future editions of this book:

Other comments:

Number of computer books I purchase in a year: ❏ 1 [12] ❏ 2-5 [13] ❏ 6-10 [14] ❏ More than 10 [15]

I would characterize my computer skills as: ❏ Beginner [16] ❏ Intermediate [17] ❏ Advanced [18] ❏ Professional [19]

I use ❏ DOS [20] ❏ Windows [21] ❏ OS/2 [22] ❏ Unix [23] ❏ Macintosh [24] ❏ Other: [25]_____
(please specify)

I would be interested in new books on the following subjects:
(please check all that apply, and use the spaces provided to identify specific software)

❏ Word processing: [26]

❏ Data bases: [28]

❏ File Utilities: [30]

❏ Networking: [32]

❏ Other: [34]

❏ Spreadsheets: [27]

❏ Desktop publishing: [29]

❏ Money management: [31]

❏ Programming languages: [33]

I use a PC at (please check all that apply): ❏ home [35] ❏ work [36] ❏ school [37] ❏ other: [38] _____

The disks I prefer to use are ❏ 5.25 [39] ❏ 3.5 [40] ❏ other: [41]_____

I have a CD ROM: ❏ yes [42] ❏ no [43]

I plan to buy or upgrade computer hardware this year: ❏ yes [44] ❏ no [45]

I plan to buy or upgrade computer software this year: ❏ yes [46] ❏ no [47]

Name:_____ Business title: [48]_____ Type of Business: [49]_____

Address (❏ home [50] ❏ work [51]/Company name:_____)

Street/Suite#_____

City [52]/State [53]/Zipcode [54]:_____ Country [55]_____

❏ **I liked this book!** You may quote me by name in future
IDG Books Worldwide promotional materials.

My daytime phone number is _____

IDG BOOKS

THE WORLD OF
COMPUTER
KNOWLEDGE

❏ YES!

Please keep me informed about IDG's World of Computer Knowledge.
Send me the latest IDG Books catalog.

Netscape®

Pl ver

Netscape®
Plug-in Power

David Wall

IDG Books Worldwide, Inc.
An International Data Group Company

Foster City, CA ◆ Chicago, IL ◆ Indianapolis, IN ◆ Dallas, TX

Netscape® Plug-in Power

Published by
IDG Books Worldwide, Inc.
An International Data Group Company
919 E. Hillsdale Blvd. Suite 400
Foster City, CA 94404
www.idgbooks.com (IDG Books Worldwide Web Site)

Library of Congress Catalog Card No.: 96-78233

ISBN: 0-7645-4009-2

Printed in the United States of America

10 9 8 7 6 5 4 3 2 1

IE/RQ/SS/ZW/FC

Distributed in the United States by IDG Books Worldwide, Inc.

Distributed by Macmillan Canada for Canada; by Contemporanea de Ediciones for Venezuela; by Distribuidora Cuspide for Argentina; by CITEC for Brazil; by Ediciones ZETA S.C.R. Ltda. for Peru; by Editorial Limusa SA for Mexico; by Transworld Publishers Limited in the United Kingdom and Europe; by Academic Bookshop for Egypt; by Levant Distributors S.A.R.L. for Lebanon; by Al Jassim for Saudi Arabia; by Simron Pty. Ltd. for South Africa; by Pustak Mahal for India; by The Computer Bookshop for India; by Toppan Company Ltd. for Japan; by Addison Wesley Publishing Company for Korea; by Longman Singapore Publishers Ltd. for Singapore, Malaysia, Thailand, and Indonesia; by Unalis Corporation for Taiwan; by WS Computer Publishing Company, Inc. for the Philippines; by WoodsLane Pty. Ltd. for Australia; by WoodsLane Enterprises Ltd. for New Zealand. Authorized Sales Agent: Anthony Rudkin Associates for the Middle East and North Africa.

For general information on IDG Books Worldwide's books in the U.S., please call our Consumer Customer Service department at 800-762-2974. For reseller information, including discounts and premium sales, please call our Reseller Customer Service department at 800-434-3422.

For information on where to purchase IDG Books Worldwide's books outside the U.S., please contact our International Sales department at 415-655-3172 or fax 415-655-3295.

For information on foreign language translations, please contact our Foreign & Subsidiary Rights department at 415-655-3021 or fax 415-655-3281.

For sales inquiries and special prices for bulk quantities, please contact our Sales department at 415-655-3200 or write to the address above.

For information on using IDG Books Worldwide's books in the classroom or for ordering examination copies, please contact our Educational Sales department at 800-434-2086 or fax 817-251-8174.

For authorization to photocopy items for corporate, personal, or educational use, please contact Copyright Clearance Center, 222 Rosewood Drive, Danvers, MA 01923, or fax 508-750-4470.